Contents: delivering the EDEXCEL GCSE Business (Building a Business) Specification Unit 3

Welcome to the Edexcel GCSE Business Studies series

The Edexcel GCSE Business Studies Series has been produced to build students' business knowledge, understanding and skills, and to help them prepare for their GCSE assessment. The books include lots of engaging features to enthuse students and provide the range of support needed. The student books in the series are:

- **Introduction to Small Business** covering Units 1 and 2 (compulsory for the Full Course) and Unit 6 (for the Short Course)
- **Building a business** (Unit 3)
- **Business Communications** (Unit 4)
- **Introduction to Economic Understanding** (Unit 5)

Building a Business

Unit 3: The specification gives the opportunity to examine how a business develops beyond its start-up phase. This book focuses on the practical methods to build up a business, including marketing, customer service and financial and people management, and also the effects of the outside world. It considers how the interactions between departments and between the business and the outside world affect the success or failure of a growing business.

How to use this book

Each Edexcel GCSE Business Studies unit is divided into topics. These books are written in the same easy-to-follow format, with each topic split into digestible chapters. You will find these features in each chapter:

Topic overview A case study sets the scene for each topic, accompanied by a series of questions. Your teacher might look at this as a starter activity to fi nd out what you already know about the subject. You'll find a summary of the assessment for the topic.

Content and objectives Each chapter starts with a case study to put the content in a context, followed by the objectives for that chapter.

Edexcel key terms are highlighted and defined in each chapter.

Test yourself question practice in every chapter contains objective and multiple choice questions.

Over to you question practice in every chapter. A short case study is followed by questions written in exam paper style.

Annotated sample student's answers and revision support to help students prepare for the exams.

Zone in: How to get into the perfect 'zone' for revision.

Planning zone: Tips and advice on how to effectively plan revision.

Know zone: The facts you need to know, memory tips and exam-style practice at the end of every topic.

Don't panic zone: Last-minute revision tips.

Exam zone: What to expect on the exam paper and the key terms used.

Zone out: What happens after the exams.

edexcel ▪▪▪

Edexcel GCSE
Business:
Building a Business

Student Book

Alain Anderton • Andrew Malcolm
Andrew Ashwin consultant editor

A PEARSON COMPANY

Acknowledgements

Pearson Education Limited
Edinburgh Gate
Harlow
Essex
CM 20 2JE
England
© Pearson Education 2009

15 14 13 12
10 9 8 7 6

ISBN 978-1-84690-497-4

Graphics by Matthew Waring-Collins
Photography Andrew Allen
Edited by Dave Gray
Proof reading by Mike Kidson
Cover photo © Getty Images/Nicholas Eveleigh
Cartoons by Alan Fraser

First edition 2009
Page origination by Caroline Waring-Collins, Waring Collins Ltd, Swordfish Business Park, Burscough, Lancs, L40 8JW
Printed and bound in China (GCC/06)

We are grateful to the following for permission to reproduce copyright material.

JVC for material and product range figures copyright © JVC, reproduced with kind permission; and The Society of Motor Manufacturers and Traders Limited (SMMT) for the figure 'Mini car production 2000-2006' *adapted from Society of Motor Manufacturers and Traders Annual Yearbook*, Motor Industry of Great Britain, 2006, reproduced with permission.

In some instances we have been unable to trace the owners of copyright material and we would appreciate any information that would enable us to do so.

The publisher and authors wish to thank the following for photographs used in the production of this book.

Action Press/Rex Features p 38 (t), Alex Segre/Rex Features p 33, Chris Ratclifee/Rex Features p 71 (b), Corel p 12, David Pearson/ Rex Features p 120, Digital Stock p 29, Digital Vision p 47, 98,Eddie Mullholland/Rex Features p 112, Geoff Robinson/ Rex Features p 14, Ilyas J Dean/ Rex Features p 8, ITV/Rex Features p 80, Jonathan Hordle/Rex Features p 100, Jupiter Unlimited Royalty-Free pp 10, 13, 15, 17, 22, 23, 24, 32, 38 (b), 40, 41, 42, 45, 48, 50, 52, 53, 54, 57, 59, 64, 65, 66, 69, 70, 71 (m, t), 81, 83, 86, 87, 90, 92, 93, 96, 99, 101, 103, 107, 110, 111, 117, 123, 125, 127, Marco Secchi/Rex Features p 114 (t), Martin Lee/Rex Features p 30, Masatoshi Okauchi/Rex Features p 28, Neil White/Rex Features p 114, Photodisc p 90, 91, 97, Ray Tang/Rex Features p 58, Rex Features p 116, Richard Jones/ Rex Features p 115, Sefton Samuels/Rex Features p 104, Shutterstock pp18, 130, 135, Sipa Press/Rex Features p 6, 7, 36, 37, Stockdisc p 98, Stockbyte pp 46, 56, 98.

Thanks

I would like to thank Dave Gray, who as usual has done a superb job publishing and editing the book, Mike Kidson for proof reading and Andrew Ashwin, who has given invaluable feedback. The page origination was sensitively accomplished by Caroline Waring-Collins. Not least I would like to thank my wife for her help with the project.
Alain Anderton 2009

I would like to extend my sincere thanks to Dave Gray for his incredible patience, support and editing skills, Andrew Ashwin for his faith and trust, my past and present students at Beaumont and Churston who never fail to make me realise why work is such fun, and last but certainly not least to Purps and Tom-Tom who are personal lighthouses who guide me safely through any rocky passages. Up the Hatters! Andrew Malcolm 2009

I would like to thank all my colleagues at Biz/ed for supporting me in doing this project, specifically Andy Hargrave, Jill Jones, Stewart Perrygrove and John Yates. There are many people who worked on the development of the qualification on which this book is based. Their faith, support, encouragement and considerable hard work and skill were crucial in getting the qualification live. As a result thanks go to Susan Hoxley, Kelly Padwick, Beverley Anim-Antwi, Derek Richardson and Lizzie Firth. No book would be produced without the dedication of the authors who combine considerable work pressures with the task of producing the book and supporting materials, mostly in their own time. The fact that the production process has been relatively trouble free is largely due to their dedication, commitment, professionalism and support. Thanks go to Alain Anderton, Ian Gunn, Keith Hirst, Andrew Malcolm, Jonathan Shields and Nicola Walker for their contributions and effort. At Pearson, Dave Gray has been a much valued publisher - his skill in handling people, deadlines, vast quantities of text and queries, whilst retaining patience and humour, has been invaluable. It has been a privilege to work with you Dave - thank you. Finally, thanks go to my family, Sue, Alex and Johnny for their patience and love. Andrew Ashwin 2009

ResultsPlus

These features use exam performance data to help you prepare as well as you can.

There are two different types of ResultsPlus features throughout this book:

Watch Out!

Many of the ways of getting customers to trial a product are the same as those for getting them to make repeat purchases. Having a special low price, for example, will encourage buying from new buyers and existing buyers. However, often the same technique needs to be adapted for the two situations. If a business is launching a new product, its advertising might emphasise its new qualities. If it is advertising an existing product, its advertising might emphasise how consistently good it is as a product.

Watch out! These warn you about common mistakes and misconceptions that that students often make.

ResultsPlus
Build Better Answers

Dunbill is a design company. It has developed a new product range of hand drawn birthday cards to suit any theme the customer wants (for example football, cooking or music). The customer can also email pictures to the business that can be reproduced as drawings. Dunbill is now looking to place the range in the market for the first time.

(a) Identify **one** way in which Dunbill might successfully product trial the cards. (1)

(b) Explain how this way might help Dunbill successfully turn the trial into repeat purchases. (3)

Think: How can a product be trialled? How can the potential customer be reached? What makes people buy products on a regular basis? What is the difference between product trial and repeat purchase? What peculiarities might there be in relation to greetings cards as opposed to any other product (application skills)?

■ **Basic** States or mentions one way, such as 'Dunbill could sell the cards cheaply at first', but offers no reasons for buying the product again. (1)

● **Good** 'One way to successfully trial the cards is to advertise online. (1) Dunbill could turn the trials into repeat purchases by

offering them for sale at a reasonable price (1) and continue to develop the product range.' (1)

▲ **Excellent** 'One way for a successful trial is to offer free samples as this allows customers to try the product to see if they like it and it it meets their needs. (1) To turn the trials into repeat purchases Dunbill should offer the cards at a price that represents value for money to the customer. (1) Given that the cards are personalised Dunbill may be able to charge a premium price, but customers must feel that the price they are paying represents value added. (1) If customers do believe they are getting value for money then they are more likely to use Dunbill's service again and so meeting customer needs at a fair price is an important way of generating repeat purchase.' (1)

Build better answers give an opportunity to answer exam-style questions. They include tips for what a basic or incorrect ■, good ● and excellent △ answer will contain.

The KnowZone 'Build better answers' pages at the end of each section include an exam-style question with a student answer, examiner comments and an improved answer so that you can improve your own writing.

Build Better Answers

Gemma Lau is a primary school teacher and is thinking about setting up her own gymnastics training school for children aged 5 – 11 in Bristol. She knows that there are lots of children in that age bracket in her local area and that many like gymnastics. She thinks she knows this because she has several friends that work in local schools. She has drawn up a questionnaire with a mixture of open and closed questions that she wants to place in all primary schools in the area. She wants to ask a representative sample of her potential customers.

(i) What is meant by the term 'sample'? (1)

(ii) Explain why Gemma may have chosen to use a questionnaire to gather information about her target market instead of other methods. (3)

Think: What is a sample? What benefits and drawbacks are there of using questionnaires? What is in this scenario to use in the answer? What alternatives are there?

Student answer	Examiner comment	Build a better answer
(i) It's the people who represent the customers.	■ A weak answer which is helped by the use of the word 'represent'. It is unclear that the student actually understands the theory.	▲ Make sure you use clear phrases such as '...a representative selection of the total number of consumers (population) in the market.' You could use an example such as '100 girls and boys aged 5-11' to back up your answer.
(ii) It is the easiest way to ask her customers.	■ A very simplistic answer that lacks depth and development for full marks	▲ Look at the marks available. This gives an indication of the number of links needed in the answer. It is clearly asking for reasons why Gemma feels a questionnaire is the best thing to use. It is clear that Gemma has access to many potential customers and probably has contacts in many schools due to her job. Many entrepreneurs find it is easiest to use a questionnaire as they can use a home computer or laptop to write it and analyse the data – this makes it cheaper to do. You could also discuss why she has chosen not to use other methods for example 'Gemma may have decided not to use a consumer panel or one-to-one interviews as these are very costly in terms of time.'

Assessment

Information on external examinations is covered in the Examzone at the end of the book. This provides details on assessment for the Unit 3 (see pages 136-137).

Topic 3.1: Marketing

Case study

Starbucks is a multinational chain of coffee outlets. Founded in 1971, it was originally a shop which sold coffee beans in Seattle on the west coast of the USA. In 1982, Howard Schultz joined Starbucks and, after a trip to Milan, Italy, advised that the company should sell coffee and expresso drinks as well as beans. In 1985, Shultz left Starbucks and set up his own coffee bar chain. Two years later, he was able to buy Starbucks from its original owners. There followed an aggressive period of expansion as Starbucks' coffee shops spread through the USA and then worldwide. By 2005, Starbucks had more coffee shops in London than in Manhattan, New York. In 2008, it had 16,120 coffee shops in 44 countries.

Starbucks is one of the world's most famous brands. Its basic product is a cup of coffee either to drink in one of its outlets or to take away. It has a range of coffees for sale from lattes and cappucinos to expressos and mochas. It also sells teas, a range of cold drinks, snacks and coffee mugs. The coffee shop is not just a place to get a cup of coffee. It is a meeting place for friends. It can also be a workplace helped by the fact that most coffee shops have internet access and places to sit.

The company is continually trialling new products. In 2009, for example, it launched an instant coffee brand. Packets of instant coffee would be sold not just in Starbucks coffee shops but also in supermarkets. Starbucks is hoping to break into the multi billion pound market for instant coffee dominated at present by companies like Nestlé with its Nescafé brand. It aims to achieve product differentiation through the high quality of its instant coffee compared to most brands. Certainly, the price of the coffee is far higher than most competitors. It hopes that once customers have trialled the product, they will be so enthusiastic about the quality of the product that they will make repeat purchases.

All new products are launched only after extensive market research. The company has its own marketing research department. It monitors a variety of quantitative data such as sales figures from its coffee shops worldwide. It also uses qualitative research data gathered, for example, from questionnaires. It takes marketing very seriously and examines all elements of the marketing mix when making decisions.

However, Starbucks has arguably stopped growing. In 2008, it announced that it was closing 600 underperforming coffee shops and cutting staff. This could mean that the Starbucks brand has moved out of its growth phase into its maturity phase. New products like instant coffee could then be seen as extension strategies for the brand. In terms of product portfolio analysis and the Boston Matrix, Starbucks has moved from being a star to being a cash cow. Howard Schultz, still with the company, is more optimistic. He has vowed to reinvigorate the brand and ensure its continued growth.

Source: information from en.wikipedia.org; www.timesonline 17.2.2009; www.guardian.co.uk 17.2.2009; www.marketingprofs.com 19.9.2006.

Topic overview

This topic examines the meaning of the term 'marketing', how market research can be collected, interpreted and used to make decisions, how businesses can break down sales into product trials and repeat purchases and how they can encourage repeat purchases, how the product life cycle, product portfolio analysis and the Boston Matrix can be used to analyse a business's products, the importance of branding and differentiation in gaining a competitive advantage and how the marketing mix can be successfully managed.

1. How does Starbucks try to understand the needs of customers?

2. Why are repeat purchases important for Starbucks?

3. Where in the product life cycle is the Starbucks core brand? Justify your answer.

4. How can Starbucks differentiate its products from rival brands?

What will I learn?

Marketing What is the meaning of the term 'marketing'?

Market research How is quantitative and qualitative research data collected? How can it be interpreted? How can research data be used to help decide on issues such as the appropriate marketing mix?

Product trial and repeat purchase What is the difference in 'sales' between product trial and repeat purchase? How can repeat purchase be maximised through customer loyalty?

Product life cycle What are the four phases of the product life cycle? What is meant by extension strategies? How does cash flow change during the product life cycle? What is product portfolio analysis in general and the Boston Matrix in particular? How are the product life cycle and the Boston Matrix linked?

Branding and differentiation Why are brands important to successful product trial and repeat purchases? Why is there a need to differentiate a product or service from others, given the level of competition in a market?

Building a successful marketing mix Why is it important to manage a brand? How can a brand be managed through the four variables of the marketing mix: product, price, promotion and place?

How will I be assessed?

This is assessed through Unit 3, a written examination lasting 1 hour 30 minutes.

The paper is divided into three sections.

Section A is a mix of mainly multiple choice questions and short answer questions with one or more questions requiring an extended answer.

Sections B and C consist of short and long answer questions based on two scenarios, one for each section, given in the paper.

Marketing

8

Nestlé is one of the world's leading food companies. In recent years, in response to growing consumer concerns about diet and food safety, it has focused on becoming a nutrition, health and wellness company. This is the idea of supporting people to lead healthier lives. Nestlé owns a wide range of brands including Shredded Wheat, Winalot, Nescafé and KitKat. In Europe, its Maggi brand is partly aimed at the 'food service sector' - chefs and the catering trade.

Objectives

- Understand the meaning of the term 'marketing'.
- Understand how to collect and interpret quantitative and qualitative research data to help decide on issues such as the appropriate marketing mix.

edexcel ⠿ key terms

Marketing – the management process that is responsible for anticipating, identifying and satisfying customer needs profitably.

Market research – the process of gaining information about customers, competitors and market trends through collecting primary and secondary data.

Primary data – information that has been gathered for a specific purpose through direct investigation such as observation, surveys and experiments.

Secondary data – information that already exists such as accounts and sales records, government statistics, newspaper and internet articles and reports from advertising agencies.

Marketing

How does Nestlé sell its Maggi products to chefs and the catering trade? First it has to develop products that they want to buy. Nestlé has to understand the needs of chefs and the catering trade and provide something that meets customer needs. Then it has to sell it to chefs and the catering trade. These customers will want to buy the products at an affordable price. Nestlé must be able to sell them at a price which gives it a profit. This whole process is called **marketing**. Marketing is the management process that is responsible for anticipating, identifying and satisfying consumer wants and needs and making a profit in doing so. This means developing products that not only meet consumer needs but which can be sold at a price consumers are willing to pay and which more than covers the cost of production.

The need for market research

To find out what customers want, companies like Nestlé engage in **market research**. Researching the market helps to reduce the risk of failure. If Nestlé does not understand the needs of its customers, it risks developing products that will not sell. Market research helps it to understand current customer needs. Market research can also help Nestlé identify when those needs are changing and so anticipate future needs. It can then develop products that satisfy those needs. When a new product is launched, it then has a greater chance of being successful. Nestlé faced a problem with its Maggi products aimed at the food service sector. Sales were falling. Market research might give some answers as to why sales were falling and what could be done about it.

Stages of market research

Market research has three main stages.

Designing the research Market research should be planned and designed. What is the research aiming to achieve? For example, Nestlé is continually engaging in market research in the hope of launching successful new products. In the case of Maggi, Nestlé wanted to understand why sales were falling so that they could redesign the Maggi range of products. How can it best conduct the research and gather information? Should **primary data** or **secondary data** be gathered? If it decided to use primary research, would it be best to use a survey or the technique of observation? Did it want quantitative or qualitative information?

Undertaking the research Once the market research has been designed, it can be carried out. Nestlé decided it wanted to gather primarily qualitative data. So it decided to ask the views of chefs and other customers who bought Maggi products. The research focussed on what customers thought about existing products. Researchers spoke face-to-face with chefs and held open discussions.

Analysing the information Once market research has been conducted, researchers can then analyse the information gathered. This means interpreting the information that has been collected. For Nestlé, were chefs and other customers saying the same thing? Or did every customer make completely different comments? Was it possible to detect trends in the answers? Did the market research give clear answers as to what Nestlé should do its Maggi range to make it more successful? Some of the data that came out of the market research was **quantitative data**. This is data that can be interpreted in a numerical way. For example, sales figures for different Maggi products is quantitative data. However, most of the data that came out of the market research was **qualitative data**. This is information about opinions, judgements and attitudes. So when existing Maggi customers said that products were 'uninteresting' and 'old fashioned', this is an example of qualitative data.

Surveys

Often, a very important part of market research is conducting a **survey**. A survey usually involves asking questions of **respondents** - people or organisations who reply to the questions asked. Nestlé, for instance, used a survey to find out what chefs and consumers thought about Maggi. The survey showed that the market was split into a number of segments. The chefs interviewed fitted into four main **market segments**. These are shown in Figure 1.

ResultsPlus
Watch Out!

Market research is useful to businesses of all sizes because it helps them to understand their markets better. However, market research can also be a barrier to understanding the market. There are plenty of examples where market research has led to new products being developed which have failed. Some of the most innovative and successful products launched onto the market, like the Sony Walkman and the Dyson vacuum cleaner, had little or no support from market research. However, their inventors thought there was a need for the product. So do not automatically assume that market research is essential for all businesses.

Figure 1 – The market segments identified in the survey carried out by Nestlé

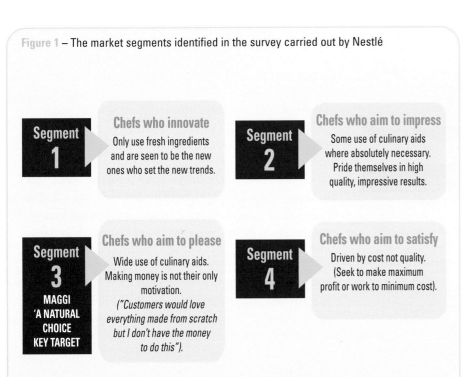

edexcel key terms

Quantitative data – data that can be expressed as numbers and can be statistically analysed.

Qualitative data – data about opinions, judgments and attitudes.

Survey – research involving asking questions of people or organisations.

Respondents – those who provide data for a survey usually by answering questions.

Market segment – part of a market that contains a group of buyers with similar buying habits.

Closed questions have definite answer.

There are different ways of conducting surveys. A postal survey, where **questionnaires** are sent through the post, or newspaper surveys, where readers are invited to fill in and return a questionnaire in a newspaper, are cheap. Telephone

edexcel ::: key terms

Sample – a small group out of the total population which is selected to take part in a survey.

Questionnaires – a list of questions to be answered by respondents, designed to give information about consumers' tastes.

Watch Out!

Market research is often costly and takes time. Sometimes, businesses are better off using their gut instincts about what is happening in a market. It is much cheaper and cuts down the time it takes to make decisions.

Watch Out!

Market research can easily give the wrong answers to what customers need and want. For example, market researchers can ask the wrong questions and they may not always be able to rely on the honesty of the answers given. They may ask the wrong people. For example, Sony concentrated its market research for its new PlayStation 3 games console on existing games players. However, the PlayStation has been outsold by the Nintendo Wii. The Nintendo Wii proved very popular with people who weren't traditional games players. Sony missed a large potential market segment for its product.

Surveys often use questionnaires and ask only a sample of people.

surveys, personal interviews and consumers' panels are more expensive because an interviewer has to be employed to interview customers. However, only a fraction of customers sent a postal survey will respond. A much larger proportion of those approached will take part in telephone and personal interviews. The interviewer can also help the respondents understand what questions mean and how they should be answered.

If the interview is in a person's home, products, packaging, etc. can also be shown so that reactions can be recorded. A **consumer panel**, where a group of people meet together, allows researchers to see how people react in a group situation to a product or idea. In the case of Maggi, the chefs and consumers were involved in open discussions about the product.

Surveys can only be useful for market research purposes if the questions asked are appropriate. For instance, sometimes it is important to ask closed questions. These are questions which have a definite answer. An example would be: 'How many cartons of Maggi did you buy last week?' Other times, the market researcher might want to find out about opinions and allow the respondent to develop an answer. It is best then to ask open questions, which have many possible answers. For instance, 'What do you like about the packaging of Maggi?' is an open question.

Sampling

A survey cannot ask every customer for their opinion. Only a fraction or **sample** of customers can be surveyed. To be useful, the sample chosen must be representative of all consumers (the population).

In a random sample, every potential respondent has an equal chance of being chosen. Random numbers can be used to do this or it can be done by 'picking people out of a hat'. It is often quite difficult to construct a truly random sample. So a cheaper and quicker method is to use a systematic sample. This is where, say, every 100th or 1,000th person on a list like a telephone directory or the electoral register is chosen. A systematic sample is not truly random though and therefore the results may be less reliable.

In a quota sample, the sample is broken down (or stratified). For example, in some research carried out by Cadbury, one of Nestle's rivals, before the launch of Fuse, the following strategy may have been used. Cadbury wanted to target 16-24 year olds in particular and 16-34 year olds more generally with its Fuse bar. It might know that 2 out of ten people who bought chocolate bars were aged 0-15, 7 out of ten were aged 16-34 and the rest were over 34 years old. So out of a sample of 100, Cadbury would ask 70 people (7 out of 10) aged 16-34 to complete a survey.

One problem with a quota sample is that any people who fit the description can be asked to complete the survey. So Cadbury wanting to find seventy people aged 16-34 to complete a survey, could ask the first seventy 16-34 year olds who came out of a McDonald's in London. This may not be very representative of all 16-34 year olds nationally.

A stratified random sample may get round this problem. It is a quota sample where all the respondents, the people being interviewed, must be chosen at random. For the sample to be random, Cadbury would have to find some way of selecting 70 people aged 16-34 through pure chance.

Decisions

The purpose of market research is to help a business come to a decision. Nestlé knew that sales of Maggi were falling. Were there problems with the marketing mix of Maggi? Did the problem lie with the price, the product, the product's promotion or place, the channels through which the product was sold? Was it a combination of factors? These questions could be answered by market research.

Based on the results of this market research, Nestlé could then make decisions about how best to act. Would it be best to leave the range unchanged? Should the Maggi range of products be adapted to make it meet consumer needs more closely? Had the products outlived their usefulness and should Nestlé consider withdrawing them altogether?

Market research showed that the problem was with the product itself. It found that the buyers of the products, chefs, thought the product was now uninteresting and old fashioned due to its dehydrated format and flavour. The market research also allowed Nestlé to group chefs into four groups or segments. One of these groups, segment 3, was made up of chefs who were most likely to buy the Maggi range. Nestlé therefore identified this segment as the target market for a 'new and improved' Maggi range. These chefs were described as 'chefs who aim to please'. They wanted to use more natural ingredients and products in their cooking. These chefs wanted to create food that was as fresh tasting as possible because that was what their customers wanted. However, these chefs needed to use products such as those in the Maggi range because they did not have the time or other resources to create everything from scratch.

So Nestlé launched the Maggi 'A Natural Choice' range. It was lower in salt and made using sunflower oil. In addition, where possible, the range had no added monosodium glutamate, was gluten free and contained no artificial colours or flavours. These were some of the main issues with the product that their research told them customers wanted addressing. Market research helped Nestlé to reverse a worrying sales trend of the Maggi products.

Source: information from ww.thetimes100.co.uk.

ResultsPlus
Watch Out!

Many students equate marketing with advertising. Advertising may be one means of making consumers aware of a product but the crucial thing to remember about marketing is that it is all about consumer needs and whether those needs can be satisfied profitably.

Test yourself

1. Quantitative data is best defined as data which

   A gives information about opinions, judgements and attitudes

   B can be presented in number form and can be statistically analysed

   C tells businesses about customer needs

   D comes only from primary research

   Select one answer.

2. Which one of the following would most likely be considered an example of marketing a product?

   A Hiring a new worker

   B Repairing a machine

   C Surveying customers

   D Sending an invoice to a customer

   Select one answer.

3. Which one of the following would be an example of market research?

   A Launching a new advertising campaign for a product

   B Cutting the price of a product

   C Persuading a large supermarket chain to sell a product

   D Surveying customers about the qualities of a product

Over to you

Malvern Safari Park carried out some research to find out why visitor numbers were falling. Visitors to the park had fallen from 56,400 in 2001 to 49,400 in 2006. A survey was carried out using telephone interviews. 1,000 telephone numbers were chosen at random from the local telephone directory. Table 1 shows answers to five key questions from the survey and Table 2 shows a selection of comments made by the people interviewed.

1. Identify the aim of the market research carried out by Malvern Safari Park. (1)
2. Explain whether the results of the research carried out by Malvern Safari Park will give quantitative or qualitative data. (3)
3. Using examples from the case study, explain the difference between open questions and closed questions in a survey. (6)
4. Using the data for Malvern Safari Park, assess the main reasons why the number of visitors has fallen in recent years. (8)

Table 2 – Comments made by some of the people surveyed

Table 1 – Answers to five questions from the survey

1. Have you ever been to Malvern Safari Park?
   YES 18% NO 82%
2. Have you ever been to any other safari park?
   YES 21% NO 79%
3. Would you visit Malvern Safari Park if it was cheaper?
   YES 44% NO 56%
4. Have you heard the radio advert for the park?
   YES 7% NO 93%
5. Have you seen the newspaper advert for the park?
   YES 29% NO 71%

Questions

What has been the main reason why you have not visited the Park in the last six months?

What do you think that the Park could do that would persuade you to visit?

Some answers

'There's no public transport to the park since the bus service was withdrawn'

'It's too expensive - it would cost me and my family over £80 to go for the day'

'There aren't any tigers in the park - that's what I would really like to see because they are so rare'

'I didn't even know there was a safari park at Malvern'

'Lower the prices - at the moment it is too expensive'

ResultsPlus
Build Better Answers

Tülay Norton has been a fashion designer for many well-known companies, designing clothing ranges for the young and trendy market. She now has her own clothing business and recently noticed the trend for 80s style legwarmers was on the rise. She thought about producing her own range of legwarmers and wants to carry out some market research to ask about the types of colours, price, advertising and buying habits consumers would have.

(a) Identify **one** disadvantage to Tülay of undertaking market research. (1)

(b) Explain how this disadvantage might affect Tülay's company. (3)

Think: What are the disadvantages to doing market research? Can Tülay afford it? Does she have the time? What useful information will come out of the research? Can she rely on the information she collects? Will it help the business make any decisions?

■ **Basic** States or mentions one disadvantage, such as '... it costs money to do', but offers no explanation. (1)

● **Good** 'One disadvantage is that market research can be expensive. (1) Tülay's business may only be a small company and may not have the funds to carry out extensive and meaningful research. (1) As a result the information she collects may only be of limited value and not be representative of the market as a whole.' (1)

▲ **Excellent** 'One disadvantage to market research is that the data collected may not be wholly accurate. (1) Producing reliable data depends on asking the right questions to the right people. (1) Unless Tülay is able to get a specialist company in to do the work for her (which will be expensive) she may get inaccurate information. (1) This might mean that if she bases decisions on inaccurate data the business may not meet customer needs and therefore might not be as successful as she hoped.' (1)

2 Product trial and repeat purchase

Case Study

In 2008, Cadbury was the world's second largest manufacturer of confectionery. In the UK, it owned the number one chocolate brand, Cadbury Dairy Milk. With retail sales of over £370 million per year, Cadbury Dairy Milk outsells every other confectionery brand. Cadbury Dairy Milk is sold in a number of different variants including Cadbury Dairy Milk itself and Cadbury Dairy Milk Fruit and Nut. In 2008, Cadbury launched two new variants of Cadbury Dairy Milk: firstly apricot crumble crunch and secondly cranberry and granola. Cadbury wanted customers to try out the new products and then become loyal customers of the two new brands.

Objectives

- Understand the concept of breaking down sales into product trial and repeat purchase.
- Understand how to maximise repeat purchase through customer loyalty.

edexcel ::: key terms

Product trial – when consumers buy a good for the first time and assess whether or not they want to buy it again.

Public relations – promotion of a positive image about a product or business through giving information about the product to the general public, other businesses or to the press.

Viral marketing – getting individuals to spread a message about a product through their social networks like Facebook or their group of friends.

Product trial

Product trial is the way in which a business persuades customers to try out a new product or service to help to raise awareness of its existence and gain feedback on its possible success. Product trial is also designed to help build loyalty to the product and thus establish repeat purchase.

If the two new variants of Cadbury Dairy Milk are to be successful, Cadbury first has to get customers to try them out. There is a large number of different ways in which Cadbury potentially could get customers to **trial** the apricot crumble crunch and cranberry and granola versions of Cadbury Dairy Milk.

Advertising Customers are more likely to trial a product if they know about it. Advertising is one way in which customers can be informed about the product. Cadbury spent approximately £2 million on a media campaign to launch the two products. The media is television, radio, cinemas, newspapers and magazines. Television advertisements or advertisements in magazines are examples of media advertising. Outside of the media, advertising can also be placed on large bill boards by the roadside.

Free publicity Free publicity or PR (**public relations**) was part of the media campaign by Cadbury. Businesses launching a product want journalists and producers in magazines, newspapers, the television and on the Internet to write about their new product. This gives the product free publicity. So journalists and producers may be invited to a launch party for the product. They may be sent articles and information which the business has written itself. Journalists can then adapt the material to use in their own publications. On the Internet, one way of getting publicity is to get people recommending a product to a friend. This is called **viral marketing** because the message is spread like a virus from one individual to another. Internet sites like MySpace, Facebook, Twitter or YouTube can be targeted in this way.

Free samples Another common way for businesses to launch a product is to give free samples. Cadbury, for example, could have chosen to give free samples to customers to try out. A special stand in a supermarket is sometimes used. For some products, such as perfume or make-up, free samples may be given in magazines.

User testing With some products, it is not possible to give out samples. However, potential customers can be offered a test trial of a product. For example, cars can be taken for a test drive by potential buyers. Games consoles can be tried out in shops or roadshows.

Low trial prices Businesses may choose to offer new products at a lower price. This strategy is known as **penetration pricing**. There is a variety of ways of doing this. A product might have a low price for the first month after launch, or there may be special offers such as two for the price of one on the new product. Coupons given away free in magazines and newspapers or over the Internet may give money off or provide a free sample.

Targeting trade buyers Cadbury does not sell Cadbury Dairy Milk directly to consumers. It sells the product to **trade buyers** such as supermarket chains and **wholesalers**. Wholesalers are businesses that buy in bulk from manufacturers and then sell in smaller quantities to **retailers** or shops like the local corner shop. Cadbury can market a new product like apricot flavoured crumble crunch Cadbury Dairy Milk to trade buyers in the same way that it sells to consumers. For example, it promoted the product by sending out advertising literature to supermarkets and wholesalers. Its sales force visited its main customers to show them the new product. New products can also be offered at low introductory prices to trade buyers. In some cases, manufacturers have to pay the large supermarket chains to stock their products. Paying a large supermarket may be the only way that a manufacturer like Cadbury can get the supermarket to give the product shelf space.

Giving out free samples is a method of trialling products.

Repeat purchase

Getting customers to buy new products can be difficult and expensive. This is especially true when customers have strong brand loyalty to existing products in the market. Retaining existing customers is, therefore, something on which many firms focus. The experience of many businesses is that the cost of retaining existing customers is far less than that of attracting new ones.

Successfully launching a new product is therefore not enough. Businesses like Cadbury have to build **customer loyalty**. They need customers to keep coming back and making another purchase. Only if there is **repeat purchase** will the product be a long-term success. There a number of ways in which businesses like Cadbury can create customer loyalty and loyalty for the Cadbury Dairy Milk brand.

Promotion Cadbury continues to spend money on promoting Cadbury Dairy Milk. Although the product was first launched over 100 years ago, Cadbury need to spend money on advertising and other forms of promotion such as point of sale displays, public relations, publicity and free samples, if it is to keep customers interested in the product. Advertising helps keep the brand image of the product in the minds of consumers. It reminds them about the product and makes them want to buy more. However, there are many other types of promotion apart from advertising. Some businesses, for example, use competitions and prizes. If you buy the product, you have a chance to win something.

Price Cadbury can increase sales by changing the price of its products. Having special offers is one way of reducing price for a short period. For example, a business may have a 'two for the price of one' offer or a '10p off' offer. Some products may use a relatively high price as a way of retaining customer loyalty especially if the business wants to convey a sense of exclusivity or prestige. Retaining the custom of high income earners can be very important to some

edexcel ::: key terms

Penetration pricing – setting an initial low price for a new product so that it is attractive to customers. The price is likely to be raised later as the product gains market share.

Trade buyers – buyers of goods which then sell those goods on to consumers or other buyers; they include supermarket chains and wholesalers.

Wholesalers – businesses which buy in bulk from a manufacturer or other supplier and then sell the stock on in smaller quantities to retailers.

Retailers – businesses which specialise in selling goods in small quantities to the consumer.

Customer loyalty – the willingness of buyers to make repeated purchases of a product or from a business.

Repeat purchase – when a customer buyers a product more than once.

businesses, for example, golf clubs, some types of hotels and restaurants.

Product Over time, businesses like Cadbury can retain customer loyalty by updating their products. For manufacturers of electronic goods like televisions and mobile phones, this means bringing out new products incorporating the latest technology. Sony or Nokia, for example, would hope that if an individual is contemplating trading in their old TV or mobile phone for a new one they will choose another Sony or Nokia product. For Cadbury, it means bringing out new variants on existing products. So the new apricot crumble crunch Cadbury Dairy Milk is a way of keeping existing customers of Cadbury Dairy Milk excited about the product.

Place Businesses must make sure that their products are available to customers when and where they want to buy them. For the two new varieties of Cadbury Dairy Milk, this means being available in supermarkets, newsagents, petrol stations and other local shops. Getting their products stocked in these places is essential if they are to sell well. So targeting trade buyers is not important just for the launch of a new product. Constantly promoting the product to trade buyers is vital to the long-term success of Cadbury Dairy Milk.

Source: information from http://www.foodnavigator.com
http://www.cadbury.com

Watch Out!

Remember that promotion is more than just advertising.

Watch Out!

Many of the ways of getting customers to trial a product are the same as those for getting them to make repeat purchases. Having a special low price, for example, will encourage buying from new buyers and existing buyers. However, often the same technique needs to be adapted for the two situations. If a business is launching a new product, its advertising might emphasise its new qualities. If it is advertising an existing product, its advertising might emphasise how consistently good it is as a product.

Over to you

How do you get your customers to keep coming back to shop with you? How do you launch a new product which will appeal to customers? Supermarket chain Tesco and its suppliers have found the answer in the data generated by the Tesco Clubcard.

Launched nationally in 1995, the card seems simple enough. It rewards customers with 1 point for every £1 they spend at Tesco. Points can then be exchanged for money off groceries at the till. Or the points can be used to get money off a range of products from a wide range of businesses. Last year, Tesco gave £250 million back to customers through Clubcard promotions. Customers are happy because their loyalty for shopping at Tesco is rewarded.

However, the Tesco Clubcard is far more sophisticated than this. Every time a Clubcard is used at a till, it sends back to a computer the record of exactly what was bought. The computer system knows whether you bought a pizza last year or last month. It knows how many pizzas you bought and at what price. It knows the brand of pizza you bought and at what store it was purchased. Pooling together billions of individual pieces of information, it can build a profile of who you are as a consumer. It also can understand the customers of any its individual stores. This helps Tesco to know what to put on the shelves of each store to encourage customers to buy. Clubcard data also allows individual customers to be targeted with offers. Every three months, it sends out a mailing to each Clubcard customer telling them how many points they have earned. More importantly, customers are given money off vouchers as a reward for their customer loyalty but also to encourage them to spend on items they don't normally buy at Tesco. The days after the mailings bring a large increase in the number of customers visiting Tesco and a big increase in sales.

The information in the Clubcard database is available to food manufacturers if they pay a fee. One such supplier is Dairy Crest, the dairy products firm. It used Clubcard data to work out that shoppers who buy mild cheddar cheese don't buy it simply because it is cheaper than mature cheddar cheese. They buy it because they like it. Families which include young children are more likely to buy mild cheddar cheese. However, less than eight per cent of mild cheddar cheese was sold under a brand name. Dairy Crest used the data to launch its own branded mild cheddar cheese, Cathedral City Mild. It was a success, particular with families with young children.

Source: information from ft.com 11.11.2006; www.loyalty.vg.

1. (a) State **three** ways in which Tesco encourages customers to come back to shop at its stores rather than at a rival supermarket chain. (3)
   (b) Explain how each of these **three** ways encourages repeat purchases. (9)

2. Explain what is meant by 'product trial' by consumers, using Cathedral City Mild as an example. (3)

3. In your opinion, what might have been the **two best ways** for Dairy Crest to encourage customers to trial Cathedral City Mild? Justify your answer. (8)

Test yourself

1. A publishing company is about to launch a new magazine aimed at female readers aged 14-20. Which **two** of the following would be direct ways in which the company could try to get potential readers to buy the first issue of the magazine? Select two answers.

   A   Keep production costs low
   B   Offer a free lipstick with the issue
   C   Take on extra staff
   D   Sell the first issue at half price
   E   Cut advertising on other magazines produced by the company

2. A car manufacturing company is worried that there is little customer loyalty amongst car buyers for its vehicles. The lack of customer loyalty is most likely to mean that:

   A   customers are buying a different make of car when they sell their existing car
   B   car sales for the company are increasing
   C   the cars the company sells are seen as being good value
   D   it would be more profitable for the company to make large cuts in the price of its cars

   Select one answer.

3. A company making frozen pizzas depends for its success on repeat purchases. Customers are most likely to make repeat purchases because:

   A   it determines the amount of profit the company makes
   B   it increases sales of pizzas
   C   the company spends heavily on advertising
   D   in the pizza market, customers have little brand loyalty

   Select one answer.

 Results Plus
Build Better Answers

Dunbill is a design company. It has developed a new product range of hand drawn birthday cards to suit any theme the customer wants (for example football, cooking or music). The customer can also email pictures to the business that can be reproduced as drawings. Dunbill is now looking to place the range in the market for the first time.

(a) Identify **one** way in which Dunbill might successfully product trial the cards. (1)

(b) Explain how this way might help Dunbill successfully turn the trial into repeat purchases. (3)

Think: How can a product be trialled? How can the potential customer be reached? What makes people buy products on a regular basis? What is the difference between product trial and repeat purchase? What peculiarities might there be in relation to greetings cards as opposed to any other product (application skills)?

■ **Basic** States or mentions one way, such as 'Dunbill could sell the cards cheaply at first', but offers no reasons for buying the product again. (1)

● **Good** 'One way to successfully trial the cards is to advertise online. (1) Dunbill could turn the trials into repeat purchases by

offering them for sale at a reasonable price (1) and continue to develop the product range.' (1)

▲ **Excellent** 'One way for a successful trial is to offer free samples as this allows customers to try the product to see if they like it and if it meets their needs. (1) To turn the trials into repeat purchases Dunbill should offer the cards at a price that represents value for money to the customer. (1) Given that the cards are personalised Dunbill may be able to charge a premium price, but customers must feel that the price they are paying represents value added. (1) If customers do believe they are getting value for money then they are more likely to use Dunbill's service again and so meeting customer needs at a fair price is an important way of generating repeat purchase.' (1)

3 Product life cycle

Case Study

The original Mini came onto the market in 1959. It caused a revolution in car design. By the 1970s and 1980s sales had fallen. BMW bought Rover, the company which manufactured the Mini, in 1994. BMW saw that the Mini was a great brand and set about designing a completely new Mini. Launched in 2001, the BMW Mini has been an outstanding success. In 2007, a new version of the BMW Mini was launched.

Objectives

- Understand the four phases of the product life cycle.
- Appreciate what is meant by an extension strategy.
- Understand the link between cash flow and the product life cycle.
- Understand product portfolio analysis using the Boston Matrix.

 **key terms**

Product life cycle – the stages through which a product passes from its development to being withdrawn from sale; the phases are research and development, launching the product, growth, maturity, saturation and decline.

Research and development – the process of scientific and technological research and then development of the findings of that research before a product is launched.

The product life cycle

The **product life cycle** shows the stages through which, it is argued, a product passes over time. A textbook product life cycle is illustrated in Figure 1. The product life cycle of the original Mini, shown in Figure 2, is similar to this.

The development stage

Products start life at the **development stage**. The Mini, for instance, first started life in 1956 when Sir Leonard Lord, chairman of British Motor Cars (BMC), ordered his designers to come up with a new small car. The **research and development** of the car took three years for the designer, Sir Alec Issigonis, and his team. This included the time needed to adapt two car plants to manufacture the Mini. Nowadays, any development of a car would also be heavily influenced by market research.

Launching the product

The product is then ready to be launched. Most products coming on the market will be backed up by some advertising and other forms of promotion. The Mini came onto the market in August 1959. It was advertised in newspapers and specialist car magazines. BMC's car dealer networks were given point of sale promotional material. Models were in the car showrooms so that customers could see the car. The aim was to get customers to trial the product.

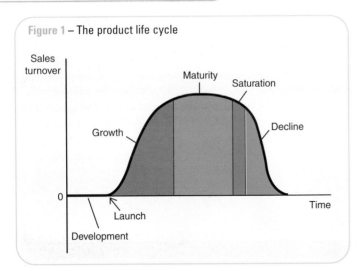

Figure 1 – The product life cycle

Figure 2 – The product life cycle of the original Mini

The growth phase

In the **growth** phase of the cycle, sales and profits will be rising. In the first full year of production, in 1960, 116,677 Minis were produced. In 1961, this increased to 157,059. More and more customers were test driving the Mini, to see whether or not they wanted to buy.

Product maturity

In the **maturity** stage, the product reaches a peak in terms of sales. Research and development costs are likely to have been paid off. The product is profitable enough to be financing the development of new products. Many buyers are now **repeat customers**, and there is **customer loyalty** for the product. For the Mini, the maturity stage probably lasted for most of the 1960s and the early part of the 1970s.

Manufacturers are likely to try to extend the maturity stage of the product for as long as possible. Producing a completely new product would involve all the start up costs again. They usually do this through developing extension strategies. This involves slightly changing the product to give it fresh appeal to its target market. Extension strategies can also help a product appeal to a new **segment** of the market.

The Mini constantly changed during its life. For instance, in 1961, a version called the Mini Cooper was launched with a more powerful engine. In 1964, a jeep-type version called the Mini Moke was first put on sale. 1967 saw a facelift of the Mini range with the new cars being called Mark II Minis. New variants of the Mini were launched in most years of its existence.

Saturation and decline

Towards the end of the maturity phase, the market becomes **saturated**. Competitors bring out products which take sales away. This means that consumers have plenty of choices of products and it becomes difficult to grow sales. For the Mini, saturation occurred in the 1970s when other car manufactures began to bring out their own small cars. These cars tended to have the advantage of being small but had more features than the Mini and took sales away from the Mini.

Eventually, a product is likely to go into decline and there are big falls in sales.

The new BMW Mini

In 1994, the German luxury car manufacturer, BMW, bought the Mini car brand. BMW decided to produce a completely new Mini, which was launched in 2001. Figure 3 shows that the car has been a great success. In 2007, BMW launched a new version of this car. This is an example of an extension strategy for the car.

Cash flow and the product life cycle

Cash flow concerns the movements of money into and out of a business. Money comes into a business, for example, when sales are made. It leaves the business when suppliers or workers are paid. Cash flow for a product changes over the product life cycle.

- During the development phase, net cash flow, the difference between money coming in and going out, is negative. Money has to be paid out to workers and for materials but no money is coming into the business from sales.
- During the launch phase, net cash flow is also likely to be negative. The costs of launch, such as the cost of promotion, are likely to outweigh money coming in from sales.
- During the growth phase, net cash flow is likely to be small. As sales grow and cash inflows increase, there are also extra costs of production. For the Mini, for

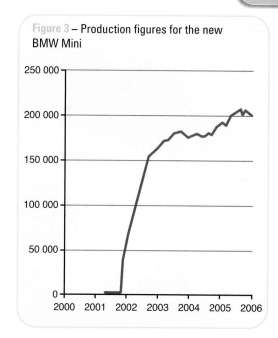

Figure 3 – Production figures for the new BMW Mini

 **key terms**

Extension strategy – method used to increase the life of a product and prevent it falling into decline.

**ResultsPlus
Watch Out!**

Every product has its own unique life cycle. Fashion items, for example, have a very short life cycle; some products never get much beyond the launch stage because it becomes obvious that they are commercial failures. A few products, like Bisto gravy (launched in 1908), Cadbury Dairy Milk (1905) and Marmite (1902), are still selling after 100 years. Many new branded products are commercial failures and are withdrawn from sale fairly quickly after launch. Only a minority of new branded products are successful and are worth the investment of an extension strategy.

Figure 4 – Managing the product portfolio by launching new products on a regular basis

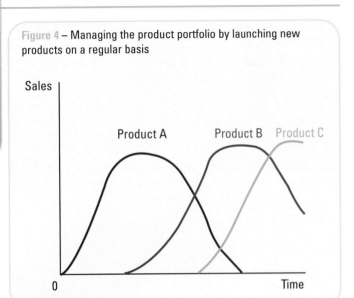

Figure 5 – The Boston Matrix

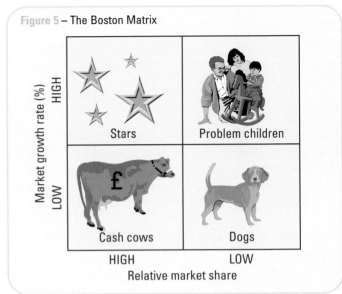

example, BMW had to invest heavily in its Oxford plant to increase production. Promotion costs may also be high during the growth phase.

- During the maturity phase, saturation and decline, net cash flow is likely to be positive. Start up and development costs have been paid. The value of sales exceeds costs of production and so net cash flow is positive. When extension strategies are planned and launched, net cash flow is likely to dip because extension strategies cost cash to put into practice.

Product portfolio analysis

Most businesses sell a **range of products**. BMW, for example, makes a number of different cars, of which the Mini is just one. This range of products represents the **product mix** or **product portfolio** of the business.

Businesses need to manage their product portfolios. To keep up overall sales, new products are launched on a regular basis. As existing products go into decline, new products are launched and grow. The new products make up for the declining sales of older products. Figure 4 shows how a business can maintain sales by launching new products on a regular basis.

A business like BMW has to make decisions about its product portfolio. The decisions are based on analysis of the

product portfolio. Which products are doing well? Which are likely to do better in the future? Should a product be withdrawn from the market? Will increased advertising improve sales? **Product portfolio analysis** helps provide answers to these questions.

The Boston Matrix

There are many ways of doing product portfolio analysis. However, one way is to use a technique called the **Boston Matrix**, a method of analysing and planning developed by the Boston Consultancy Group. The Boston Matrix is shown in Figure 5.

The Boston matrix can be closely linked to the product life-cycle. In the Boston Matrix, a product is described in two ways.

- How fast is the whole market for the product growing? The whole market for the BMW Mini could be seen as the market for luxury cars. So BMW has to ask itself: 'How fast is the luxury car market growing?' In the Boston Matrix, a product can be put into one of two categories: high market growth and low market growth. High market growth is where the percentage increase in sales year on year is high and possibly rising . Low market growth means that sales are only rising by a relatively small percentage. In the Boston Matrix, the low market growth also includes markets where sales are falling and so less is being bought over time.
- How strong is the product within its market? What market share does it have? A product may have a relatively high market share or it may have a relatively low market share. What is the market share of the BMW Mini in the luxury car market?

Using these two descriptions, a product like the BMW Mini can be placed in one of four categories shown in Figure 5. Each of these categories is given a name – stars, cash cows, problem children and dogs – to show their value to the business.

edexcel ⠿ key terms

Product portfolio or product mix – the combination or range of products that a business sells.

Product portfolio analysis – investigation of the combination of products sold by a business.

Boston Matrix – a model which analyses a product portfolio according to the growth rate of the whole market and the relative market of a product within that market; a product is placed in one of four categories - star, cash cow, problem child or dog.

Stars A star is a product whose market is growing fast and it has a relatively high market share. Stars are very successful products. Sales and profits will be growing. On the other hand, the business will be spending money on new equipment and machinery to make the extra output. It may also be spending heavily on promotions such as advertising to encourage the growth in sales. Stars are often in the growth phase of their product life cycle. They will be big profit earners in the future. Current net cash flow, however, is likely to be small. Money coming from growing sales is matched by costs of production and the cost of extra investment.

Cash cows A cash cow is a product with a relatively strong market share. The product is often in the maturity phase of its product life cycle. However, the market itself has relatively low growth or indeed sales may be in decline. This means that sales of the product are unlikely to grow much in the future. Cash cows are products which give good levels of profit. Since they have a high market share, they tend to be popular products within their markets. Customer loyalty to the product is high and customers make repeat purchases. However, because their sales are not growing very quickly, if at all, there is little need for new investment in production facilities. Cash cows therefore are products which have strong positive net cash flows for the business. This positive cash flow can be used to invest in developing new products to update the product portfolio. Extension strategies for the product can help keep sales and profits high.

Problem children A problem child is a product with relatively low market share in a fast growing market. It is a problem for the business because it is unclear what should be done with the product. It is a product which may not have been successful within its own market because it has a relatively low market share. However, it may have some promise but for some reason may not have taken off just yet. Its net cash flow is likely to be small. Should the business get rid of the product? Or should it invest more in the product in the hope that it can be turned into a star? For example, it could spend money on bring out a new version of the product. Or it could spend heavily on advertising and other promotion in the hope of raising sales.

Dogs A dog is a product with relatively low market share in a low growth market. Not only is the product unsuccessful in its market, but the prospects for the whole market are poor. There is usually little point in investing in this product. If it is profitable, and it generates some positive net cash flow, it could stay on sale. If it is unprofitable and net cash flow is negative, the product should be withdrawn from sale.

The BMW Mini is probably a star. Between its launch in 2001 and 2008, the luxury car market was growing strongly. There are many different cars for sale in the luxury car market, but the Mini quickly became a best seller within the market. So it had relatively high market share. This helps to explain why BMW invested heavily in extra production facilities at the car plant in Oxford where the car is made.

Source: information from Rover Group Ltd, Society of Motor Manufacturers.

Test yourself

1. In which phase of the product life cycle is a business most likely to experience a negative cash flow? Select one answer.

   A *Development phase*
   B *Growth phase*
   C *Maturity phase*
   D *Decline phase*

2. A company makes a brand of toothpaste. Which one of the following is most likely to be an example of an extension strategy for the brand? Select one answer.

   A *Increasing advertising spending on the toothpaste*
   B *Launching a new flavour for the toothpaste*
   C *Launching a new brand of soap*
   D *Increasing production of the toothpaste*

3. A business has 25 products in its product portfolio. It has classified one of these as a star, using the Boston Matrix. This means that

   A *the other 24 products are dogs*
   B *the markets for the 25 products are all growing very fast*
   C *sales of the product are higher than sales of any of the other 24 products*
   D *the product has a relatively high market share*

Select one answer.

Over to you

Bisto gravy developed from an idea by two women for a product that would guarantee perfect gravy every time. It was first created in 1908. 100 years later, the Bisto brand is still going strong with a market share of between 60 and 70 per cent. Most of the rest of the market is made up of own label gravy products sold by the major supermarket chains.

There is a great history in the product, the result of investment and advertising. During this time, there have been enormous changes to what people eat. Bisto has had to keep ahead of the game, battling against competitors and developing the product.

Bisto granules were introduced in 1979. Bisto Best, giving a fuller flavour than the standard granule, was introduced in 1991. It is a premium product sold in a glass jar to give it an air of quality as well as convenience. More recently, a ready-made Bisto Heat and Pour gravy has been launched. This comes in plastic pouches suitable for heating. In 2004, the Bisto brand was extended into chilled and frozen products with the introduction of Bisto Roast Potatoes, Bisto Crispies, Bisto Yorkshire Puddings and Bisto Frozen Mashed Topped Pies. Bisto also makes a range of sauces including white sauce, cheese sauce, curry and parsley sauce in granulated form, as well as a range of casserole sauces all in glass jars.

In 2009, the owners of Bisto, Premier Foods, announced plans to further develop Bisto. Premier Foods had been encouraged by a successful £20 million relaunch of another traditional product, Hovis bread, which had increased sales by 12 per cent. A relaunch of Bisto could both increase sales and profits.

Table 1 – Bisto history

1908 - Bisto powder launched

1919 - Bisto Kids adverts born

1979 - Bisto Granules launched

1984 - Relaunched granules and new onion granules

1991 - Bisto Best is launched

2004 - Launch of chilled and frozen products under the Bisto brand name

Source: adapted from news.bbc.co.uk; en.wikipedia; *Daily Express*, 14.1.2009.

1. (a) Draw a product life cycle diagram for Bisto gravy. (7)
   (b) Explain where Bisto was on the product life cycle in (i) 1908, (ii) 2009. (6)

2. (a) Give **two** examples of ways in which the owners of the Bisto brand have used extension strategies. (2)
   (b) Explain **one** possible reason why the producers of Bisto introduced these extension strategies. (3)

3. (a) List the names of the **four** categories used in the Boston Matrix to classify products. (4)
   (b) In which category do you think Bisto was in 2009? Justify your answer. (6)

Build Better Answers

Windemer is a traditional manufacturing firm in the UK which has been producing traditional windbreaks for use on the beach for many years. It has always produced a range of colours (pastels, stripes and plain) for its products, colours that people throughout the years have come to associate with this product. Sales in the last few years have been in decline due to less UK based holidays being taken by travellers. The chairman of the company, Edward Windemer, has recently read several reports that UK based holidays may be on the increase due to the global financial crisis and the relative weakness of sterling.

(a) Identify at what stage of the Product Life Cycle you feel the windbreak products are. (1)

(b) Explain how extension strategies may help the business turn things around. (3)

Think: What are the stages of the Product Life Cycle? What have the sales been like for the windbreaks? What may affect the sales of the windbreaks? What possible extension strategies would be suitable for the product?

■ **Basic** Identifies where the windbreaks are on the Product Life Cycle, such as 'They are in decline', but offers no extension strategies. (1)

● **Good** 'The windbreaks are likely to be in the decline stage of the Product Life Cycle. (1) One way to extend the life of the product is to expand the range of colours available (1) or develop the range of products to include an umbrella perhaps.' (1)

▲ **Excellent** 'The windbreaks are a traditional product and are likely to be in the saturation phase of the product life cycle and moving into decline. (1) An extension strategy could be to develop a range of products that complement the windbreaks (1) and perhaps make them more up to date with funky colours, pictures or patterns. (1) This should attract new and lapsed customers to the firm who can then take advantage of the potential upturn in UK based holidays.' (1)

Branding and differentiation

Case Study

JVC is a global design, development and manufacturing company. In 1976 it invented the VHS video system and produced the first VHS home recorder. Today it manufactures a range of consumer electronic goods, including LCD TVs and projectors, video cameras and audio systems.

Objectives

- Appreciate the importance of brands as an aid to product trial and repeat purchase.
- Understand the need to differentiate a product/service from others, given the level of competition.

edexcel ∷ key terms

Brand – a named product which consumers see as being different from other products and which they can associate and identify with.

Generic product – a product made by a number of different businesses in which customers see very little or no difference between the product of one business compared to the product of another business.

Own brand – a product which is sold under the brand name of a supermarket chain or other retailer rather than under the name of the business which manufactures the product.

Branding

Every business would like to own strong **brands**. A branded product is a product which in the eyes of customers is seen to be different from other, often similar, products. A brand has an image and/or an identity that consumers can associate with. It triggers images, thoughts, emotions and attachments and as a result is more likely to be purchased over rivals if those feelings are all positive. Many consumers, for example, see JVC products as different from those of other electrical manufacturers such as Sony, Bush, Phillips or Toshiba.

Many businesses seek to develop a number of brands as part of their product portfolio. For example, Viennetta ice cream, Timotei shampoo, Pot Noodle, PG Tips, Marmite and Lynx are all brands owned by the multinational firm Unilever. Each brand may be targeted at a different market segment. For example, in the personal hygiene goods category, Unilever sells Lynx, Sunsilk, Sure and Impulse. Consumers will not be aware that they are buying a product from Unilever but brands help the business to increase its overall market share.

Brands can also develop from things that are not physical goods. Star Wars, Dr Who, Mr Bean, James Bond and Harry Potter are all brands which can be exploited in association with a range of products and merchandise.

A business will often try to find a legal way of preventing others from copying or getting benefit from its brand name – which it often will have spent many years and large sums of money developing. These legal ways include registered trademarks and trade names.

Table 1 shows the top 30 brands in the world. There will be many that you will recognise but also a number that you may not. You might also be surprised that some famous names are not in this list – names such as Sony, Nike, Marks & Spencer, IKEA and Amazon.

The opposite of a branded product is a **generic product**. Potatoes are generic products. Consumers generally don't see any difference between the same type of potatoes produced on one farm compared to those of another farm. Coal, steel, milk and bananas are other examples of generic products.

Today, many brands are faced with strong competition from **own brands**. These are products which carry the brand labels of retailers such as Tesco, Sainsbury or Asda. Own brands are usually cheaper than the branded products from manufacturers.

Branding and purchases

Strong branding means that a business is more likely to get customers both to trial products and make repeat purchases.

Product trial Companies with strong, well known brands have an advantage over other companies when it comes to product trial. When customers want to buy a television set or a DVD player, they are more likely to try out a product with a brand name like JVC than those with weaker or unknown names. The same is true for other products from cars to chocolate to clothes.

Repeat purchase Customers tend to make repeat purchases of strong brands. The owner of a JVC television, for example, might buy a second JVC television. A consumer who buys one jar of Nescafé is likely to buy another jar of Nescafé when the coffee has been all been used. There is a great deal of research being carried out by some large firms into the links between the way the brain works and purchase decisions. A strong brand can help to influence a purchase decision because consumers associate a brand with positive feelings and so are more likely to choose the same brand again. This brand of marketing is called 'neuromarketing'.

The product range

JVC sells a range of products. In 1976 it invented the VHS video system and produced the first home recorder. This is still part of the company's total **product mix**. Today it manufactures a wide range of electronic products. For example, it produces video cameras, Blu-ray/DVD players and recorders, televisions and audio products used in the home and in vehicles. These are shown in Figure 1.

JVC produces a range of televisions, for example, because different consumers want different products. JVC can then sell more and make more profit by satisfying different consumers' wants.

Table 1 – Top 30 brands ($ million)

	Brand	Brand value
1	Google	66,434
2	GE (General Electric)	61,880
3	Microsoft	54,951
4	Coca Cola	44,134
5	China Mobile	41,214
6	Marlboro	39,166
7	Wal-Mart	36,880
8	Citi	33,706
9	IBM	33,572
10	Toyota	33,427
11	McDonald's	33,138
12	Nokia	31,670
13	Bank of America	28,767
14	BMW	25,751
15	HP	24,987
16	Apple	24,728
17	UPS	24,580
18	Wells Fargo	24,284
19	American Express	23,113
20	Louis Vuitton	22.686
21	Disney	22,572
22	Vodafone	21,107
23	NTT DoCoMo	19,450
24	Cisco	18,812
25	Intel	18,707
26	Home Depot	18,335
27	SAP	18,103
28	Gillette	17,954
29	Mercedes	17,813
30	Oracle	17,809

Source: adapted from http://www.brandz.com/upload/BrandZ_2007_Ranking_Report.pdf.

Figure 1 – JVC product mix

JVC The Perfect Experience

Televisions
•Full HD Super Slim LCD TV
•Full HD LCD TV
•LCD TV

•DVD Players

Home Entertainment
•Blu-ray Network Media System

Full High-Definition D-ILA Front Projector

Audio Systems
•DVD Compact Component Systems
•Micro Component Systems
•DVD Micro Component Systems
•CD Micro Component Systems
•Portable Audio Systems

Mobile Entertainment
•AV Navigation system
•AV Centers
•CD Receivers
•Amplifiers
•Subwoofers
•Speakers

Accessories
•In-Ear Headphones
•Headphones
•Cables
•Portable Speakers
•Bluetooth Accessories

Everio
•HD Hard Disc Camcorder
•HD Memory Card Camcorder
•Hard Disc Camcorder
•Memory Card Camcorder

The Perfect Experience   1

Product differentiation

Producing a range of televisions, for example, allows JVC to **differentiate** its products. Each television will be different. For instance, JVC manufactures a 119cm, full high definition LCD, widescreen television with superior sound features. This might be bought for the home by a film or music enthusiast. Its 48cm, widescreen television might be bought by a family that wants a flat screen television in the kitchen, or a student living in a flat. Consumers in Europe often buy televisions with only basic features.

Ways of differentiating the product

There is a number of important ways in which businesses make their products different from each other.

Design, formulation and function The different products manufactured by JVC have different characteristics. Televisions are made with different sized screens. Some are 19 inch, some are 26 inch and some are 47 inch. Headphones have different designs. Some cover the ears and others are in-ear designs. Amplifiers manufactured for vehicle sound systems have different outputs. Some are 370 watt and some are 1,800 watt. AV Centers have different functions. Some allow MP3 players to be connected and some have receivers with motion sensor and touch pad. Each year JVC introduces new designs with improved visual and audio functions, cosmetic features and improved functionality.

Similarly, car manufacturers produce a range of cars. Each car model may have hundreds of different feature combinations, from the colour of the car to the engine size to whether or not it has a fitted sunroof. McDonald's sells a variety of foods, from Big Macs to Chicken Nuggets to coffee. More expensive up-market products are likely to be of better quality than a better selling but cheaper mass market product.

Name Different products have different names. The name of the product is important if it is to sell. Calling a coffee 'Cafe stink', for example, is likely to be a disaster in sales terms. Some products have names which are easy to remember and say something positive about the product. 'Gold Blend' coffee, for instance, links something valuable (gold) with a soft word (blend) which implies mellowness. Audio products often have abstract names designed to create a technical image, like the JVC Alneo range of MP3 players.

However, the name is only a small part of the **marketing mix** of the product. No marketing company would have advised a UK baked bean manufacturer to brand its product 'Heinz', and yet Heinz baked beans is one of the most successful brand names in the UK today.

Packaging Packaging is used to deliver products safely to the consumer. For instance, JVC manufactured products are delivered in cardboard boxes with polystyrene padding and plastic wrapping inside. This keeps the products clean and secure before they are taken out to be used. Packaging can also prevent products from being scratched.

Packaging also gives information to the customer about the product. JVC packaging may contain information about where to place the product for best results and electrical information on the correct voltage to be used. It may give instructions on how to recycle packaging. It may contain details of any awards won by the product, such as the EISA Best Product award 2008-2009 won by its DLA-HD100(projector), GZ-MG330(Video Camera), KD-AVX44(in Car Head Unit) and LT-42SD9(Green TV Award). Food products contain nutritional information and cooking times are given as well, as how long the packet can safely be kept.

Packaging has other uses though. It is a way of promoting the product. Colours, designs and letters attract the customers' attention. For example, the JVC logo is placed on all product packaging. This can attract customers to the product.

Differentiating across the value chain The value chain refers to all the stages that a product goes through during production before it reaches the final consumer. Businesses may find a way of differentiating themselves at any stage of this process and it may not be something that the final consumer ever sees or notices but it can give the business a competitive advantage. For example, Federal Express (FedEx) invested in the way in which it receives and transports parcels and packets across the globe. This made it very different to other couriers.

edexcel ⠿ key terms

Product differentiation – making one product different from another in some way, for instance through the quality of a product, its design, packaging or advertising.

**ResultsPlus
Watch Out!**

It is easy to think that any business would be successful if only it sold branded products. In practice, there are relatively few strong brands in the world economy. Most consumer markets tend to have one or two strongly branded products that have high sales. Weak brands are often not very successful. Then there are the non-branded products such as own label brands sold by supermarket chains. These can sell extremely well because of their relatively low price. It is very difficult to create a successful new brand. This is the reason why most businesses do not sell strongly branded products.

The advantages of branding

There is a number of advantages to a business of branding.

Premium prices Strong branding means that a business may be able to charge a **premium price** for the product. This is a price that is higher than those of competitors. There are two reasons why customers are willing to pay premium prices for branded products. First, the quality of the product is usually higher (or perceived as higher). For instance, the JVC brand statement is 'The Perfect Experience'. It places emphasis on the quality of its products in all its easy operations for customers. Consumers might see JVC products as higher quality than other audio products of competitors as a result. Second, brands tend to be advertised heavily. This helps increase both the sales of the product and the willingness of customers to pay a higher price.

Greater consumer awareness Brands tend to be advertised heavily. Advertising and other forms of promotion mean that customers are more aware than they would otherwise be of the claimed advantages of the product. This may affect their decision when making a purchase.

Increased sales and market share Strong branding also means that sales are likely to be higher than if there were no branding. Customers are more likely to make repeat purchases of branded products. This helps maintain strong sales. It can also mean that a firm is able to increase market share.

Branding and market maps

A market map is a diagram that shows the range of possible positions for two features of a product, such as low to high price and consumer perceptions of low to high quality. Market maps can be used to illustrate the differences between a strongly branded product and a weakly branded product or one with no branding at all.

Figure 2 shows a market map for television sets. The price of television sets is shown on the vertical axis. Consumer perceptions of quality are shown on the horizontal axis. Branded televisions like Sony, Toshiba and JVC tend to be perceived as being higher quality than brands such as Bush and Goodman. On the other hand, they tend to be higher priced. Lowest prices and lowest

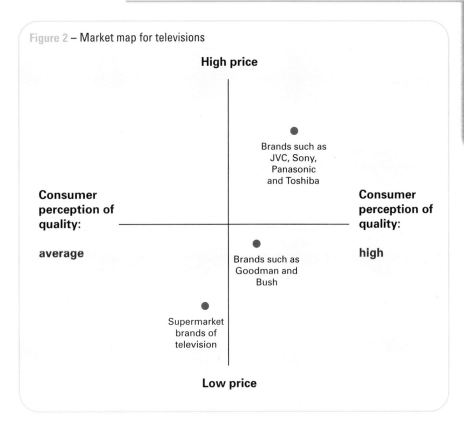

Figure 2 – Market map for televisions

perceptions of quality tend to be brands of television which are only sold by supermarkets like Tesco, Asda and Sainsbury.

Most strongly branded products, whether they are televisions or baked beans or cars, tend to be in the higher price/higher quality part of a market map.

Source: information from JVC.

Premium price – a price which is above the average for products of a particular type.

 Watch Out!

Branded products are not just 'expensive' label brands like Armani, Boss, Ralph Lauren and so on. A brand is one which has an identity. So businesses such as Poundstretcher, Aldi, Ryanair and Travelodge, all associated with low cost products, are also important brands.

Test yourself

1. A manufacturer of chocolates wants to more clearly differentiate its brand of chocolates from brands sold by competing businesses. The most likely way in which it could do this is by:

   A increasing production
   B changing the packaging design
   C increasing sales
   D changing its suppliers

   Select one answer.

2. Which one of the following is most likely to be an advantage for a business of owning a nationally recognised brand? The business can:

   A cut costs of production
   B launch own label brands
   C sell generic products
   D charge a premium price for the brand

   Select one answer.

3. A manufacturer of coffee launches a new brand of instant coffee. Which one of the following is most likely to aid product trial? Select one answer.

   A Negotiating a high price for the brand with supermarket chains
   B Trialling a new production method
   C Spending a significant amount of money on advertising the brand
   D Cutting trial launch costs of the brand

Over to you

In 2008, 1.21 billion mobile phone handsets were sold worldwide. This is approximately one mobile phone handset for every six people alive today. By far the largest manufacturer of mobile phones is the Finnish company Nokia. In 2008, nearly two in every five phones sold was a Nokia phone. Nokia has been making mobile phones from the earliest days of the mobile phone market.

However, the star of 2008 was not Nokia but a company that up until 2007 had never sold a single mobile phone. Yet in 2008 it came from nowhere to make 1 in every 100 mobile phones sold worldwide. The company was Apple and the phone was the iPhone.

The success of the iPhone is partly linked to the strong Apple brand image. Apple computers and the Apple iPod are cult consumer products. Apple has gained a reputation for designing stylish, easy to use products. However, branding would not have been enough to break into the fiercely competitive mobile phone handset market on its own. Apple came up with a product that is easy to use and has many features not found on most other mobile phones. With the Apple iPhone, it is relatively easy not just to make a phone call or text but also to do things like email, go onto the Internet, play games and listen to music.

Getting 1 per cent of the world market is even more surprising since the iPhone is relatively expensive. The cost of the handset is well above the market average. Annual contracts to pay for the cost of phone calls and other usage are also relatively high.

Apple can look forward to even better news in the future. If Apple computers and iPods are anything to go by, iPhone users are likely to stay with Apple as they change their old handsets for new handsets. With more customers trialling the product, Apple sales and profits are likely to increase substantially.

Source: information from www.pcadvisor.co.uk.

1. What is meant by a 'brand'? Use Apple as an example in your answer. (3)

2. Explain why branding can help Apple (a) to get consumers to trial its iPhone and (b) to make repeat purchases. (6)

3. Identify **three** possible ways in what Apple has differentiated the iPhone from other products. (3)

4. Explain **one** possible advantage to Apple of selling a branded product such as the iPhone. (3)

5. How, in your opinion, should Nokia react given the successful launch of the iPhone? Justify your answer. (6)

ResultsPlus
Build Better Answers

Newton Beers, a regional, independent brewing company based in the South West, has recently expanded its product mix from 5 to 15 beers, lagers and ciders. All the products have the company name on them and the distinctive logo of an outline map of the South West of England overlaid with a traditional beer mug. The company has been going for many years and sells its products in a variety of places, including two national supermarket chains, two national off licence companies and 46 independent stores. It also has stalls at farmers' markets and trade fairs.

(a) Explain **one** advantage of developing a branded range of products. (3)

Think: Why do companies need a branded range? How does this benefit them?

■ **Basic** States a benefit such as 'People can recognise products'. (1).

● **Good** 'Branded products create an identity that people can recognise on the shop shelf (1) and this helps to develop brand loyalty.' (1)

▲ **Excellent** 'Having a branded range of products means that a customer is likely to recognise products and relate them to other products from the same company (1) which develops brand loyalty and repeat purchase. (1) The potential for premium pricing through branded products means that quality can be maintained and used as a Unique Selling Point.' (1)

Building a successful marketing mix

Case Study

Heinz Beanz is one of the most instantly recognised brands in the UK. Launched over 100 years ago in 1901, it is a familiar sight in most grocery and supermarket stores. In 2009, it had an approximate market share of the baked bean market of 65 per cent. Heinz, the US company which owns Heinz Beanz, has actively managed the brand over its 100 year history.

Objectives

- Understand the importance of managing a brand through the key variables that make up the marketing mix: product, price, promotion and place.

The marketing mix

Businesses like Heinz want to sell products to satisfied customers and make a profit. Heinz Beanz is a brand which is over 100 years old. So, to make the product up to date and attractive to today's consumers, Heinz must make regular adjustments to its **marketing mix**. This is the combination of factors which will help the business meet customer needs more successfully and thus sell its product. The four elements of the marketing mix are product, price, promotion and place.

Product

The basic baked bean product is made of haricot beans baked (i.e. stewed) in a tomato sauce. Heinz uses high quality raw haricot beans for its product. It also has a unique tomato sauce **formula**. This formula is a closely guarded secret. Only four people in the world know the whole formula. Having a secret formula for a product is not unique to Heinz. Successful products such as Coca-Cola and Benedictine liqueur also are made to closely guarded, secret formulae.

Formulae, however, often have to be updated and changed to suit the different tastes of different consumers. For example, in recent years, Heinz has reduced the amount of both sugar and salt in its baked beans. This is because of growing awareness that too much salt and sugar in a diet is unhealthy. The formula for Heinz Beanz sold in the USA is different from the one used for UK consumers. The US product is both sweeter and mushier than the UK equivalent.

Almost every business has to change and adapt its product over time. Car manufacturers bring out new models. Clothes manufacturers bring out new fashions every season. Hair salons change the styling of hair.

Packaging is also important. Baked beans normally come in a can. However, in 2008 Heinz introduced Snaps Pots. These are similar to yoghurt pots. Their great advantage over a can is they can be put straight into a microwave oven and heated. The beans can then also be eaten straight from the pot. This adds convenience to the product.

Different varieties of a brand can be introduced as customer preferences change. For example, you can buy a tin of Organic Beanz, catering to customers who prefer organic products. For those worrying about their weight, there is Weight Watchers No Added Sugar Beanz which has fewer calories than the original formula. For those who want to less sugar and salt, there is Reduced Sugar and Salt Beanz. To cater for those who enjoy ethnic products, there are four

edexcel ⠿ key terms

Marketing mix – a combination of factors which help a business to take into account customer needs when selling a product, usually summarised as the 4 Ps (price, product, promotion and place).

varieties: Jalfrezi, Mexican, Sweet Chilli and Tikka. There are also a number of different Heinz Bean Meals including Baked Beanz with Chicken Nuggets and Baked Beanz with Pork Sausages.

The **name** of the brand may also change over time. In 2004, the name was changed from Heinz Baked Beans to Heinz Baked Beanz. This was to reinforce the image created by one of the UK's most successful advertising campaigns ever in the 1960s which had the slogan 'Beanz Meanz Heinz'. In 2008, the name was changed again to 'Heinz Beanz'. It was felt that the new two word name would make it easier to pronounce the product brand name. At the same time, the packaging label was also altered to give more emphasis to the nutritional benefits of the beans.

Price

Branded products, such as Heinz Beanz, can be sold at a higher price or **premium price** compared to rival non-branded products. There are four main reasons for this.

- The cost of production is usually higher than that of non-branded products because branded products tend to be higher quality.
- The cost of marketing the product is often higher. Branded products are often backed by advertising and other forms of promotion. Non-branded products do not have these costs.
- Charging a higher price in itself suggestions to customers that it is better quality. Experiments have shown that consumers are often suspicious of the quality of low priced goods. For example, although supermarket own brand beans are much cheaper, Heinz has kept its high market share over the years.
- A higher price allows the business owning the brand to earn a higher profit. Successful brands are highly valuable because they enable their owners to earn more profit per item sold than the typical non-branded products. One of the reasons why supermarket chains like Tesco and Asda can sell non-branded baked beans at such a low price is because the manufacturers of the baked beans make low profits on each tin sold.

Companies like Heinz use a variety of pricing techniques to increase sales. For example, a pack of four cans of Heinz Beanz is typically sold at a lower price than four individual cans. This is to encourage customers to buy in bulk. Heinz might run a special offer, lowering the price for a short period. If it is launching a new variety, it might offer a low price at launch to encourage customers to trial the product. Heinz is constantly reviewing its pricing policy to see whether it can gain an advantage by changing its price.

Promotion

Strong brands, like Heinz Beanz, tend to be backed by successful promotion. One example of promotion is advertising. Supporting a brand with regular advertising typically increases sales. If an advertising campaign captures the customers' interest and imagination, it can considerably boost sales. The most famous Heinz Beanz set of adverts was in the 1960s when it ran the 'Beans Meanz Heinz' campaign. In 2009, Heinz reused the 'Beans Meanz Heinz' catchphrase in a new £1.4 million marketing campaign.

Promotion is often targeted at particular market segments (i.e. groups of customers). In 2008, Heinz ran a series of advertisements targeting young single men. They are likely customers for baked beans because baked beans are relatively cheap and easy to prepare. The new Snap Pots and adult flavours such as Mexican Beanz are aimed at this market.

ResultsPlus
Watch Out!

Many think that it is easy to create a brand. Most new brands launched into the market fail. Only around one in five are successful enough not to be withdrawn from sale. Even then, most of these new brands will only be moderately successful. It is very difficult to challenge existing strong brands in the market.

Promotion is much more than advertising. Changing the packaging design is a form of promotion. So too are competitions and prizes. PR (public relations) campaigns aim to get free positive publicity for a product.

Place

Place is about having a product available to customers when they want it and where they want it. For Heinz Beanz, this means ensuring that the product is available in all the major supermarkets and in local grocery shops. Because the brand is so popular, the standard can of Heinz Beanz is a product that is likely to be available in nearly every grocery store.

However, Heinz would like grocery stores also to stock all the variants of Heinz Beanz such as Organic Baked Beanz and Beanz with Chicken Nuggets. Most individual supermarket stores do not stock the full range of Heinz Beanz, let alone the small corner grocery store. If the product is not on the shelves, customers cannot buy it. So Heinz is working all the time to get more of its products stocked by retail outlets.

Businesses have a variety of ways of getting their products to customers.

- For food products like Heinz Beanz, food manufacturers sell directly to supermarket chains. They also sell in bulk to **wholesalers**. These wholesalers then sell in smaller quantities to small retailers like a local corner shop. Promoting the product to supermarkets and to wholesalers is therefore very important in reaching out to the eventual consumer.

- Some products are sold by producers directly to consumers rather than through shops. Examples are Stannah Stairlifts or Avon Cosmetics. Producers employ a sales force to sell directly to the individual consumer. In the case of Avon Cosmetics, it uses agents. An agent receives a commission from the producer for every item sold. The Internet has also made it far more possible for businesses to sell directly to consumers.

Source: www.heinzbeanz.com; www.telegraph.co.uk 18.7.2008; en.wikipedia.org; www.heinzfoodservice.co.uk; www.dailymail.co.uk 12.9.2006; thegrocer.co.uk 31.10.2008.

Results Plus
Watch Out!

Brands need very careful maintenance if they are to retain their market share. Heinz Beanz went through a difficult period in 2005-06 when rival Branston launched a new brand of baked bean which quickly took nearly 10 per cent of the market. Sales of Heinz Beanz fell as a result. One appeal of the Branston beans was that the beans were served in a sauce with 30 per cent tomato content compared to Heinz with 27 per cent tomato content. Heinz responded by changing their formula to a 33 per cent tomato sauce. With more marketing, Heinz stopped losing market share to Branston and has since regained market share mostly at the expense of own label products. If Heinz had done nothing, it would be selling fewer beans today.

Results Plus
Build Better Answers

Streamline Transfers is an airport transfer company based in Slough. It specialisea in airport transfers from the major airports in the South East, picking up and returning passengers to and from their homes and the airport. It currently sells its service as 'luxury transfers' mainly to the business market and has a fleet of vehicles that can take up to 12 people. All cars are black in colour with tinted windows. The business advertises in local papers and using word of mouth. Its prices are competitive with other firms and are seen as giving value for money by customers.

Explain one way in which Streamline Transfers might adjust its marketing mix to improve its brand awareness. (3)

Think: What are the elements of the marketing mix? What are the advantages to changing each element?

◼ **Basic** States **one** method, for example 'Streamline Transfers might promote itself to more customers'. (1)

⬤ **Good** 'Streamline Transfers might improve the promotion of its service. (1) Promotion helps a company by letting customers know what products it has for sale. Promoting more widely can increase sales.' (1)

▲ **Excellent** 'Streamline Transfers might improve the promotion of its service. (1) Promotion is a key part of the marketing mix as it informs potential and actual customers of Streamline's service. Streamline Transfers might consider setting up its own website and paying for its name to appear high in any search in Google. (1) This might attract a wider target market than it currently has and improve its sales.' (1)

Over to you

KFC, Kentucky Fried Chicken, is one of the world's largest fast food chains. In 2009, it announced that, over the next five years, it would open between 200 and 300 new outlets in the UK and Ireland to add to its existing 760 chain of restaurants in the two countries. Approximately 60 per cent of these new outlets will be run as franchises.

KFC is proving popular with customers. Sales in existing stores were up 5 per cent in 2008, 9 per cent in 2007 and 6 per cent in 2006. A drive-through outlet that opened in Worcester in January 2009 smashed KFC's previous UK record for first week sales. It sold £100,531 of food and drink compared to the previous best total of £88,000.

The fast food chain is popular with customers partly because it offers low prices. A bargain bucket of food which will feed a family of four, for example, costs just £10 to take out. In response to growing health fears about fast food, KFC has been adapting its recipes. In 2005, for example, it was the first fast food retailer to stop pre-salting its fries. It is also adding new products to its range. It has plans, for example, to offer grilled chicken. It has also responded to environmental concerns about packaging. From 2009, it has pledged to reduce its packaging by 1,400 tonnes a year. Fillet and Zinger burgers will be packaged in paper wrappers rather than cardboard 'clamshells'. Classic chicken meals – the Colonel's Meal and Variety Meal – will also move from cardboard boxes to paper bags. The paper bags are made from 100 per cent renewable sources from sustainably farmed European forests, and are 100 per cent recyclable, biodegradable and made in the UK.

KFC backs its products with extensive promotion. In 2008, for example, it ran an advertising campaign which reused the slogan 'Finger Lickin' Good'. The advertisements were placed

on posters, billboards, phone booths and on London Underground escalator panels.

Source: adapted from www.telegraph.co.uk; www.guardian.co.uk 23.4.2008; www.timesonline.co.uk 16.2.2009; www.packagingnews.co.uk 26.1.2009.

1. State **three** elements of the marketing mix. (3)

2. Explain how the brand image of KFC might make its new stores successful. (3)

3. Analyse **two** possible advantages and **two** possible disadvantages to KFC of using franchising to expand its business. (8)

4. Over the next five years, what do you think is the most important element of the marketing mix which will make KFC successful in the UK? Justify your answer. (10)

Test yourself

1. A company manufactures clothes and sells them using a brand name. It introduces a new range of clothes each season. This is most likely to be because

   A   *it is cheaper to change the range each season*
   B   *each season it increases the price of its products*
   C   *of the importance of place in the marketing mix*
   D   *it needs to respond to changing consumer tastes*

   Select one answer.

2. A company manufactures toys and sells them under its famous brand name. It charges a premium price for its products. This means

   A   *it charges a higher price than many of its competitors*
   B   *the quality of its products is always higher than that of its competitors*
   C   *it is always more profitable than its competitors*
   D   *its sales are higher than those of all its competitors*

   Select one answer.

3. A manufacturer of electronic products such as television sets is worried because one of the larger UK supermarket chains has decided to stop stocking its products. This is most likely to be an immediate problem for the company because

   A   *its total manufacturing costs will now rise*
   B   *it harms 'place' in its marketing mix*
   C   *it will have to cope with wider distribution of its products*
   D   *the cost of distributing its products will rise*

   Select one answer.

In this topic you have learned about: the importance of market research and how it allows a company to find out about a customer's needs and wants which help businesses to make decisions, the need for product trial and the necessity to turn those trials into repeat sales, the role of the Product Life Cycle and the Boston Matrix, the value of branding and having differentiation within the product mix, how to develop and maintain a successful marketing mix.

You should know…

- [ ] Any business must identify and understand its actual and potential customers' needs and wants.

- [ ] The price set for a product must enable a business to make a profit in the long term.

- [ ] The planning of market research should have specific aims and objectives so that it is focused and has direction.

- [ ] Surveys are a key part of market research and involve asking questions. People who are questioned in a survey are called respondents. The questions asked must be appropriate to reach the aims and objectives of the task and not misleading or biased

- [ ] Sampling is used in market research as not everyone can be questioned. There are several types of sample – random, systematic, quota and stratified random.

- [ ] Market research is a key element that helps businesses come to decisions. These decisions can shape the future for existing and potential products within a business's product portfolio.

- [ ] The drawbacks to effective market research are time and money.

- [ ] Market research is limited by the accuracy of the information generated – if decisions are based on inaccurate information the business might not benefit from it.

- [ ] A product trial is a way of getting a product to the market in its infancy. It often allows potential customers to try the product with limited expense to the business. It is important to turn the product trials into repeat purchases.

- [ ] Repeat purchase is often backed up by a range of strategies that ensures the product's success. These include advertising campaigns, effective pricing strategies and product development.

- [ ] Advertising an existing product often focuses on the reliability or consistency of the product's features.

- [ ] The product life cycle is made up of distinct areas – Development, Launch, Growth, Maturity, Saturation and Decline. Every product has its own unique product life cycle.

- [ ] Product portfolio analysis helps provide answers to questions that are concerned with the success or failure of the range of products sold by a company.

- [ ] The Boston Matrix helps a company look at its products in terms of their actual and potential value to the business and is an aid to planning. It is made up of 4 key areas – Stars, Cash Cows, Problem Children and Dogs.

- [ ] Branding often helps develop new products and brings customers to trial and repeat purchase more quickly. Branding may allow a business to charge a higher price for its products.

- [ ] Many own brands (i.e. supermarkets) are now as strong as branded products themselves in customer awareness and recognition.

- [ ] The product mix is the range of products a business sells.

- [ ] It is important to differentiate products from the competition through design, formulation, function, name or packaging.

- [ ] Logos are often a great way of setting a product apart from the competition. They create instant recognition.

- [ ] Market maps are a way of analysing the market to illustrate the differences between strong brands and unbranded products.

- [ ] The marketing mix is made up of 4 key elements – Product, Price, Place and Promotion.

- [ ] Each part of the marketing mix works both separately and in harmony, to maximise the product's recognition and sales.

- [ ] It is not easy to create a brand that lasts. Many fail early on with only a few remaining for a long time in the market.

- [ ] Brands must be maintained and the marketing mix must be constantly reviewed in order for it to be successful.

Support activity

- Identify the needs and wants of your family and friends in relation to the amount and type of food they eat in a week. How do these wants and needs differ between individuals?

- Collect several different types of packaging from some everyday household products like cereals, washing machine powders/liquids etc. shampoo, toothpaste, food cartons and so on. Construct a table to outline what message you think the business is trying to give to consumers to try to differentiate the product.

- What attracts you to the type of things you buy? Write a list of things that attract you to products and things that make you steer clear of other products.

Stretch activity

- Identify one independent convenience store and one local branch of a national supermarket chain. Compare and contrast how they satisfy the needs and wants of the local market by writing a short report.

- Find 3 examples of surveys being used by companies. Identify what the aims and objectives of the market research are for each one.

- Choose one product that you are familiar with. Think about the elements of the marketing mix that the business which sells it uses and write a short report of no more than 500 words analysing its marketing mix.

Gemma Lau is a primary school teacher and is thinking about setting up her own gymnastics training school for children aged 5 – 11 in Bristol. She knows that there are lots of children in that age bracket in her local area and that many like gymnastics. She thinks she knows this because she has several friends that work in local schools. She has drawn up a questionnaire with a mixture of open and closed questions that she wants to place in all primary schools in the area. She wants to ask a representative sample of her potential customers.

(i) What is meant by the term 'sample'?(1)

(ii) Explain why Gemma may have chosen to use a questionnaire to gather information about her target market instead of other methods. (3)

Think: What is a sample? What benefits and drawbacks are there of using questionnaires? What is in this scenario to use in the answer? What alternatives are there?

Student answer	Examiner comment	Build a better answer
(i) It's the people who represent the customers.	■ A weak answer which is helped by the use of the word 'represent'. It is unclear that the student actually understands the theory.	▲ Make sure you use clear phrases such as '…a representative selection of the total number of consumers (population) in the market.' You could use an example such as '100 girls and boys aged 5-11' to back up your answer.
(ii) It is the easiest way to ask her customers.	■ A very simplistic answer that lacks depth and development for full marks	▲ Look at the marks available. This gives an indication of the number of links needed in the answer. It is clearly asking for reasons why Gemma feels a questionnaire is the best thing to use. It is clear that Gemma has access to many potential customers and probably has contacts in many schools due to her job. Many entrepreneurs find it is easiest to use a questionnaire as they can use a home computer or laptop to write it and analyse the data – this makes it cheaper to do. You could also discuss why she has chosen not to use other methods for example 'Gemma may have decided not to use a consumer panel or one-to-one interviews as these are very costly in terms of time.'

Practice Exam Questions

Mandy McColl was becoming increasingly bored in her job as a sales manager for a national food wholesaler. She had always dreamed of opening her own restaurant serving good quality, locally sourced food at prices that represented value for money. She felt that there was a gap in the market for this type of business but never had the nerve to actually go for it. One evening she was having dinner with friends in their favourite restaurant and the conversation turned to the economic situation in the country. At the time, the economy was slowing down. One friend commented that he 'would have to start going out less as he couldn't afford to eat out as much as he used to be able to', another felt that 'restaurants in the area hadn't realised that they would have to adjust their prices to keep customers coming back', whilst a third said that she 'was getting bored of the same old restaurants week in week out'.

These three comments finally convinced Mandy to hand in her notice and start the process of opening her own restaurant. Over the following two weeks she looked into the legal aspects of starting a business and where she might get her financial backing from. Mandy realised that she needed to find out 4 key things:

(1) exactly what the potential market might want from a new restaurant;
(2) what she should charge for her food;
(3) where she should locate her restaurant;
(4) how she should promote her business.

She also understood the need for anyone that might come in and try the restaurant to come back regularly and become repeat customers. Mandy understands that she needs to focus on the needs and wants of the customers in order to be a success.

(a) Mandy realises that repeat customers will be essential to the success of the restaurant. Which **two** of the following best describe why repeat custom is important to Mandy? (2)

A There will be a greater chance of long-term success for the restaurant
B Staff will feel more motivated to work at the restaurant
C Customer loyalty means that Mandy may be able to develop the product range
D Customers might try the restaurant for the first time
E It helps to determine the price paid for ingredients

(b) Mandy could use the Boston Matrix as a means of analysing the range of menu items she provides.. Explain how using the Boston Matrix might help Mandy plan ahead more effectively. (3)

(c) Analyse **two** benefits to Mandy's business of focusing on the needs and wants of her customers (8).

Topic 3.2: Meeting customer needs

Topic overview

This topic considers the effects of design and research and development on product differentiation and meeting customer satisfaction, how stock control can be managed effectively, the methods used to keep productivity up and costs and prices down to allow business to be competitive, how effective customer service can be achieved and the effects of legislation on business.

Case study

Apple is a US technology company. It makes a variety of products including Apple computers, MP3 players (iPods) and mobile phones (iPhones). Key to its success is its software which powers these products.

The company is at the leading edge of technology. The markets in which it operates, such as computing and mobile phones, are very fast changing. Companies which fail to bring out new products quickly lose sales and in the long term can disappear. For this reason, Apple spends hundreds of millions of pounds each year on design and research development. It has gained a reputation for excellent design. Its products look stylish whilst at the same time being highly functional. The iPod in conjunction with the iTunes website where music can be downloaded, for example, dominates its market because of its stylish looks and ease of use. Effective customer service means that Apple customers are highly loyal, making repeat purchases of company products.

Like any company, Apple has to make a profit to survive. This means providing great value products that customers want to buy at affordable prices. Apple managers are always keeping an eye on costs to help keep those prices affordable. For example, it maximises productivity by ensuring that its workers have the right equipment for the job. It also has plants round the world to take advantage of differences in wage, land costs and taxes between countries. iPods and iPhones are manufactured in China rather than the USA partly because of lower wage costs in China. Apple computers are assembled in Ireland in the town of Cork. Ireland is a highly attractive location to US firms because of low taxes and a highly skilled labour force. It is also inside the European Union which makes exports to other EU countries easier than if products are coming from the USA or China.

The Cork factory was first set up in 1980. It is a highly efficient plant employing the latest manufacturing techniques. For example, where possible, it uses Just In Time (JIT) systems to manage stock. Where stock has to be made and stored, the buffer stock kept is the smallest amount consistent with efficient production.

In the UK, consumers buying Apple products are fully protected by law. For example, under the Sale of Goods Act, consumers have a right to a refund or repair if the product they buy is faulty. Consumers are also protected under the Trade Descriptions Act from any retailer who attempts to mislead customers about the products it sells - including those from Apple. In addition to these rights, Apple also gives customers a warranty or guarantee.

Source: information from www.businessweek.com 12.10.2004; www.rgaros.nl 1996; www.macobserver.com 19.08.2008.

1. Why is design and research important for Apple?

2. How does Apple control its stock at its Cork factory?

3. Why must Apple managers always keep an eye on costs?

4. What could be (a) the financial and (b) legal penalties for Apple if it offered poor quality products?

What will I learn?

Design and research development Why is design a key approach to product differentiation? What is meant by the 'design mix'? Why is there a need for scientific research to provide the basis for product development?

Managing stock and quality What is a bar gate stock graph? How does stock control work in theory? How should a bar gate stock graph be interpreted? Why is there a need for the use of Just In Time (JIT) stock control?

Cost-effective operations and competitiveness How can productivity be increased? How can costs be lowered? Why are higher productivity and lower costs important in managing overall costs? How do lower costs feed through to lower competitive prices?

Effective customer service Why is it important for a business to provide customers with the service level they want, when they want it? What is the link between effective customer service and repeat purchase levels? What are the disadvantages of poor customer service for a business?

Meeting consumer protection laws What is the purpose of Trade Descriptions and Sales of Goods legislation? What effect does this legislation have on a business?

How will I be assessed?

This is assessed through Unit 3, a written examination lasting 1 hour 30 minutes.

The paper is divided into three sections.

Section A is a mix of mainly multiple choice questions and short answer questions with one or more questions requiring an extended answer.

Sections B and C consist of short and long answer questions based on two scenarios, one for each section, given in the paper.

6 Design and research development

Case Study

James Dyson is the inventor of the Dual Cyclone bagless vacuum cleaner, more commonly known as a 'Dyson'. In the late 1970s, two ideas came together. First, he was vacuuming a room in a house he was renovating. He noticed that dust blocked the airflow of the cleaner and suction dropped rapidly as a result. Second, he visited a local sawmill. It had a machine that sucked sawdust out of the air using a giant cyclone. Could the problem with his vacuum cleaner be solved by cyclone technology? Five years later, having gone through many prototypes, he had a machine that would become the world's first commercial bagless vacuum cleaner.

Objectives

● Appreciate design as a key approach to product differentiation.

● Appreciate the design mix.

● Understand the need for scientific research to provide the basis for development

Design and product differentiation

Design helps a product stand out from it competitors. It is a very important form of **product differentiation**.

In the first half of the 1980s, James Dyson tried to persuade the major manufacturers of vacuum cleaners such as Hoover to buy the rights to manufacture his revolutionary vacuum cleaner. They all turned it down. The Dyson bagless vacuum cleaner first went on sale in Japan in 1986. Coloured pink, it sold for the equivalent of £2 000 and became a cult object. In 1991, it won the International Design Fair prize in Japan. By being different from its competitors, it was able to sell in the Japanese market despite its very high price. The money earned from Japanese sales allowed James Dyson to set up a factory in the UK to manufacture his machine. It went on sale in 1993 in the UK at a price of £200, at the top end of the price range for vacuum cleaners. Within two years, despite the high price, the Dyson was the UK's best-selling vacuum cleaner. The revolutionary design strongly appealed to UK customers. Design was the key to the Dyson's success.

There are many other examples of products which are successful because of their design. These include Apple's iPod, Porsche cars, Boeing 747 (the Jumbo) aircraft, Nike and Converse trainers or Chanel perfume.

Many products, such as cars, trainers and MP3 players, are successful because of their designs.

Design mix

There are three elements to successful design. This design mix is made up of three variables: function, cost of production and appearance.

Function Function is about how well a product works and the extent to which it does what it supposed to do. Will a washing machine clean clothes properly? Will a car be reliable and not have to have repairs? Will a pair of shoes last a long time? Will a television set give a good colour image? In the case of the Dyson vacuum cleaner, there is a number of aspects to its functionality. First, it did clean better than most of its rivals because of its cyclonic design. Being bagless also helped maintain suction over time. Second, it was easy to use. Emptying the dirt out of the machine was easier than having to replace a bag in a conventional vacuum cleaner. Third, it was very strong. It was impossible to break the plastic parts of the cleaner in normal circumstances. Very importantly, the company has continued to improve the functionality of its vacuum cleaners through research and development. Good design is about being one step ahead of the competition.

Cost The cheaper the cost of producing an item, the better. Designing a product which has a cost of production lower than that of its rivals will give a business a competitive advantage. Over time, for example, the cost of producing motor cars has fallen because of improved design. Less and lighter steel is used and machinery is far more sophisticated than 20 years ago. Producing the lowest cost item, however, is not necessarily the best strategy. James Dyson's vacuum cleaners cost more to produce than the typical vacuum cleaner sold by rival companies. Partly this is because the cost of research and development of the product has been high. A business like Dyson has to weigh up the competitive advantages of producing a high quality but high production cost item against making a lower quality but lower production cost item.

Appearance Stylish, elegant, beautiful products are more likely to sell than products that have no style. Appearance is therefore very important in design. The Dyson vacuum cleaner, with its bright, bold colours and modern styling has been a design success.

Scientific research

There are many products which are based on the use of traditional materials such as wood and cotton. For simple products like wooden toys or wooden furniture, it may be possible to create beautifully designed products without the need for science. However, scientific research is at the base of the majority of products made today. A plastic toy, for example, is made from a product - plastic - which has been scientifically developed. A modern car, with its advanced bodywork, sophisticated engine and electronic systems is full of scientifically engineered parts. Some businesses have their own research and development teams and departments. Other businesses buy in components and materials that have been developed by companies using science.

Dyson is a company that has a very strong record of using science to develop its products. The original Dyson cleaner only made it into commercial production after 5,126 **prototypes** had been made. A prototype is a working model of a possible finished product. Dyson has a large **research and development (R&D)** centre in Wiltshire where it continues to develop existing products and work on new products.

Source: information from en.wikipedia.org; www.dyson.co.uk.

ResultsPlus
Watch Out!

It is easy to think that market research will always give better information than the hunch of one individual. This is not always true. When developing the Dyson vacuum cleaner, market research suggested that customers would not want a transparent container for the dust that was collected. James Dyson and his team decided, however, that it would be a great advert for the cleaner if customers could see just how much dirt was collected. So they used a transparent container. This has become a distinguishing feature of the Dyson design and helps sell the product.

edexcel ::: key terms

Design mix – the range of variables which contribute to successful design: they are function, cost and appearance.

Test yourself

1. A manufacturer of freezers designs its latest model with more insulation than other freezers on the market. This results in it being the most energy efficient freezer sold. This is an example of

   A *appearance as part of the design mix*
   B *product trial*
   C *product differentiation*
   D *repeat purchase*

   Select **one** answer.

2. Function in the design mix is about how

   A *good a product looks*
   B *much it costs to produce*
   C *good is the brand image of the product*
   D *well a product works*

   Select **one** answer.

3. A car manufacturing company has a large R&D department. R&D stands for

   A *research and development*
   B *research and discovery*
   C *resources and development*
   D *resources and discovery*

   Select **one** answer.

ResultsPlus
Build Better Answers

A significant proportion of products that are made today comes from the process of scientific research. Which of the following best describes 'scientific research'? Select **one** answer.

A   The collection of data using a scientific process to determine the needs and wants of a market

B   Application of scientific development to the advance of a product design

C   The third element in the design mix, along with cost and appearance

D   A working model of a possible finished product developed using a scientific approach

E   The scientific study of the physical efficiency of an individual worker

Answer B

Technique guide: There is a number of choices available so first:

Think: What link is there between products and science? How might a business use science and its advances? What is the relationship between production and scientific research?

Then: Consider each alternative.

Go through these:

A is incorrect. Data collection on market habits is part of market research - whether using scientific means or not. ■

C is unlikely. The answer could be this, but the function of a product is more likely. ■

D is incorrect. A working model of a product is a prototype, which businesses develop to test out what the product is and does. ■

E is incorrect. This may be a scientific study, but related to human resources management rather than product development. ■

This leaves B as most likely. The question indicates products and making them and scientific development helps to produce new products. ▲

Over to you

Thirty years ago, London had its own unique design of bus. Called the Routemaster, it had been the result of ten years of research and development in the 1940s and 1950s. By the 1980s and 1990s, it was clear that the Routemaster had to be replaced. Its engine was too polluting. The cost of production was too high. It needed a conductor on board to collect fares as well as a driver making each bus costly to operate. It also had no disabled access and parents with young children and push chairs found them difficult to get on and off. Yet, many Londoners loved the friendly, welcoming design of the bus with its rounded edges. They also liked being able to hop on and off the bus between stops using the open platform at the back.

The Routemaster was replaced by buses which were in use all over Europe. Cheap to buy, they have never caught the imagination of Londoners. In the 2008 election for the Mayor of London, buses became an electoral issue. The winner of the election, Boris Johnson, disliked 'bendy buses' - two single-decker buses put together - and promised the return of a new 21st century Routemaster.

Boris Johnson created a competition for the design of a new Routemaster. The competition was jointly won by Capoco Design and a combined entry by Aston Martin and architects Foster and Partners in 2008. The winning designs included 21st century technology such as a zero emissions engine, solar panels built into a glass roof, lightweight structure and warm lighting. They returned to the past by imitating the curved design of the old Routemaster and using wood for the flooring.

The next stage is to get bus manufacturers to develop a final design and to get a prototype bus on the road. Transport for London, responsible for London's buses, hopes to award a contract to build the bus by the end of 2009 with the first vehicles on the streets by 2011.

If the cost of production were competitive enough, the distinctive new Routemaster would then be well placed to win contracts from bus operators outside of London. Could the new Routemaster become a world-beating design in use all over the globe?

Source: adapted from www.thisislondon.co.uk 24.12.2008; www.timesonline.co.uk 19.12.2008; www.guardian.co.uk 19.12.2008.

1. State **two** elements of the design mix. (2)

2. Explain **one** advantage and **one** disadvantages of the design of the old Routemaster compared to more modern buses. Use the elements of the design mix to help you structure your answer. (6)

3. (i) Define the term 'scientific research'. (1)
   (ii) Explain why scientific research is likely to be important in the design of the new Routemaster. (3)

4. The new developers of the Routemaster are hoping that the changes it makes will differentiate the bus. They are hoping that this will enable them to sell the bus to buyers outside London. In your opinion, will the changes make it easier for the developers to do this? Justify your answer. (8)

7 Managing stock

Case Study

Aldwyn Plastic Products is a company that manufactures plastic components. With £8 million sales a year, it has thousands of customers worldwide including in Poland, Turkey, China and Australia. These customers are other businesses that use the plastic components in their finished products. The plastic components range from knobs on electrical and musical equipment to thermostats, to wash basins and mouldings for ventilation systems. Like most businesses, Aldwyn Plastic Products keeps stocks of raw materials.

Objectives

- Interpret bar gate stock graphs to see how stock control should work in theory.
- Understand the need for the use of Just In Time (JIT) stock control.
- Appreciate the advantages and drawbacks of different stock control methods.

Stocks

Most businesses hold stocks. These stocks are of three main types.

- There are stocks of materials which have been bought from other businesses. For example, Aldwyn Plastic Products buys bags of plastic pellets from its suppliers. The plastic pellets are fed into machines that produce the finished plastic component. A car manufacturer would hold stocks of steel to make car panels. A coal fired electricity power station would hold stocks of coal.
- There are stocks of materials that have been semi-finished by the producer. For example, Aldwyn Plastic Products makes parts for ventilation systems. Some of these parts are made up of several different components. Aldwyn Plastic Products would make one of these components and they would then become stock. Another of these components would then be made, and so on. At the end, the different components are put together to make the finished part for the ventilation system.
- There are stocks of finished goods. These are products that have been made and are waiting to be delivered to customers.

Stock control

How does a business like Aldwyn Plastic Products know when to buy in new stocks of raw materials? One way is to set maximum, minimum and re-order levels of stock, shown in Figure 1. This is sometimes called a **'Just In Case'** method of stock control. The diagram is called a bar gate stock graph or chart.

edexcel ::: key terms

Stocks – materials that a business holds. Some could be materials waiting to be used in the production process and some could be finished stock waiting to be delivered to customers.

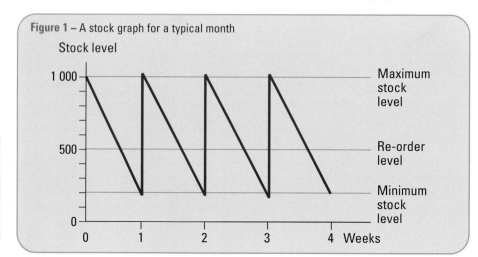

Figure 1 – A stock graph for a typical month

Maximum stock levels The maximum stock level is the largest amount of stock the business has decided to keep at any one time. Aldwyn has decided that its maximum stock level for plastic pellets is 1000 bags.

Re-order level The re-order level is the level of stock at which the business orders new stock. So at Aldwyn's, the company places a new order for plastic pellets when stocks have fallen to 500 bags.

Minimum or buffer stock levels The minimum stock level is the lowest level of stock that the business wants to hold. At Aldwyn's, the minimum stock level is 200 bags of plastic pellets. The minimum stock level is also known as the buffer stock level. If stocks fall below this level, Aldwyn's might have problems making an unexpected order that has suddenly been placed by a customer. Equally, if there is an unexpected delay in getting new stock, the buffer stock allows Aldwyn's to carry on production. The buffer stock is important because, if stock levels fell to zero, Aldwyn's would have to stop production.

These different stock levels are shown in Figure 1. Aldwyn's uses 800 bags of plastic pellets each week. It has set itself a buffer stock or minimum stock level of 200 bags. The maximum stock level is 1,000 bags. When stocks fall to 500 bags, the company re-orders 800 bags of plastic pellets. They take around 3 days to arrive. So the new stock arrives when stocks have fallen to 200 bags. The 800 bags are added to the stock and so stock levels go back up to 100 bags.

Uncertainty

In practice, stocks and production don't change exactly in the way that Figure 1 suggests. Mainly this is because production at Aldwyn's changes from week to week. Some weeks, more stock is used up than in other weeks. Equally, stock orders do not always arrive on time. So the new stock going into Aldwyn's does not always come on the same day of the week or month.

Figure 2 shows a stock graph for the month of November. In the first week, there is a rush of orders to make and so stocks are used up more quickly than usual. The result is that stock levels fall below the desired minimum stock level. In the second and third weeks, though, production is lower than usual. Stocks are not used up as quickly. Hence the order time for stock is much longer than in the first week. Stocks are higher than the minimum when the stock delivery takes place. In the last week, production is normal and new stocks are delivered on the day when the minimum stock level is reached.

Just In Time stock control

Holding stock is costly to a business like Aldwyn's. For this reason, some businesses have, where possible, changed to a different system of stock

Results Plus
Watch Out!

Just In Time stock management systems are often seen as better than other types. However, most businesses cannot make Just In Time work for them. Their orders for stock are too small to make it cost effective to receive stock Just In Time. Only very large companies, such as car manufacturers, tend to be in a position to exploit Just In Time to the full.

43

edexcel ⠿ key terms

Maximum stock level – the highest amount of stock to be kept by a business.

Re-order level – the amount of stock held by a business at which an order for new stock is placed with suppliers.

Buffer stock level or minimum stock level – the lowest amount of stock to be kept by a business.

Just In Time (JIT) – a stock management system where stocks are only delivered when they are needed by the production system, and so no stocks are kept by a business.

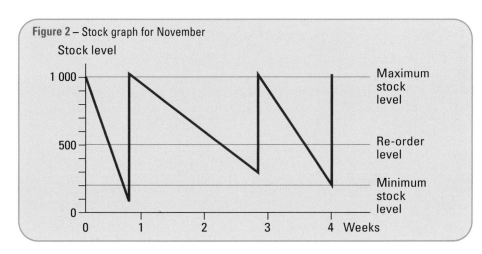

Figure 2 – Stock graph for November

management. This system is JIT or Just In Time stock management. With JIT, the business holds no stocks. When raw materials or components are needed, they are delivered to the business at exactly the time when they are to be used. JIT is widely used in car manufacturing on production lines. Businesses which supply components to the car manufacturer deliver parts to the production line as and when they are needed. This means there are frequent deliveries of stock.

Advantages and disadvantages of different stock control methods

What is the minimum level of stock that a business should hold? Should it hold any stock at all? When should stock be reordered? The answers to these sorts of questions depends on the individual business and how it can be run most efficiently.

Cost Stocks cost money to hold. For example, Aldwyn's holds an average of £100,000 of stock at any one time. It has to borrow the money to pay for this stock. At an interest rate of 10 per cent a year, it means that it is costing Aldwyn's £10,000 a year just in interest to hold this amount of stock. For a large company like a world car manufacturer, the cost of interest on holding stock could run into hundreds of millions of pounds a year. So holding the least amount of stock possible cuts costs. However, there are other costs to keeping stocks. Stocks have to be stored somewhere. The less stock is held, the less space a business needs to occupy. This saves on the cost of buildings, rent and insurance. Stocks also require workers to handle them. Some businesses have sophisticated systems for putting stock into storage and then taking it out again. Cutting stock can reduce the need to employ workers like warehouse managers or stock managers. In some industries, stock can also perish. Food companies, for example, have to use food stocks within very short periods of time or else the stocks have to be thrown away. Having the least amount of stock can minimise this sort of wastage.

Production needs Holding too little stock could lead to a loss of production and sales. For example, occasionally Aldwyn's is contacted by a customer to see whether it could complete an order within 24 hours. If Aldwyn's does not have the raw materials in stock to make the order, it has to turn the order away. Equally, sometimes a supplier fails to make deliveries on time. Very occasionally, this has meant that Aldwyn's has run out of stock and been forced to stop production. The less stock that is kept, the more likely these sorts of problems will occur. For companies that operate Just in Time production methods, a failure to deliver stocks will mean an immediate stoppage in production. An example of this occurred in 1997 in Japan. The car company Toyota bought all its components for brake valves from one single factory which suffered a devastating fire in 1997. The result was that production at most of Toyota's car plants was stopped within 24 hours. It took over a week to get production of the brake parts back to normal levels and for Toyota to resume production of cars.

Price Sometimes, businesses are able to negotiate discounts to prices if they order a certain amount from a supplier. The more that is ordered, the lower the price per item. So some businesses buy in bulk and put the materials into stock. So it could be cheaper for a business to do this than buying smaller amounts more frequently.

The advantage of Just In Time stock control is that the cost of holding stock is minimised because no stock is held. However, the business is then vulnerable if it cannot get hold of stock when it needs it. The business may also lose out on bulk buying discounts from suppliers.

The advantage of holding a buffer stock of materials is that sudden unexpected orders can be made. Problems with delivery from suppliers are also far less likely to cause problems. Holding stock means that the best price can be got from suppliers if they charge lower prices per item for larger deliveries. On the other hand, it is costly to run a system where the business holds stocks.

Overall, there is no correct stock management system for every business. Each business has to weigh up the advantages and disadvantages of different methods and decide which is the best for them.

Test yourself

1. A business aims to keep at least 2,000 metal sheets in stock at any one time. This stock is called

   A   a stock check
   B   a buffer stock
   C   the maximum stock level
   D   the re-order level of stock

   Select **one** answer.

2. A company does not keep stocks. Its suppliers deliver material and components as and when they are needed. This system of stock management is called

   A   Just In Time
   B   Just in Case
   C   Just When Needed
   D   Just In Stock

   Select **one** answer.

3. The managing director of a company has a policy of not ordering stock unless it is absolutely necessary. However, all too frequently, work has to come to a stop because there is not any stock of components in the factory. As a result, output is lost and time is wasted. This would suggest that

   A   the maximum stock level is too low
   B   the re-order level is too high
   C   the minimum stock level should be lowered
   D   the buffer stock level should be raised

   Select **one** answer.

Over to you

Jollife Metals is a company that makes products from metal sheets. The metal sheets are purchased monthly from a steel wholesaler. Demand fluctuates during the year and is greater in the winter months than in the summer months. The pattern of stock holding is shown in Figure 3.

The steel wholesaler, with its base only a few miles away from the Jollife Metals factory, has been very reliable in terms of deliveries. Jollife Metals is concerned that the wholesaler is not always offering the lowest price available in the market. Some of the competitors to Jollife Metals have been cutting costs by ordering directly from steel manufacturers in Turkey and the Ukraine. However, there have been reports that deliveries from these manufacturers have been unreliable and often late.

1. Explain, using an example, what is meant by (a) the maximum stock level and (b) the re-order level. (6)

2. Explain what is meant by the 'buffer stock level'. In your answer, give the number of metal sheets that make up the buffer stock level for Jollife Metals. (3)

3. At the end of the working day on 1 June, Jollife Metals had 2,000 sheets of metal in stock. By 31 July, this had fallen to 400 sheets. How many metal sheets were in stock at the end of the working day on (a) 1st August; (b) 31st August; (c) 1st November? (3)

4. (a) What happened to stock levels in June and July compared to September? (2)
   (b) What does this indicate about sales in those months? (2)

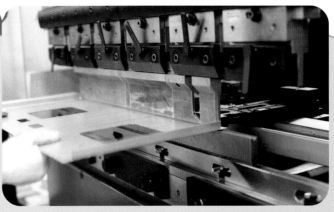

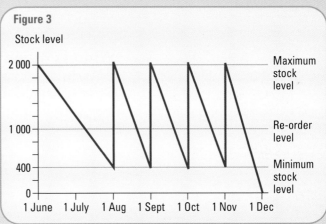

Figure 3

5. In late November there was a sudden unexpected rush of orders. How can you tell this from the stock graph? (3)

6. Do you think that Jollife Metals should hold a larger buffer stock of metal sheets? Justify your answer. (8)

ResultsPlus
Build Better Answers

Many large manufacturing firms hold stocks. These are necessary to complete the production process. There are more than just raw materials that can be counted as stocks. The larger the quantity of stocks held the larger the amount of storage needed.

(a) Identify **two** other types of stocks than raw materials. (2)

(b) Explain **one** disadvantage of a traditional stock control method (Just In Case), (3)

Think: What can be defined as stocks? What are the different types of stock control systems? What are the differences between them? Why do some firms move away from a traditional stock control system?

(a) Part-finished goods and finished goods. (2)

(b)

■ **Basic** States or mentions one disadvantage, such as '... it is expensive to store', but offers no explanation. (1)

● **Good** 'One disadvantage is that it ties up capital. (1) This capital could be used elsewhere in the business and so represents an opportunity cost.' (1)

▲ **Excellent** 'One disadvantage is that large amounts of storage are needed to hold the stocks. (1) This can be expensive, particularly if land or buildings are expensive to buy or rent. (1) The cash needed to pay for this storage could be better used elsewhere in the business such as investing in more productively efficient technology.' (1)

8 Quality

Case Study

The GSM Group employs over 300 people in five self-contained companies in the UK and a wholly owned subsidiary based in Germany. Examples of some of the products supplied by the group include metal, plastic and digitally printed labels, fascias and overlays; treadplates, interior trims and labels for the motor industry; and label printing software, barcode scanners and portable data capture systems. The group has a reputation for providing a friendly helpful service at competitive prices.

Objectives

● Understand the nature of quality control and compare this to a culture of quality assurance.

A good quality product meets the standards set by customers.

edexcel ⁝⁝⁝ key terms

Quality – achieving a minimum standard for a product or service, or a production process, which meets customers' needs.

Quality control – ensuring that a product or service meets minimum standards, often through testing of sample products once they have been made.

Quality assurance – ensuring that quality is produced and delivered at every stage of the production process, often through making quality the responsibility of every worker.

What is quality?

Which has the better quality: a Rolls Royce car or a Ford Fiesta? Or a shirt mass produced in China compared to a handmade, made-to-measure shirt manufactured in England? The Rolls Royce car and the made-to-measure shirt have more features than a Ford Fiesta or a mass-produced Chinese shirt. However, in business terms, they are not necessarily of better quality. This is because quality in business is about comparing a product to a particular standard. One standard for cars is that they should not break down. If the Rolls Royce car breaks down once every year, but the Ford Fiesta only breaks down once every three years, then the Ford Fiesta is better quality.

A good quality product is one which meets the standards set by customers. A poor quality product is one that does not meet the standards set by customers. It is likely to be one that has faults or does not work correctly.

GSM has some high profile customers which include Ford, General Motors and Nissan. GSM's approach to quality is that it finds out what its customers want and then provides it. The customers set the standards for quality. GSM provides the products that meet those standards.

Traditional quality control

The approach to quality has changed in the last thirty years. The traditional approach saw quality control as part of the chain of production. A product would be designed and the materials to be used would be chosen. The design would be handed over to the production department. It would decide how the product should be made and set about making it. The product would be tested for quality at the end of the production process by quality controllers or inspectors, whose responsibility it was to check for quality. If the product didn't meet the quality standard, it would have to be altered or made again. In some factories, goods that didn't meet quality standards might be thrown away or sold as 'seconds'. Quality inspectors would also test materials bought in from suppliers. There was no guarantee that they would be of the right standard.

Quality assurance

The modern approach to quality is called quality assurance. Quality control relies mainly on tests being carried out once a product is made. A culture of quality assurance in a business relies on building quality into every stage of the production process. It is about building quality into how a product is made. Every part of the production process must lead to a quality, no-faults product. So when a product is sold to a customer, the business can **assure** the customer that it is a quality product.

Quality assurance has many implications for a business.

Quality as part of every process Quality assurance means that quality must be part of every process. So quality is not tested just at certain stages of the production process. It is built into production. For example, quality is important at the design stage. GSM appreciate this and takes the trouble to visit customers when they are designing future products.

Quality is everyone's job With quality control, quality is the responsibility of the quality inspector. With quality assurance, every worker is responsible for quality. This may mean that a worker or group of workers does the job that a quality inspector did before. It may mean that quality is being tested at a stage of the production process where it wasn't being tested before. If products are not of the right quality, then it is important that the problem can be identified quickly so that it can be put right. Training and teamwork is very important. At GSM, every employee signs a contract to say that they are a member of a team. At each site there are six teams. Team leaders have to demonstrate good quality communication skills. Training in communication is also given. GSM spends 1.4% of revenue on training and every employee has a personal development plan.

Customers and suppliers To help build quality into the production process, workers need to recognise the needs of customers. Suppliers must take into account the requirements of businesses, their customers. Workers in sales must take into account the needs of the public or other businesses buying their products or services. By recognising that their work affects customers, workers become more responsible for what they do. They see their importance in the overall work of the business. GSM found that in the electronics market, customers wanted one supplier for all non-electronic parts. GSM is now making everything that customers were buying from lots of different suppliers. Continuing down the supply chain, GSM itself has cut down the number of suppliers it has, searching for single source arrangements wherever possible.

Kaizen Kaizen means 'continuous improvement' in Japanese. It is a technique which was originally used in Japanese factories and has now spread throughout the world. To achieve the highest possible quality standards continuous improvements are necessary. Kaizen is very active throughout GSM. At GSM's Thirsk site, more than 4,000 suggestions for improvements were made over a four year period alone. One example of Kaizen was the elimination of the wrapping process at GSM. This saved money in wrapping materials and made it easier for the customer when receiving orders.

Zero defects The ultimate aim of a business using quality assurance techniques like GSM is to have zero defects. This means that all its work meets the required quality standards at every stage of the production process. To reach this, the business may set itself intermediate targets where it aims to reduce defects to a certain level within, say, the next year.

The role of management Although every worker is responsible for quality, it is the responsibility of management to set up systems which will ensure this quality. For instance, if a worker or group of workers is producing faulty goods, then there must be a system for identifying the nature of the problem. It could be they are working with inadequate machinery. It could be that they haven't been trained sufficiently to do the job. It could be that there is inadequate lighting where they work or that machines are poorly spaced out on the factory floor. Then the system must put the problem right. At GSM, management is very involved in quality assurance. For example, there is a team leaders' conference every six months where objectives are reviewed and ideas discussed. Although decision making is

Watch Out!

There are many meanings of the word 'quality'. In Business Studies, quality has only one meaning. It is about whether a product or production process meets a minimum standard. Standards for products may change. The overall standard for a meal in a top restaurant is higher than in a fast food outlet like McDonald's or KFC. However, one of the reasons why McDonald's and KFC are so popular is because they produce a product which meets their standards.

Quality assurance means every employee is resonsible for quality.

not democratic, there is a feeling at GSM that the views of workers are heard.

Quality standards

Many products are made to standards which are laid down by independent organisations. The British Standards Institution (BSI), for example, is an organisation which draws up standards for a wide range of products from beds to nails. Some consumer products like kettles are sold with Kitemarks on them. This shows that they have been made to a standard drawn up by the British Standards Institution. Other examples are the British Electrotechnical Approvals Board (BEAB), which tests and approves electrical products, and The British Toy and Hobby Association which grants a Lion Mark for approved toys. Product standards measure the quality of a product once it has been made. They are therefore linked to quality control.

However, there are also standards for the quality of production systems. These are used to assess quality assurance. There are an internationally recognised set of quality assurance standards called ISO (International Organisation for Standardisation) standards. ISO 9000 is the basic standard for quality management systems. There are further standards such as ISO 9001 which covers quality assurance in design, development, production, installation and servicing.

There are two main advantages for a company like GSM in meeting ISO 9000 standards. First, GSM was forced to review its quality procedures and make improvements to them. Second, because ISO 9000 is an international standard, it is widely recognised by GSM's overseas customers such as Ford, Nissan and GM. By buying from GSM, they know that the company is committed to and able to deliver quality products. This helps GSM to sell its products.

Source: adapted from GSM web site http://www.gsmgroup.co.uk/ and dti: *from quality to excellence.*

It is important that toys meet quality standards as children handle them.

Over to you

How do you get a customer satisfaction rate of 96 per cent? For Peel Northern, it was about quality assurance. Peel Northern is a security company. Started only two years ago, it provides a range of services including guarding sites and site protection as well as CCTV (closed-circuit television) products and installation. Based in Halifax, West Yorkshire, you might see its security officers patrolling a local construction site, factory premises or car park. It employs 10 office staff and between 50-100 security officers depending on the volume of work. Customers have included construction companies such as Mowlem and Carrillion and supermarket chains such as Asda and Tesco.

Quality assurance at Peel Northern is about checking everything the company does for quality. This goes from staff training to logging phone calls and monitoring efficiency. Quality is the responsibility of every individual worker in everything they do. Inevitably, there are cost implications. The company has spent £300,000 in changing its practices to improve quality. For example, new software was installed to provide real time, instantaneous, monitoring of security guards on all their sites.

Gaining certification of quality standards has been essential to Peel Northern's success. From the start, the company worked towards gaining ISO 9001 certification. The British Standards Institute (BSI) awarded certification having rigorously checked through all Peel Northern's procedures. Peel Northern has gone on to gain ACS status. ACS stands for Approved Contractor Scheme. This is a government benchmark for quality. ISO 9001 and ACS are essential for Peel Northern if it is to win any work with major companies and local authorities.

Andrew Peel, who founded the company, says that the company's success is down to a continual passion for good quality. 'You are only as good as your last day's work and we always put quality first', he says. 'Our policy is to strive to continually improve.'

Source: information from www.bsigroup.co.uk, June 2008.

1. Explain what is meant by 'quality', using Peel Northern as an example. (3)

2. A firm in competition with Peel Northern checks for quality by getting its security guards to phone in if there has been a break in at a site they are protecting. Why would this be an example of quality control? (3)

3. What is the difference between quality control and quality assurance? In your answer, use examples from Peel Northern. (3)

4. Identify **three** advantages for Peel Northern of having gained ISO 9001 and ACS certification. (3)

5. Is quality assurance more important for Peel Northern or for its customers? Justify your answer. (8)

ResultsPlus
Build Better Answers

Draw five lines to link each statement about quality assurance on the left with its correct description on the right.

A 'Quality is everyone's job'

B 'Workers and suppliers must think about customers'

C 'Kaizen means "continuous improvement"'

D 'Zero defects are the ultimate goal'

E 'Management must listen'

(i) A technique originally used in Japanese factories after World War II

(ii) The customers' needs must be taken into account

(iii) All work meets the required quality standards

(iv) Workers' ideas and thoughts should be acknowledged and discussed

(v) All staff are responsible for levels of quality

Answer

A - (v)

B - (ii)

C - (i)

D - (iii)

E - (iv)

Technique: you have 5 statements that link to the concept of Quality Assurance (QA). Look at the list and try and see if there are any clear links between the statement and the descriptions and likewise ones that do not match at all.

Think: What are the main areas of QA? What is the role of the worker? What is the role of the supplier? Where did it originate? What is the goal?

Decide:

'...everyone's job' talks about people so A = (v)

Thinking about 'customers' links to customers' needs. So B = (ii)

'Kaizen' is a Japanese term, therefore C = (i)

'Zero defects' is where nothing is 'wrong', which means that quality standards must be maintained. So D = (iii)

This leaves the management 'listening' to staff to acknowledge their ideas. So E = (iv)

9 Cost-effective operations and competitiveness

Case Study

Rolls-Royce is a multinational company. It makes power systems for use in aeroplanes, ships and power stations. Rolls-Royce engines, for example, can be found on many Boeing and Airbus aeroplanes. In 2008, it sold £9 billion worth of products to customers all over the world. Rolls-Royce's success is based on being highly competitive. Part of this is producing better products than those of its rivals. However, it also needs to be price competitive. It needs to keep its costs down to be able to offer its customers competitive prices.

Objectives

● Understand that improving productivity is likely to lead to lower costs.

● Appreciate that managers must keep costs down to ensure cost-effective operations.

● Appreciate that lower costs allows for more competitive prices.

Productivity

In a highly competitive world, Rolls-Royce's success depends crucially on continually raising the productivity of its workers. Productivity is output per worker. It measures how much each worker produces over a period of time. As a formula:

$$\text{Productivity} = \frac{\text{Total output}}{\text{Number of workers}}$$

In the 2000s, the average rise in productivity per employee at Rolls-Royce was over 7 per cent per year. This meant that each year the amount of what the average Rolls-Royce worker produced went up by over 7 per cent.

For example, assume that a team of 100 workers can produce 500 engines each year. Productivity of the team is therefore 5 engines per worker per year (500 engines ÷ 100 workers). The next year, the same 100 workers produce 600 engines. The productivity of the team therefore rises to 6 engines per worker (600 engines ÷ 100 workers).

Productivity is important because if workers increase the amount they produce, assuming that no costs of production have changed, then the cost per item produced will fall.

There is a number of ways in which Rolls-Royce can raise productivity.

Training It costs money to train workers in the short-term. However, in the long-term, better trained workers tend to be more productive. They are better at doing their job. They may also be able to perform new tasks with a higher level of output. For example, say that a group of 10 workers can produce 40 engines a month. Their productivity is therefore 4 engines per worker per month (40 engines ÷ 10 workers). They now receive training and as a result their output increases to 50 engines per month. Their productivity will now be 5 machines per worker per month (50 engines ÷ 10 workers).

Better equipment Workers will be more productive if they are provided with better equipment. Rolls-Royce spends hundreds of millions of pounds each year replacing old equipment and adding to its stock of equipment in order to improve productivity. For example, say a group of 20 workers produce 300 engines every year. Their productivity is 15 engines per worker. (300 engines ÷ 20 workers). The company now replaces their out-of-date machinery with the latest state of the art machinery. As a result, they now make 400 engines per year. Their productivity has increased to 20 machines per worker per year (400 engines ÷ 20 workers).

More effective work practices Businesses tend to find over time that they can improve how people work. Inefficiencies in the system become apparent. Reorganising workers can mean that the same amount of work can be achieved using fewer workers. Or higher levels of output can be gained using the same number of workers.

In 2009, Rolls-Royce announced it was cutting up to 2 300 managerial, professional and clerical staff in Europe. Investment in IT (information technology) meant that data management systems had improved, reducing the need for some staff. Improved management skills also meant that productivity had increased, reducing the need for staff. Improved productivity meant that fewer staff were needed and so costs could fall.

Other ways of reducing costs

Improving productivity is just one way in which a business like Rolls-Royce can reduce its costs and become more competitive. There are many other ways by which management in a business can put downward pressure on its costs and make its operations cost-effective.

Improved purchasing Businesses like Rolls-Royce can change their purchasing over time. For example, they may be able to change their supplier to get a lower price on the components and materials they buy. Or they might be able to find a supplier that provides a higher quality component at a slightly higher price. In such cases overall quality and reliability can be improved. A business may also be able to negotiate a lower price with an existing supplier. Firms that buy in larger quantities (bulk buying) may find they can get lower prices.

Relocation Some businesses can relocate part of all of their activities to reduce costs. For example, a business might decide to close a factory in the UK and shift the work to Eastern Europe or the Far East. The advantage of making a move like this is that the cost of land and buildings is likely to be lower. Taxes may be lower in the new location. Also, local workers are likely to be paid far less than even the lowest paid UK workers. However, there can be disadvantages to relocation. Moving can be highly disruptive to production in the short-term. Also, workers in Eastern Europe or the Far East may not have the skills of UK workers. So the quality of work may be lower. If you are making cheap clothes, this may not be too much of a problem. If, like Rolls-Royce, you are making parts for aeroplane engines, lower quality may be totally unacceptable.

Better design Better design can reduce costs. A new design for a product may use fewer or better quality or better designed materials to achieve the same effect. Alternatively, a new design may be easier to make or manufacture, leading to lower labour costs.

Results Plus
Watch Out!

It is a mistake to think that buying at a lower price is always in the best interests of a firm. Price is just one of the factors that a firm should take into consideration when buying. For example, a lower priced item may not be of the same quality. Or it may take more time to deliver.

Cutting overhead costs Overhead costs are costs not directly related to production. For example, at Rolls-Royce, there is the cost of running headquarters for each of its manufacturing divisions. There is a research and development programme. There is the cost of marketing its products. If some of these costs can be cut, then overall costs will also fall.

ResultsPlus
Watch Out!

Do not confuse 'productivity' with 'production'. Productivity measures output per worker (or machine) per period of time whereas production refers to the total amount produced by a business over a period of time.

Competitive prices

Businesses like Rolls-Royce face a competitive challenge. They need to sell their products to be successful. There are many factors which decide whether or not a customer will buy a product. Price is one very important factor. When competing against rival companies, Rolls-Royce has to be price competitive. If its prices are too high then, however good the product, it will not sell. Getting the price right is crucially dependent on keeping control of costs. Like any private sector business, Rolls-Royce needs to make a profit to survive in the long-term. So it needs to be able to sell its products for more than they cost to make. If costs can be cut, then Rolls-Royce can offer its customers lower prices. In the long-term, this will give it a competitive advantage provided it can sustain the advantage and its rivals would find it hard to imitate or copy its ideas.

Source: information from www.rolls-royce.com.

Test yourself

1. Ginifer's is a company which manufactures television sets. Last year, labour productivity rose by 10 per cent. This means that

   A sales rose by 10 per cent
   B labour costs rose by 10 per cent
   C output per worker rose by 10 per cent
   D output rose by 10 per cent

   Select **one** answer.

2. Belk's is a company that operates a chain of sandwich shops. It wants to increase the productivity of its workers. Which **one** of the following is most likely to achieve this?

   A Opening a new sandwich shop in London
   B Installing new coffee machines which make coffee faster than old machines
   C Hiring 20 new workers
   D Tightening health and safety regulations in the company's outlets

   Select **one** answer.

3. Bollam's is a company that owns a chain of health and fitness centres. Which **one** of the following is most likely to lead to a significant fall in costs for the firm? A fall in the

   A the number of workers employed by Bollam's
   B the annual membership fee charged to customers by Bollam's
   C the number of people applying for jobs at Bollam's
   D the prices charged by firms in competition with Bollam's

   Select **one** answer.

Over to you

RHZ Containers is a large shipping company. It specialises in transporting containers round the world. Competition in the container shipping market is intense and firms are continually seeking ways to improve productivity and cut costs.

Between 2002 and 2007, RHZ Containers experienced increasing demand for its services. The worldwide boom saw a 20 per cent increase per year in the number of containers the company carried. Like many of its competitors, RHZ Containers ordered a number of new, larger ships. These ships were far more cost effective to operate. For example, the number of crew needed to work one of the new, larger ships only increases by 10 per cent when the number of containers carried increases by 50 per cent.

However, the worldwide recession that started in 2008 has seen a slump in demand for container transport. This has started a fierce price war between companies. Prices for carrying a container have fallen dramatically. RHZ Containers, like its rivals, has been forced to cut its costs to survive. For example, ships now travel at slower speeds because this saves on fuel. The oldest, least efficient ships have been laid up in ports round the world. The company has only been using its more modern, more efficient ships. Inevitably, workers have lost their jobs. Crews on the ships no longer being used have been laid off. There has been a 30 per cent cut in jobs at head office. All investment in new ships has been cancelled.

Despite all this cost cutting, RHZ Containers recorded a loss in 2008 and expects to see an even larger loss in 2009. However, the pain is being shared by all its competitors. At the moment, the focus of management is on the survival of the business. Can RHZ Containers get through this difficult period and still be in existence when world trade begins to grow again?

1. (a) Explain, using an example, what is meant by labour productivity. (3)
   (b) Explain why productivity is likely to be higher on larger container ships than on smaller container ships. (3)

2. Analyse how RHZ Containers is cutting costs to cope with a slump in demand. (6)

3. Discuss whether cutting costs now will make RHZ Containers more competitive in the short term and in the long term. Justify your answer. (8)

 ResultsPlus
Build Better Answers

Rikki Bekele is the production manager for an independent brewery in the West Midlands. It produces 6 different beers for 37 pubs in the local region. Rikki wishes to improve his productivity.

(a) Explain **two** ways in which Rikki can raise the productivity levels in the brewery (6)

Think: What is productivity? How can productivity be increased?

■ **Basic** States up to two methods of improving productivity but with no development. (1-2)

● **Good** Identifies two methods and offers some explanation behind them. For example 'Rikki could buy better equipment. (1) This would mean that the production would be more efficient. (1) He could also train the staff (1) to be more efficient at operating the machinery to get more out of them. (1)

▲ **Excellent** Clear identification of two methods with a good explanation of each. Links to the outcome from each method are

discussed. For example 'Rikki could purchase some new brewing equipment (1) that works more efficiently than the current ones. (1) This would mean that the productivity rates would rise as more would be made over the same period of time. (1) Rikki could also look at the working practices of the staff (1) and re-organise them so that they work in a more efficient manner. (1) This may mean that the same amount of production could take place with fewer workers or higher levels of production could result in the same time period, depending on available space. (1)

10 Effective customer service

Case Study

54

trent barton is a small independent bus company in the UK. It employs nearly 1,000 people in various parts of Derbyshire, Leicestershire and Nottinghamshire. It has a fleet of around 270 modern buses that run on a network of local routes. It is proud of the personal service it provides to customers and is continually looking at ways in which it can improve this service.

Objectives

- Understand the meaning of the term 'customer service'.
- Understand that effective customer service means providing customers with the service level they want, when they want it.
- Appreciate the link between effective customer service and repeat purchase levels.
- Understand the disadvantages to a business of a poor customer service.

edexcel ⠿ key terms

Customer service – the experience that a customer gets when dealing with a business and the extent to which that experience meets and exceeds customer needs and expectations.

Providing customers with excellent service

Successful companies are ones that provide customers with the products and service levels they want. Customer service refers to the methods a business uses to enhance or improve the experience that a customer has in using the goods or services of the business. It is a way in which the business builds a relationship with the customer that creates trust and loyalty. Satisfied customers will keep coming back to the company to buy more products. They will also tell their friends and family about the products. Word about good customer products and services spreads without the need for any paid advertising.

A number of factors contribute to excellent products and service.

Meeting the needs of customers Customers will buy a product if it meets their needs. So getting the product right is essential for the success of any business. trent barton has found from market research that its customers look for four main characteristics in a bus service. These are reliability, friendliness, a clean bus interior and comfort. Less important are accessibility, convenience of stops, information and price. *trent barton* works hard to provide its customers with a bus service that satisfies these needs. For example, all buses are intensively cleaned overnight at their depots. However, in addition, buses are also cleaned during the day. Cleaners are stationed at major departure points to sweep out the buses and finish off with an aerosol spray.

Quality In business, quality is meeting a standard that satisfies customer needs. *trent barton* does everything possible to achieve a quality service. To achieve quality, it has one of the highest levels of investment per £ of sales in the bus industry. It invests in new buses, extensive staff training and customer care.

Excellent service for transport businesses can mean buses arriving on time or good facilities being provided on planes.

On time service Getting a product to the customer when they want it will encourage repeat purchases. For *trent barton*, having a bus turn up at the bus stop on time and completing the journey on time is one of the four most important priorities for customers. *trent barton* regularly reviews its bus timetables to make sure this happens. The main problem it faces with reliability is traffic congestion, particularly at the rush hour. Sometimes it will add an extra bus to a route to deal with this problem. In some cases, it has reduced the number of times the bus stops because each stop increases the journey time. However, *trent barton* recognises that reliability during the rush hour is too often out of its control. This is the reason why it would like to see the government take action to reduce the use of cars and stagger working hours. Some aspects of customer service, therefore, are out of the hands of the business but many are something that businesses can control.

Innovation Businesses must innovate to stay ahead of the competition. This is true even if the product being sold was first developed a long time ago. For example, although Coca Cola first came onto the market in 1886, Coca Cola the company is continually working to bring out new variants of the drink. Coca Cola has also diversified into producing a range of soft drinks. trent barton is continually innovating too. It has invested heavily in new buses. This means that all its buses now have low floors for easy-access to all passengers. Over the years, *trent barton* has introduced new services where it saw a customer need. For example, in 2008, it introduced a limited stop, fast service between Alreton and Derby called F1. It aims to cater for shoppers who want to take advantage of shopping in the attractive Westfield shopping centre in Derby, which had only just opened.

Collaboration Businesses like *trent barton* operate in a competitive environment. However, sometimes there are opportunities for collaboration with other firms, with government agencies or with pressure groups that will improve what is being offered to customers. For example, in the UK, bus companies have the opportunity to negotiate Bus Quality Partnerships with local authorities. trent barton has negotiated Bus Quality Partnerships with Nottinghamshire County Council, Derby City Council, Nottingham City Council and the Highways Agency. In return for *trent barton* guaranteeing a certain level of service, the government authorities provide investment funds for improvements. For example, the local authorities working with *trent barton* paid for new bus shelters along particular routes. The Highways Agency paid for a bus lane to be constructed along the busy A52 route. Local authorities have also funded real time electronic information displays at bus shelters. These show when the next bus is due. The information is based on the actual position of the next bus at that point in time. All these things help to improve the customer experience and make it more likely that passengers will use their services again.

Spotting problems Successful businesses are ones which can identify problems as they arise and respond to them. Bus drivers are in the frontline of the service at *trent barton*. They are often the first to notice problems. So *trent barton* listens to its drivers. They take part in regular seminars, which take a detailed look at service quality. Their ideas are taken into consideration when deciding how to resolve problems that arise. Those working with customers are often far better placed to understand the problems and the possible solutions than managers. Management may not always see the problems and issues at first hand on a regular basis.

Listening to customers Any business that wants to provide products that customers want must listen to them. If the business wants to expand its customer base, it must also listen to potential customers who at the moment are not buying the product. One way of listening is to conduct market research. trent barton has

What is meant by effective customer service differs from industry to industry and business to business. Effective customer service, for example, is different for Kellogg, the maker of breakfast cereals, than for British Telecom, the phone company. Make sure you think carefully about the needs of customers for a particular product when you write anything about effective customer service.

edexcel ::: key terms

Innovation – the process of transforming inventions into products that can be sold to customers.

Some businesses may not have customer service at the very top of their agenda. In some cases, the business exists simply to provide the lowest prices possible and as a result customers may not get the quality of service that exists elsewhere. Discount shops, for example, may have basic levels of customer service only but the prices are very low and the range of goods on offer is very wide. For customers, there is a trade off - lower prices and limited customer service or higher prices and excellent customer service.

Listening to customers and dealing with their questions helps a business to provide effective customer service.

been using market research since the late 1980s. It regularly interviews customers on a route by route basis. It also interviews people who make the same journey by car instead of bus to find out why they are not using the bus. It was market research that highlighted the four main requirements that its customers had.

Dealing with complaints How a business deals with complaints is very important for repeat business. If customers have a complaint and do not feel that it has been dealt with properly, then they may not buy again. Customers must feel they have been fairly treated. The customer may not always be right but they have to feel that they have been treated properly and have been listened to by the business. Good customer service involves trying to find solutions to problems that satisfy customers and are affordable for the business.

Staff training Only properly trained staff can deliver a quality product. Training is essential for every aspect of a business. Staff at *trent barton* receive regular training. For example, bus drivers are trained to deal with customers who are using the bus for the first time. The quality of this first time experience is often crucial for repeat purchases. If the first time experience is good, the customer will be tempted to use the bus again.

Going beyond what is expected Some businesses acquire a reputation for excellence in their customer service. This can be a major selling point for the business and encourage repeat purchase. Many businesses today say that one of their aims is to 'exceed customer expectations'. One of the ways in which trent barton exceeds customer expectations is the relationship between bus drivers and their customers. Bus drivers are recruited partly for their customer skills. Many bus drivers are on first name terms with their regular

passengers. The bus driver is the main point of contact between the company and its customers. If bus drivers are friendly and helpful, this goes beyond what many bus customers expect.

The disadvantages of poor customer service

Poor customer service will almost inevitably hit sales. Customers will find substitute, competing products to buy. Bus companies which provide poor customer service, for example, find that travellers switch either to rival bus companies or rail or to the car. Repeat purchases are lower than they would be if customer service were good. Lower sales means lower profits. So providing a poor level of service can hit a business hard. If competitors are providing good customer service, it could even force a business to close down as it loses sales. At its most extreme, the very survival of a business depends on its level of customer service.

Source: information from http://www.trentbarton.co.uk.

Over to you

Pelstone Hotels is a chain of hotels in the South of England. It owns 3 hotels in central London. Over the past few years, its marketing department has worked hard to win contracts from US travel firms. The marketing department has emphasised the good locations of the hotels and the cheap prices. As a result, US travel firms have placed a large number of bookings with Pelstone, helping to fill the hotels.

However, American visitors to England have not been impressed with their stays at Pelstone Hotels. The hotel chain has gained a reputation for poor customer service. Hotel rooms too often have equipment such as kettles or bedside lights that do not work. The cleaning of rooms and bathrooms is often poor. The quality of food served at breakfast is well below the standard that Americans expect. Hotel staff are too often unhelpful. The hotels also seem to employ too few staff to cope with the number of people staying the night.

This year, bookings at Pelstone Hotels have fallen dramatically. The whole hotel industry has been badly affected by the worldwide recession. Fewer British tourists are taking a holiday or weekend break because they cannot afford it. The number of US visitors has also dropped because the USA is in recession. However, Pelstone Hotels has suffered a much larger drop in the number of overnight stays than the industry average. US travel firms are booking their clients into other hotels. They are taking advantage of the drop in prices for hotel rooms across the UK hotel industry.

1. Explain, using Pelstone Hotels as an example, what is meant by 'poor customer service. (3)

2. Assess **two** ways in which poor customer service might affect Pelstone Hotels. (8)

3. Do you think that improving customer service would bring back American visitors to Pelstone Hotels? Justify your answer. (8)

Results**Plus**
Build Better Answers

Many people visit fast-food restaurants. Often these types of businesses are criticised for their poor levels of customer service.

(a) Identify **one** disadvantage of good customer service. (1)

(b) Explain how poor customer service might affect a business such as a fast food restaurant. (3)

Think: What is customer service? Who is responsible for customer service? What does good customer service give to a company? Where have I experienced good and bad customer service?

■ **Basic** States or mentions one disadvantage, such as ... 'people might not come back again', but offers no explanation. (1)

● **Good** 'One disadvantage is that customers might go elsewhere to buy their food. (1) This means that sales will be lower and profits will fall. (1) The lack of profits might mean less opportunities for future development.' (1)

▲ **Excellent** 'One disadvantage is that customers will not become repeat purchasers.' (1) This might lower sales and profit

levels. (1) It may also lead to a loss of reputation and market share. (1) The drop in revenue and profits will hinder any future development of the business, making it more difficult to regain market share. (1)

11 Meeting consumer protection laws

58

Case Study

Topshop is a chain of over 400 fashion stores in the UK and internationally. Launched in 1964, it aims to sell into the female 16-25 age segment of the market. It has an international reputation for being at the cutting edge of fashion. The company is owned by Arcadia which also owns well known high street businesses such as Burton, Miss Selfridge and Wallis.

Objectives

● Appreciate the purpose of Trade Descriptions and Sale of Goods legislation.

● Understand the effects of this legislation on business.

edexcel ⠿ key terms

Sale of goods legislation – gives consumers rights to compensation if a product they buy is not of merchantable quality, not as described or not fit for purpose.

Trade Descriptions legislation – makes businesses liable for prosecution and fines if products are sold in a misleading way.

Protecting the consumer

In the UK, there are two main types of law that protect the consumer. One type of law, civil law, helps consumers get compensation when things go wrong. One of the examples of civil law is the Sale of Goods Act. The other type of law, criminal law, lays down rules by which retailers like Topshop must operate. If they break these rules, then they can be prosecuted and fined. One example of criminal law is the Trade Descriptions Act which has been updated by the Consumer Protection from Unfair Trading Regulations in 2008.

An Act is an Act of Parliament. The Parliament sits at Westminster. Members of Parliament (MPs) create new laws or change existing laws when they pass an Act of Parliament. The Sale of Goods Act was first passed into law in 1979. It has been changed and updated a number of times since then. The Trade Descriptions Act was first passed into law in 1968. Most of it was replaced in 2008 by the Consumer Protection from Unfair Trading Regulations. The law is very important both for businesses and consumers. It sets down the rights and obligations of both buyers and sellers. Businesses and consumers who act contrary to the law can be taken to court and either ordered to pay compensation or be fined.

The Sale of Goods Act

The Sale of Goods Act helps consumers get compensation when things go wrong. According to the Sale of Goods Act, when a business like Topshop sells a product to a customer, a contract is established between the seller and the buyer. The seller, the business, has to make sure that products have three characteristics.

Match the description Goods must match the description given to them. For example, if the label on a skirt sold at Topshop says that the skirt is made out of 100 per cent cotton, then the material must indeed be 100 per cent cotton. If the label on a pair of shoes says 'leather', then the shoes must be made of leather.

Merchantable quality Goods must be of merchantable or satisfactory quality. What is meant by satisfactory quality varies from product to product. It also varies according to the price that is paid. For example, clothes sold at Topshop must have a good appearance and finish. They must be free from defects such as rips or holes (unless, of course, the rips or holes are part of the design). For some businesses, safety is very important when it comes to merchantable quality. For example, a television set must be electrically safe to use if it is to be of merchantable quality.

Fit for purpose Goods must be fit for purpose. This means they must do what would normally be expected of such a good. For example, you must be able to walk in shoes sold at Topshop. Clothes must be washable unless it clearly states on the label that they are dry clean only. They should also last a reasonable length of time. You could expect a coat to last a long time even if it is worn every day. In contrast, you would reasonably expect a pair of tights to last much less time if worn every day.

What happens if a consumer buys a product that does not meet any one of these three characteristics? In law, the business selling the product to the consumer must then either give a refund, a replacement or a repair.

Many retailers, like Topshop, give additional rights to customers. These are rights over and above what they need to give by law. For example, say a shopper bought a coat but decided when she got home that she did not like it. In law, she has no automatic right to take the coat back to the shop for a refund. However, Topshop allows its shoppers to bring back clothes so long as they have a receipt and the tags are still on the clothes.

The Trade Descriptions Act and Consumer Protection from Unfair Trading Regulations

The Trade Descriptions Act is different from the Sale of Goods Act. The Sale of Goods Act helps a consumer get their money back if there is a problem. The Trade Descriptions Act, updated by the Consumer Protection from Unfair Trading Regulations, makes a number of different actions illegal. Businesses selling to consumers that offend against these laws can be taken to court and fined.

Under the law, it is illegal for a business to engage in a number of unfair practices.

Giving false information It is illegal for a business to give false information about a product. For example, if Topshop says that a coat is made of wool, then legally it must be made of wool. A retailer that sold a coat advertised as wool but in fact made of another material would be breaking the law.

Failing to give important information Some businesses fail to give important information in order to increase their sales. For example, a shop may advertise mobile phones for sale in a local newspaper. Consumers would reasonably expect that these were new mobile phones. However, if the shop only sold second hand mobile phones, it would be breaking the law unless the advertisement specifically mentioned this. Another example of a business breaking the law would be a car park where drivers could not see the car parking charges before they entered the car park. Drivers might have made a different decision about where to park if they had seen the charges.

Acting aggressively Some businesses, unfortunately, act aggressively towards potential customers in order to get them to buy their products. For example, a garage might do work on a car in for repair that has not been agreed with the customer. If the garage refuses to hand back the car unless the bill is paid, then it is acting illegally. Some sales people from firms that visit people's homes to sell products, like double glazing or burglar alarm systems, also act aggressively towards their customers. Elderly people are particularly vulnerable to this sort of illegal selling.

There is also a list of specific selling practices that are banned outright. For example, it is illegal for a business to advertise to children and tell them to get their parents to buy the product.

The reason for consumer protection

In the past, consumers have been exploited by some businesses. To increase their profits, businesses have sold shoddy goods. To increase sales, businesses have

Shoes should be fit for purpose. Running shoes should be suitable for this sport.

Food should be match the description. Fish sold as 'Fresh, caught today' must be caught that day.

MP3 players must be capable of playing music in this format.

60

used high pressure selling tactics.

Individual consumers are at a disadvantage once they have bought a product. What happens, for example, if you have a bought a computer game and the disk does not work? If the shop from where you bought it refuses to give a refund, what can you do now? Without consumer law, you will have lost your money.

Consumer protection is particularly important in areas of health and safety. Every year, people become ill from buying food which is not fit for human consumption from shops and restaurants. These shops and restaurants are acting illegally in selling this food and risk being prosecuted. The problem, though, would be far worse if there were no consumer laws protecting us from these sorts of businesses. Food is not the only example, though, of products that can be dangerous. Everything from electrical goods to clothes, toys and paint potentially can be harmful. Hair dryers that have not been wired properly and give an electric shock when used, or toys that have nails sticking out which could harm a child are just two examples.

These are the reasons why governments have passed laws to protect the consumer from businesses that would otherwise sell poor quality goods.

The effects of consumer legislation on business

Businesses have to comply with consumer protection law. There is a number of effects of these laws on businesses.

Knowing the law Businesses have to understand the law. Very large businesses like Tesco or Arcadia, the company which owns Topshop, will employ their own legal experts. Small businesses tend to rely on reading leaflets and books. When changes to consumer protection laws are introduced, businesses must understand what those changes will mean for their particular operations. Government departments like the Department for Business, Enterprise and Regulatory Reform (BERR) and bodies like the Office of Fair Trading provide information and advice for businesses to help them understand the law and how it affects a business.

Compliance costs Complying with the law leads to extra costs for businesses. Many businesses would, if there were no consumer laws, give consumers fewer rights than they

have with the current laws. Having to give refunds, for example, is costly. So too is making sure that all products being sold are totally safe. Compliance costs can be very heavy for businesses in the food industry. There are very strict regulations about storing food and preparing food for grocery stores and restaurants. Every year, hundreds of grocery stores and restaurants are prosecuted for failing to comply with consumer protection laws.

Revenues and profits Businesses, like Topshop, which follow the law very strictly can turn this into a marketing advantage, especially if they give their customers more rights than the legal minimum. They can gain a reputation for taking care of their customers and giving value for money. This leads to greater customer loyalty, higher sales, more revenues and larger profits. On the other hand, businesses which get into court can have a lot of bad publicity. Their reputation can be damaged and so they lose sales and profits.

Source: information from www.acadiagroup.co.uk.

Test yourself

1. **One** of the purposes of Trade Descriptions legislation is to

    A *prevent businesses from giving false information in advertisements*
    B *force businesses to offer low prices on their products*
    C *make businesses give detailed descriptions of products on packaging*
    D *offer compensation to consumers when products are faulty*

    Select **one** answer.

2. **One** of the purposes of Sale of Goods legislation is to

    A *encourage shops to have regular sales when they mark down prices*
    B *stop shops from refusing to sell goods to customers at low prices*
    C *allow consumers to get compensation if a product is faulty*
    D *prevent businesses from selling out of products*

    Select **one** answer.

3. Which **one** of the following is most likely to be an effect of consumer protection legislation on businesses? It

    A *reduces their costs*
    B *leads to bad publicity if a business is taken to court*
    C *leads to a fall in the number of their customers*
    D *gives businesses greater freedom when selling products*

    Select **one** answer.

ResultsPlus
Watch Out!

It is important to understand the difference between Sale of Goods legislation and Trade Descriptions legislation. Sale of Goods legislation gives consumers rights to obtain compensation for faulty products. Trade Descriptions legislation makes businesses liable to prosecution by the government if products are misleadingly sold.

Over to you

Marc Stringer has been awarded £5,925 in compensation after he had taken a 'holiday from hell' in the Dominican Republic. He had booked himself on a package tour with the holiday company MyTravel which has since merged with Thomas Cook. Staying at a five-star hotel, 'after a couple of days we started to notice we were getting ill' he said. There were cockroaches in his hotel room and there were often flies on the restaurant food which was left out uncovered for several hours.

Within three days of arriving, he was in hospital with acute diarrhoea. When he came back to the UK, he was ill for a further eight months. He only got his compensation after taking legal action against the tour company.

Source: adapted from news.bbc.co.uk 24.7.2008.

Sophie King has been awarded £7,200 compensation after the heel on one of her brand new £35 Dolcis stiletto heeled shoes snapped. She broke her ankle, had to have an operation and was put in plaster. The compensation was awarded for her pain, suffering and loss of ability to work. Michael Hardacre, who represented Sophie King, said: "In English law, she was well protected under the Sale of Goods Act, so it was relatively straightforward.'

Source: adapted from www.guardian.co.uk 9.7.2008.

A Devon caravan seller has been fined £7,200 and ordered to pay £2,400 in costs by a Devon court for offences under the Trade Descriptions Act. LK Caravans had given misleading information about the age of 12 caravans in advertisements. One caravan, for example, was described as being manufactured in 2003 when in fact it was made in 1996.

Source: adapted from www.devon.gov.uk

1. Explain the purpose of (a) Trade Descriptions legislation and (b) Sale of Goods legislation. In your answers, give examples from the data. (6)

2. Assess **two** effects of consumer protection laws on businesses such as Thomas Cook or LC Caravans (8)

3. Would businesses like Thomas Cook be better off if there were no consumer protection legislation? Justify your answer. (8)

Results Plus
Build Better Answers

The majority of businesses comply with the law, in other words they follow the rules. However total compliance can result in negatives for a firm as well. Which of the following can be viewed as a disadvantage of compliance to a business? Select **two** answers.

A Customers will be more likely to use the business if they have such protection

B Making sure that the products meet safety guidelines can be expensive

C Staff may demand a higher wage

D Being compliant may lead to an enhanced reputation

E Refunds can be costly in both time and money

Answer B and E

Technique guide: There is a number of choices available so first:

Think: What is compliance? How does it benefit a business? What are the negatives of compliance?

Then: Consider each alternative and firstly look for the most obvious wrong answer.

C is clearly not the right answer as wage increase demands from staff are not linked to consumer laws. ◾

Now: Go through the remaining options.

A is incorrect. This is clearly an advantage, as happy customers tend to be repeat customers. ◾

D is incorrect. Anything that improves a business's reputation is a good thing. ◾

B is highly likely. If a product is going to comply with the laws laid down then businesses need to check the products themselves. ▲

E is very likely. Refunds are part of consumer law and this would mean a business has to return the payment to the customer, losing revenue and possibly adding to costs as well. ▲

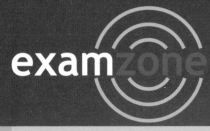
In this topic you have learned about: The importance of design and research and the link between research and product development; the use of bar stock graphs and the benefits of JIT; the necessity for cost management and reduction and how they link to competitiveness; why effective customer service is important for achieving and satisfying the needs and wants of the customer; what is involved in meeting consumer protection laws and the effect of these laws on a business.

You should know...

- [ ] Design is a key approach towards product differentiation. The design mix is made up of function, cost and appearance.

- [ ] Scientific research is at the heart of the majority of product manufacture.

- [ ] Prototypes are working models of possible finished products.

- [ ] Market research does not always give the best information; a 'hunch' is sometimes just as important.

- [ ] Stocks can be made up of materials bought from other businesses, semi-finished goods and finished goods.

- [ ] Stock control is made up of maximum stock levels, re-order levels and minimum stock levels (or buffer stock). Efficient stock control tries to minimise the uncertainty surrounding stock levels.

- [ ] Just In Time is one method of stock control and attempts to minimise the levels of stocks held at any one time.

- [ ] Levels of stocks held are dependent on key variables - storage cost, production needs, purchase price and the nature of stock.

- [ ] A business must decide on the stock control method that best suits it.

- [ ] A good quality product meets the standards set by the customer.

- [ ] Quality control is the traditional method of ensuring that quality remains constant in manufacture, where a quality controller would check for quality levels .

- [ ] The modern approach is quality assurance, where quality is built into every part of the production process. It is everyone's responsibility to maintain quality. The aim is to have zero defects.

- [ ] Kaizen is a Japanese quality concept that has been adopted throughout the world by many businesses.

- [ ] Quality standards are set by international organisations (i.e. BSI, ISO) so products can meet agreed levels of quality.

- [ ] Productivity is measured as output per worker per period of time. It can be raised by training, better equipment or more effective work practices.

- [ ] Improving productivity is one way of reducing costs. Other ways include improving purchasing, relocating a business, improving the design of a product and cutting overheads.

- [ ] In competitive markets, prices must be competitive.. Buying at lower prices is not always the best option.

- [ ] Successful companies give customers products they want.

- [ ] Satisfied customers tend to return to buy more products. They also tell people about the products as well.

- [ ] Several factors can affect the delivery of excellent products or services - meeting customer needs, on-time service, innovation, collaboration, identifing problems early, listening to customers, dealing with complaints efficiently and properly trained staff.

- [ ] Poor customer service will affect sales, as repeat purchases will not be as good. Lower sales = lower profits.

- [ ] Consumer law gives a level of rights to the consumer if things go wrong with their products or services.

- [ ] Sale of Goods is a civil law and leads to compensation. Trade Descriptions is a criminal law and leads to fines and prosecution.

- [ ] Adhering to laws can be expensive in both time and money for businesses.

Support activity

- In your opinion which businesses design and manufacture high quality products? Make a list and compare it to one of your friends' lists. Are they similar or different? Why?

- Choose one product that you have in your home. Put it on a table and look at it from all possible angles. Now try and write down all the things that you could do to it to improve it and possibly reduce the cost or make it meet the customers' needs even better.

- Now look at your list and put it in order from the most realistic option to the least realistic. How feasible do you think your number one choice is? Justify your answer.

Stretch activity

- Pick one shop or restaurant that you visit regularly. Think about the members of staff that work there. What training do you think they need?

- Now create a table with 12 columns to write a training plan that would give them a year's worth of training allowing for about 4 hours per month.

- Make a decision on what areas of training you would choose to concentrate on.

- Finally, discuss the cost implications to the firm of such a training plan.

Ionnaou Electricals has recently completed a review of its stock control systems and feel that it is holding too much stock. It has decided that the best course of action to resolve this situation is to implement a Just In Time stock control system. This, it thinks, will give the business the chance to cut costs and increase its competitive advantage.

(i) What is meant by the term Just In Time stock control? (1)

(ii) Explain how Just In Time stock management might benefit a business (3)

Think: What is stock control? What is Just In Time (JIT) stock control? What are the differences between a traditional method and JIT? What advantages does using JIT bring?

Student answer	Examiner comment	Build a better answer
(i) It's where a firm orders its stock just when they need it.	■ A very simplistic answer that is helped by using the word 'just'. The examiner will not be sure if the candidate actually understands the term.	△ Use clear phrases such as '...raw materials are delivered to a firm exactly when they need them' or '...there are more frequent deliveries of stock'.
(ii) A business will be able to reduce its costs.	■ A basic comment which, whilst correct, is not developed and will not achieve full marks.	△ Identify a clear benefit and then develop it. The marks available indicate the number of points needed for an effective answer. The development is the outcome from the point that is made. For example 'The firm will be able to reduce its costs by employing a Just In Time method (1) because it will reduce the cost of storing large quantities of stock. (1) Storage costs money and the money that is being spent on storage at the moment could be used elsewhere. This is a case of opportunity cost.' (1)

Here the student has linked in other business concepts as well. Other benefits may include the ability to get the product to the consumer on time, or that using JIT means the components will be the latest type or freshest in the case of perishable goods.

Practice Exam Questions

Ricky Moss was frustrated. Every time he opened the business's post there seemed to be yet another letter of complaint from a customer about quality. The firm, Growing Success, makes greenhouses and has been doing so since 1972. Recently they changed suppliers of the raw materials as it made sense financially and the quality of the goods remained the same. From this information Ricky could assume that the quality issues did not arise from this change in supplier.

Ricky called an emergency management meeting to discuss the increasing levels of complaints about quality. At the meeting his production manager, Julie, indicated that she felt the quality issue was possibly to do with the staff being de-motivated. In discussions with staff she had discovered that they felt as if they didn't have any responsibilities and were not trusted by management to get on with their jobs without someone looking over their shoulders.

Following the meeting it was agreed that the company should initiate some form of quality assurance programme. Ricky had done some research and liked the idea of the principle of Kaizen. He felt that the responsibility that everyone should have would be a good response to the frustrations shown by the workers.

(a) Ricky realises that quality assurance might be the way forward for the company. Which **two** of the following **best** describe the benefits of quality assurance? (2)

A It takes time to get quality assurance to work in a firm

B Staff will feel empowered and responsible for their own quality

C Profits will increase

D The company can charge a higher price for the products

E New markets can be exploited

F The business can assure the customer that each and every product is a quality one

(b) Ricky is aware that the role of the management is a key issue to the success of this venture. Explain, using examples, one approach that might be taken by the management at Growing Success to improve the likelihood of success. (3).

(c) Analyse the difference between quality control and quality assurance (8).

Topic 3.3: Effective financial management

Case study

Skillen's is a small chain of indoor play zones. Typically, it leases a building on an industrial estate and fits it out with an indoor play area aimed at 3-11 year olds. It is popular with parents giving birthday parties for their children and for somewhere to go during the school holidays or at a weekend. There is a small bar and kitchen area in each outlet for the sale of tea, coffee and soft drinks to parents and children. Party food is also prepared and served, mainly for birthday parties.

Topic overview

This topic examines how to improve cash flow and profit, analyses break-even charts and their use, considers how changes in price and costs can affect the break-even point and examines the different internal and external sources of finance that are available to businesses to finance growth.

The company has firm policies about payment designed to maximise cash inflows and minimise cash outflows. Parents booking parties have to pay a 20 per cent deposit on booking and then pay the balance a week in advance. Parents who bring their children individually pay at the door. Sometimes, a local business will book a party. Skillen's treats them like any other customers and does not give any credit. On the other hand, it has an unwritten policy of paying as many invoices as late as possible. It knows which suppliers put pressure to pay roughly on time and which suppliers are very lax in chasing up invoices.

Management at Skillen's knows that maximising cash inflows is key to also maximising profit. The manager of each outlet is expected to keep the outlet as busy as possible. For example, parents of children coming to birthday parties are given money off vouchers if they come with their children as individuals. Parents can buy season tickets. Less popular evenings are promoted in local newspapers with low entry prices. With high fixed costs, getting as much revenue as possible through flexible pricing is essential.

The main cost that can be varied is the labour cost. Most of the workers in the outlets are employed on the minimum wage. They tend to be young girls or working mothers. Many are casually employed. It is up to the manager to have the minimum level of staffing needed at any time in order to minimise cost. So the manager has to call in casual staff as and when they are needed. This has its disadvantages. Managers of outlets complain they spend too much time sorting out staffing. Casual workers also often lack training and commitment. This can lead to customers getting less than satisfactory service.

When considering whether to open a new outlet, management prepares a business plan including break-even analysis. The rent on industrial units differs in different locations. So too do a variety of other costs. This affects the break-even point and the margin of safety. New outlets are expected to reach break-even point within six months. If they are not showing a profit after a year, they are closed down. Closing down a poorly performing outlet has only happened once fortunately. It was a reminder that choosing a good location is also important to success.

The business was initially financed from a mix of bank loans and equity (share capital) put in by the two founders of the business. These two shareholders want to keep control of the company and so would not contemplate issuing new shares to raise finance for expansion. The company is now heavily reliant on retained profit to finance the opening of new outlets. Bank borrowing is kept to a minimum in an effort to minimise risk to the business.

1. **How does Skillen's maximise cash inflows?**
2. **Why does employing casual staff help minimise costs for the business?**
3. **How do promotions and special offers help increase profit?**
4. **Why does Skillen's use break-even analysis when considering whether or not to open a new outlet?**
5. **What internal and external sources of finance are used by this business?**

What will I learn?

How to improve cash flow What are the key aspects of financial management? How can establishing more favourable credit terms with customers and suppliers improve cash flow? How can the practice of de-stocking improve cash flow? What is the difference between increasing cash inflows and reducing cash outflows?

How to improve profit How might cutting costs and increasing revenues improve profit? What is the impact of price changes on profit?

Break-even charts and break-even analysis How are break-even charts drawn? How can break-even charts be analysed? How can the break-even point and margin of safety be calculated? How do changes in price and costs affect the break-even point? What is the value to a business of using break-even analysis?

Financing growth How can a business be financed from internal sources such as profits and assets sales, and from external sources such as share capital and debt? What is meant by a stock market flotation?

How will I be assessed?

This is assessed through Unit 3, a written examination lasting 1 hour 30 minutes.

The paper is divided into three sections.

Section A is a mix of mainly multiple choice questions and short answer questions with one or more questions requiring an extended answer.

Sections B and C consist of short and long answer questions based on two scenarios, one for each section, given in the paper.

12 How to improve cash flow

Case Study

Duxton is a manufacturer of pet food. It has its own range of pet foods that it supplies to small independent retailers and garden centres, mainly through wholesalers. However, much of its output goes to large supermarket chains as own label products.

Objectives

- Understand key aspects of financial management such as how to establish more favourable credit terms with customers and suppliers and the practice of de-stocking.

- Understand how to analyse the difference between increasing cash inflows and reducing cash outflows.

edexcel ::: key terms

Cash flow – the flow of cash into and out of a business.

Financial management – deliberately changing monetary variables like cash flows to achieve financial objectives such as improved cash flows.

Cash flow

Cash flow is the movement of money into and out of a business. For example, Duxton has a variety of types of money flowing into and out of the business.

Cash inflows Its main inflow of cash comes from customers who have bought its products. So when a supermarket chain buys its dog food, Duxton sends out cans and packets of food and in return receives a cash payment. However, it has other, much smaller cash inflows. For example, it holds some money in a bank account on which it receives interest. So each year it gets an interest payment from the bank. It also has a factory unit on its main manufacturing site which it does not need itself. So it rents it out to another business. The rent it gets is part of its cash flow.

Cash outflows Businesses like Duxton have a number of cash outflows. One large cash outflow is wages paid to workers of the firm. Another is payments to other businesses for materials. For example, Duxton buys meat from companies as one of the ingredients of its products. It has to buy the tins in which the product is packaged. It also pays out money on administration items such as paper, telephones, and postage, as well as heating and lighting and insurance. Another important cash outflow is taxes paid to the government such as Value Added Tax, income tax for its workers and business rates. Duxton owns its factory but many businesses have to pay rent for their premises. Duxbton pays out money monthly on a mortgage for the premises it owns.

Financial management

A business like Duxton has some control over its finances. It can, within limits, change the levels of cash inflow and cash outflow for example. Deliberately changing monetary variables like cash flows is known as **financial management**. Businesses like Duxton use financial management to achieve their financial objectives. For example, the top managers at Duxton decided 12 months ago that the economy was going into recession. They were afraid that consumers would cut back on buying pet food. If this happened, then cash inflows would fall. If this was not matched by falling cash outflows, the company could get into serious financial difficulties. So the management decided to look at how Duxton's cash outflows could be reduced. The overall financial objective was at least to match any fall in cash inflows with a fall in cash outflows.

There are many ways in which the management of a business can change both cash inflows and cash outflows.

Changing cash inflows

Cash inflows are cash coming into a business. Usually, businesses are concerned with increasing the amount of cash coming into a business rather than reducing it. Increasing cash inflows tend to be linked to other positive indicators such as increased profit or increased financial security. There are many ways in which a business like Duxton could increase its cash inflows.

Increasing sales revenues In most cases, the most financially desirable way of increasing cash inflows is to increase sales revenues. Sales revenues are the average price of products times the quantity sold. Strategies for increasing sales revenues are explained in more detail in Subtopic 13.

De-stocking Duxton is constantly receiving deliveries of raw materials like meat, grains and seeds. It uses these to make its products. Completed tins and packets of pet food are stored ready for delivery to customers. Raw materials waiting to be processed and finished products waiting to be sent out to customers are examples of stocks. One way of increasing cash inflows is for the business to make a one-off reduction in its stocks of finished products by selling them off. This is called **de-stocking**. For example, Duxton sells on average £100,000 worth of pet food each month. It could hold a sale where it offered reduced prices to customers for a limited period. The result is that customers buy more and there is an increase in monthly sales to £140,000. During the month of the sales, cash inflows have increased by £40,000.

Improving cash flow from customers Duxton sells its products to other businesses and offers **trade credit**. This means that, when it sends out its products, it also sends out an invoice for payment in the future. Most of its customers have 30 days to pay the invoice or bill. Its supermarket customers have negotiated with Duxton to give them 60 days to pay. There is a number of ways to increase the cash inflows from customers.

- One is to chase up the businesses which pay late far more vigorously. Typically, Duxton finds that most of its customers pay late. On average, non-supermarket customers pay only after 60 days, not the 30 days they are given. So if Duxton could cut this time to just 50 days, it would see a one-off improvement in cash inflows.
- Another way to improve cash flow is to reduce the time given to customers to pay. If Duxton reduced the time to 20 days, hopefully customers would pay more promptly compared to when it offered 30 days credit. The danger with this strategy is that Duxton might lose customers to competing firms that offered longer payment periods.
- Duxton could employ a factor. This is a financial company, often a bank, that will advance the money that a business is owed by its customers. It will typically advance 90 per cent of the value of invoices immediately. However, there is a drawback. The factor charges a fee for its services.

Long-term solutions Businesses like Duxton have a number of ways of making large one-off improvements to their cash flow.

- Duxton could take out a loan from a bank. If it borrowed £100,000, there would be a once and for all cash inflow of £100,000. This would then mean that the net cash flow going forward from month to month would be £100 000 larger than it would otherwise have been. However, the loan has to be repaid with interest. If it is being repaid monthly at a rate of £2,000 a month, each month there would be a cash outflow of £2,000.

ResultsPlus
Watch Out!

This chapter builds on the work you will have covered in Unit 1 of the course.. It is advisable to go back through the work you have done on this section and ensure you understand the main principles. You can review subtopic 16, **Forecasting cash flows**, in *Business: Introduction to Small Business* before reading this subtopic. You will be expected to interpret a cash flow forecast and then explain how net cash flow could be improved. It is important, therefore, that you are confident in handling cash flow forecasts.

ResultsPlus
Watch Out!

When talking about 'cash flow', do not be confused into thinking that cash is notes and coins. For most businesses, hardly any of the cash flowing into and out of the firm is made up of physical cash like this. Almost all cash is various forms of bank transactions, like cheques, automated bank transfers, direct debits and credit card payments.

edexcel ::: **key terms**

De-stocking – reducing the level of stocks in a business.

Trade credit – where a supplier gives a customer a period of time to pay for a bill (or invoice) for goods or services once they have been delivered.

- Another way of improving cash flow is for a company to issue new shares. Investors pay cash for the shares. The cash is a cash inflow for the company.
- Duxton might have physical assets which it can sell. The most obvious sellable asset is land or property. If land is sold, cash flows into the business. Sometimes, businesses negotiate a sale and leaseback arrangement. The business sells its premises to a property company. The property company then leases (i.e. rents) the premises back to the business. The sale generates a large one-off inflow of cash. However, each month or year there is a much smaller cash outflow which represents the rent paid to the property company.

Changing cash outflows

There is a number of ways that a business like Duxton can improve cash outflows.

Orders for new materials and stocks One simple way of reducing cash outflows is to order fewer materials from its suppliers. In a typical month, Duxton orders £30,000 of materials. If in one month it cut this to £20,000, then cash outflows would be reduced by £20,000. Reducing the amount of raw materials is likely to have an effect on production levels. If the company has fewer stocks of raw materials, it is unlikely to be able to produce as much as before. So cutting orders and stocks of raw materials tends to be a strategy used as a response to falls in sales. On the other hand, a one off fall in orders for new stocks could be a sign that the business is becoming more efficient in its use of stocks. A move towards more Just In Time production methods, for example, could lead to a one-off improvement in cash flow.

Delaying paying invoices Duxton, like most businesses, owes money to its suppliers. Typically, it receives materials and then has 30 days to pay the invoice for those materials. Most businesses pay their invoices late because this improves their cash flow position. The longer Duxton waits to pay an invoice, the longer the time that cash does not flow out of the business. So Duxton could improve its cash flow position by further delaying payments to suppliers. There is a risk, though, with this strategy. Suppliers could refuse to sell the company any more products, at least until all the money they

are owed is paid. Some businesses also offer discounts on the invoice for prompt payment. Duxton would lose these and end up paying more because it is paying late.

Leasing rather than buying If Duxton were to buy a machine costing £30,000, there would be a cash outflow of £30,000 on purchase. However, sometimes it is possible for businesses to lease or rent a machine. Then, the monthly outflows will be much smaller and spread over a period of time. If the lease were £800 a month, then in the first year of leasing, there would be an outflow of £9,600 compared to the £30,000 with purchase.

Test yourself

1. Plante is a business which manufactures lawnmowers. It takes out a loan from a bank repayable over four years. For Plante, this will lead to an immediate large cash

   A *inflow and smaller cash outflows over a period of time*
   B *inflow and smaller cash inflows over a period of time*
   C *outflow and smaller cash inflows over a period of time*
   D *outflow and smaller cash outflows over a period of time*

   Select **one** answer.

2. Gaweda is a company which manufactures parts for DVD players. De-stocking by Gaweda of both raw materials and finished products occurs in February. Between February and April, this is most likely to lead to

   A *improved cash flow because more raw materials will be ordered*
   B *improved cash flow because fewer raw materials will be ordered*
   C *improved cash flow because fewer finished products will be sold*
   D *a deterioration in cash flow because more finished products will be sold*

   Select **one** answer.

3. Which **one** of the following is most likely to lead to improved cash inflows for a business?

   A *Increasing the amount of materials bought from suppliers*
   B *Increasing the level of stocks of raw materials held by the business*
   C *Reducing the length of time customers are given to pay their invoices*
   D *Reducing the amount of time taken by the business to pay its suppliers*

   Select **one** answer.

Over to you

John Fazil has run a restaurant for the past ten years. It took him a couple of years at the start to earn a profit but since then he has been able to earn a reasonable living from his business. This was until a year ago. The economy began to do badly, unemployment rose and his customers began to think twice about going out for a meal. Sales of ready prepared meals in supermarkets boomed whilst John Fazil saw his customer numbers decline.

John was reluctant to take any serious action. He hoped the economy would recover quickly and everything would get back to where it was before. However, his bank has just phoned to say that they are worried about his overdraft. A cheque that he wrote to a food supplier would have taken him over his overdraft limit. The bank has therefore bounced the cheque (i.e. it has refused to pay out the money on the cheque).

Bouncing cheques means that John has got to take action. He looked at his cash flow for last week. This was a fairly typical week for him. In the restaurant trade, the general rule is that the cost to the restaurant of food ingredients should be around one third of the prices charged to customers for an item on the menu. Drinks can be sold for between three and five times their cost price to the restaurant. Restaurants are typically staffed by permanent and temporary workers. The temporary workers tend to be low paid doing jobs such as waiting tables and cleaning dishes in the kitchen. John employs both permanent and temporary workers.

Looking at his cash flow position, John does not know whether he should try to increase his sales to bring in more cash or cut his costs to reduce his cash outflows. He has thought about changing the prices he charges. Would cutting prices attract more customers into the restaurant and increase the amount of cash coming into the business? Maybe he should increase his prices and pitch for high quality food; would this increase his cash inflow? Should he perhaps have one or two evenings a week where he offers lower prices, or perhaps have a 'happy hour' say between 6 and 7 in the evening when prices are lower? Should he cut his costs? What about making some of his

Table 1 – Cash flow, last week

	£
Cash inflow	
Food sold	1,800
Drink sold	700
Cash outflow	
Food ingredients	800
Drink supplies	200
Wages and other staff costs	1,200
Rent	400
Gas, electricity, telephone	320
Other costs	80

permanent staff redundant or reduce the use of temporary staff? Could he save on food ingredients?

In the short term, John has decided that some of his suppliers will have to wait longer to be paid. John's business is now in crisis and it demands radical action.

1. Using Table 1, calculate the following figures for John Fazil's restaurant for last week.
   (a) Total cash inflows. (1)
   (b) Total cash outflows. (1)
   (c) Net cash flow. (1)
2. Explain why John Fazil's business is facing a cash flow crisis. (3)
3. John has decided that he will make suppliers wait longer for their payments. Explain how this will improve his cash flow position. (3)
4. John is angry about the amount of food that his head chef wastes. Do you think that cutting back on orders of food could improve cash flow without affecting the quality of meals in the restaurant? Justify your answer. (6)
5. Would making staff redundant be the best way for John to solve his cash flow problems? Justify your answer looking at other possible alternatives. (8)

 Results Plus
Build Better Answers

Cash flow is the movement of money into and out of a business. It is made up of inflows and outflows of cash.
(a) Identify **two** types of cash outflow. (2)
(b) Explain **two** ways a business could use to improve its cash inflow. (6)

Think: what is the difference between cash inflows and cash outflows? What can have an impact on these? What can be changed to get more money in and more quickly?

(a) Wages, payments to suppliers, taxes, rent, vehicle running costs, advertising. (2)

(b)

▪ **Basic** 'A business could ask its customers to pay on time (1) meaning that the money comes in faster.' (1)

● **Good** 'One method is to take out a loan from the bank. (1)

This will inject cash into the business. (1) Another way is to reduce the amount of time a customer has to pay their bill. (1) This means that cash enters the business at a quicker rate.' (1)

▲ **Excellent** 'One method is to de-stock. (1) De-stocking means reducing the amount of stock held by selling it off. (1) Selling stock at lower prices would be likely to increase demand and sales would mean that more cash flowing into the business not to mention lowering the cost of storing the stock.(1) Another way is to use the services of a factor. (1) By using a factor a business gets access to the money it is owed quickly. The factor then chases the debts on behalf of the business. In return the business would have to pay a commission to the factor for their services. (1) If the business is owed £5,000, for example, the factor may charge the business £500 to make sure the debt gets paid but the business is able to get access to £4,500 quickly to help its cash flow.' (1)

13 How to improve profit

Case Study

Observer Standard Group Media was a company that published 20 weekly free newspapers including the Leamington Observer and the Warwick Observer. With revenues of £9 million a year, it employed 150 staff. However, in 2009, it went into administration. This meant that the company was unable to pay those it owed money to (its creditors) – it had 'gone bust'. However, the newspapers continued to be published whilst new owners for the business were sought.

Objectives

● Understand how cutting costs and increasing revenues can improve profit.

● Appreciate the impact of price changes on profit.

edexcel ⋮⋮⋮ key terms

Profit – occurs when the revenues of a business are greater than its costs over a period of time.

Revenues – the amount of money received from selling goods or services over a period of time.

ResultsPlus
Watch Out!

Remember to not get confused between the terms 'price' and 'cost'. In everyday life we tend to use the two terms interchangeably but in this subject we must be sure to use the two terms more accurately.

Profits, revenues and costs

For any business like Observer Standard Group Media, long-term survival depends on being able to make a **profit**. This means that over a period of time, **revenues** have to be greater than costs because

$$Profit = Revenue - Costs$$

When a business begins to make a loss, its costs become greater than its revenues. The longer the time it makes a loss, and the larger the losses it makes, the greater is the danger that it will be forced to close down.

This is what happed to Observer Standard Group Media in 2009. Between 2007 and 2009, local newspapers throughout the UK came under increasing financial pressure. The main problem was that their revenues were falling. Most, if not all, of a local newspaper's revenues come from the sale of advertising space in the newspaper. However, the UK economy went into recession over this period. This meant there was less spending in the economy. There was a large fall in the number of businesses wanting to take on new workers. There was a large drop in the number of cars being bought. The housing market also suffered badly. House prices fell by a quarter and the number of houses bought and sold fell dramatically. The three largest categories of advertising for local newspapers are jobs, cars and houses. Employers, car dealers and estate agents all cut their spending on advertising. As a result the newspaper group saw its revenues fall whilst its costs remained the same.

If a firm is making a loss, it needs to take action to get back into profit. It can do this by increasing its revenues relative to costs. For example, a newspaper might be able to move back to profit if it could sell substantially more advertising space. Or it could cut costs by making staff redundant and closing offices. Equally, if a firm is already making a profit, it can make an even larger profit by making revenues larger compared to costs.

Cutting costs

One way to increase profit is to cut costs. However, cutting costs is not easy and often there are effects of these cuts on the performance of a business.

A business, such as Observer Standard Group Media, has a number of different types of costs that can be cut.

Materials costs Businesses buy in materials from other firms. Observer Standard Group Media, for example, paid printers to print its newspapers. It had ordinary bills like telephone and postage bills, as well as gas and electricity for its offices. Sometimes, it is possible to cut material costs through better buying. For

example, a company might be able to find a cheaper provider of electricity. Some companies can cut costs by changing the product itself; for example, some ice cream manufacturers reduced the size of their tubs and chocolate manufacturers slimmed down their bars. This can reduce production costs. Or it might be able to get a better price on materials by buying in greater bulk or seeking out different suppliers. These reductions in costs can make the business more efficient. Sometimes, however, cutting costs will make a business less efficient or have an effect on quality which might affect sales. For example, forcing reporters on a newspaper to make fewer phone calls to save on phone costs will limit their ability to write stories. Closing an office to save on rent might mean that reporters are further away from their customers. For a printer, not ordering paper this week to save on costs might mean production delays and ultimately lost orders.

Labour A major cost for many businesses is employing workers. So making workers redundant, cutting the number of hours worked, or not replacing workers that leave are important ways to cut costs. Sometimes, a business has too many workers to be efficient. In this situation cutting the number of workers may have little or no impact on the amount that is produced. Sometimes, however, reducing the number of workers will lead to a fall in output. For example, in November 2008, Observer Standard Group Media made 20 per cent of its workforce redundant in a bid to cut costs. This included 8 workers in the editorial department. This is likely to have affected the quality of what was being published by the newspaper. News coverage is likely to have been reduced. Making workers redundant also has an effect on the motivation of the workers that remain. They are likely to be told to do more work to cover at least some of the work done by the workers that have left. This will make the remaining workers resentful. Also, they will be afraid that they might be next to lose their jobs. This can be demotivating and also affect production.

Newspapers can increase revenues by selling advertising space and improving the quality of their product, for example including glossy extras.

Investment Businesses invest in research, the development of new products and in equipment. They also invest in their workers through training. An easy way to cut costs is to cut back on investment. This reduces costs in the short term. However, it may affect the competitiveness of the business in the long term. For example, Observer Standard Group Media gradually increased the number of newspapers it distributed over time. It invested in a website too. Cutting back on opening new newspapers saved costs in the short-term. However, this meant there were smaller revenues from advertising being received in the long-term.

Newspapers can reduce costs by cutting back on investment in new machinery.

Marketing Most businesses spend on marketing. They conduct market research, run promotional and advertising campaigns and employ a sales team, all of which can be a costly process. A firm can cut costs by cutting back on its marketing expenditure. However, this has its drawbacks. Cutting back on marketing might affect sales. Less advertising, for example, may lead to fewer products being bought and so revenues will fall and if a firm does not keep up with the changing needs of its customers it may lose competitiveness.

Firms have to think very carefully, therefore, before cutting costs. Invariably there is a trade-off involved and a business will have to weigh up the costs and benefits of the decisions that it will have to take and where it might decide to cut costs.

ResultsPlus
Watch Out!

Cutting costs might seem to be good for the profit of a business. However, cutting some costs can have a serious impact on other costs and on revenues. Cutting the amount of stock held, for example, may cause production problems if there is a sudden rush order to bring out. Using poorer quality materials may damage the reputation of a product and lead to lower sales. Sometimes, profit can increase by increasing some costs. If increased costs in some areas leads to more efficient production, overall costs may fall. Or higher costs may lead to a better quality product or service and higher sales.

Increasing revenues

Profit can also be increased by increasing revenues. The sales revenue of a business is the number of products sold times their average price.

Revenue = Number of products sold x Average price

This is sometimes shown by the formula

$$TR = P \times Q$$

where TR = total revenue, P = price and Q = the quantity sold.

So a business could increase revenue by either changing price in some way or boosting sales (or a combination of the two). A business can do this in a number of ways.

Improved marketing If products are marketed better, they are likely to sell more. For example, a local business in Warwick might have been able to increase its sales by advertising in the Warwick Observer newspaper. Observer Standard Group Media might have been able to increase the number of advertisements it sold by increasing its sales force. More sales workers could have spent more time ringing round local businesses to persuade them to place advertisements in the newspapers run by the group.

Better products If a business can improve its product range, then it is likely to sell more. For example, Observer Standard Group Media increased its sales over a twenty year period by launching more and more newspaper titles covering different local areas. A chocolate manufacturer can increase its sales by launching a new chocolate bar. However, changing the product range will not necessarily bring success. New products often fail. Successful businesses are ones that bring out new products that customers want to buy.

Price, revenue and profit

The relationship between price, revenue and profit is complicated. If a business like Observer Standard Group Media wanted to increase revenues and profits, should it have increased its prices, left them the same or reduced them?

The price of a product directly affects the quantity bought. The higher the price, the less will be bought for almost all products. For example, if Observer Standard Group Media had cut the price of advertising in its newspapers, more advertising space would have been bought. If Nintendo cuts the price of its Wii games console, it will sell more games consoles. Equally, if Mars puts up the price of Mars Bars, it will sell fewer Mars Bars.

ResultsPlus
Watch Out!

Cutting prices will almost certainly increase sales in the short term. However, this will not necessarily increase total revenues. Whether revenue increases or falls depends on the responsiveness of sales volumes to prices (price sensitivity). If prices fall and there is a big impact on sales, then revenue will rise. If prices fall and there is only a small impact on sales, then revenue will fall.

However, selling more at a lower price does not necessarily mean higher revenues. The impact of a change of price on total revenues depends on the sensitivity of sales to changing prices.

Assume the Observer Standard Group Media charged £200 to place a boxed advert in one of its newspapers. At this price it normally sells 50 adverts a week. Its total revenue, therefore, would be 200 x 50 = £10,000 per week. If it cut this price in half to £100, what will be the impact on revenue?

- If it sells 10 per cent more advertisements (so the number taken out rises to 55), then revenue will fall (100 x 55 = £5,500) It has halved the price but only sold one tenth more. If this were to happen then reducing price by this amount would actually reduce revenue!
- If it sells three times the number of advertisements (150), then revenue will rise (100 x 150 = £15,000). It is only getting half the amount of revenue per advert compared to before. But sales volume has increased three times. This means its revenues will be increase by one half or 50 per cent.

Sometimes, businesses can increase their revenues by raising their prices. For example, say Observer Standard Group Media had raised the price of advertisements by half or 50 per cent to £300 per advert. If sales fall by just one tenth or 10 per cent, then its revenues will go up (300 x 45 = £13,500).

A business thinking of changing prices, therefore, will need to think about the percentage change in the price and the corresponding percentage change in the sales that might result. In general, if a small percentage price cut leads to a much larger percentage rise in sales, then revenues will go up and vice versa.

The impact on profit is more complex. If a business cuts its price and wins extra sales, production costs are likely to rise. If Observer Standard Group Media had sold more advertising space, it would have had to increase the size of its newspapers by adding more pages. This would have increased printing costs. If a business raises its price and loses sales, its costs of production should fall.

So the overall impact of a change in price on profit depends on what happens to the quantity of sales and to costs. For Observer Standard Group Media, it would have changed the prices charged to customers for advertisements if it had thought that this would increase profit. There are always limits to how far prices can be changed and consumers do not always react in the way expected. Observer Standard Group Media may have found that even reducing prices significantly would not have generated extra sales simply because businesses placing adverts were also facing difficulties. In this situation, there is very little more the business can do and it may be forced to cease trading.

Source: adapted from
http://www.observerstandard.com, http://www.guardian.co.uk.

Test yourself

1. Which **one** of the following would lead to an increase in profit for a business? Select **one** answer.

   A An increase in costs with a fall in revenues
   B An increase in costs with a smaller increase in revenues
   C A fall in costs with a larger fall in revenues
   D A fall in costs with a rise in revenues

2. Arroba is a company that designs and makes computer games. It is struggling financially and has decided to make a quarter of its workers redundant. Which **one** of the following is most likely to be a **disadvantage** of this decision for the company? Select **one** answer.

   A Remaining workers will become more motivated
   B Costs are likely to rise in the medium term
   C It will be more difficult to produce new computer games
   D Arroba will have to increase the prices of its products

3. A bus company, faced with rising costs, decides that it has to increase its bus fares to keep its profit stable. A rise in bus fares will only increase total revenues if

   A costs also fall
   B more people travel on the buses
   C profits do not fall
   D the fall in the number of bus passengers is less as a proportion than the rise in bus fares

   Select **one** answer.

ResultsPlus

Build Better Answers

Cost control is a key aspect in a successful business. Which **one** of the following is **least likely** to lead to an immediate increase in costs? Select **one** answer.

A Taking the staff on a paintballing weekend to help them bond
B Redesigning the product now so that it is improved in some way
C Cutting back on marketing activities
D Buying better desks for the staff to work on

Answer D

Technique guide: There is a number of choices available so first:

Think: What things cost money? What areas can be trimmed to reduce costs? What is essential for businesses to operate?

Then: Consider each alternative.

Go through these.

A is unlikely. This exercise will cost money immediately, although it may improve motivation, which may lead to some reduction in costs. ▪

B is unlikely. The new product may be more efficient to produce, reducing costs in future, but will have a cost attached to it in terms of research and development and also possibly needing new or re-tooled machines to produce it. ▪

D is incorrect. This is a cost outlay and would add to overall costs, although better desks may lead to some slight reduction in costs if they worked better. ▪

C is most likely. Marketing is expensive and cutting back on these activities would reduce overall costs. ▲

Over to you

JustYou is a fashionable nightclub in the centre of Manchester. Established five years ago, it was a very popular place to meet friends and dance. Over the past year, however, numbers coming into the club have declined. Part of the problem has been increased competition from a couple of other nightclubs that have recently opened nearby.

The normal cost of entry to the nightclub is £5 per person. Monday night, the club is closed. Tuesday and Wednesday nights, which are the quietest nights, are free. On a typical week, around 50 people might come in on a Tuesday and Wednesday. At the weekend, around 300 people used to come per night but this has fallen to 200 in recent months. Charging people to come in is not the main source of revenue. More money is made from the sale of drinks at the bar. Costs have been increasing. The landlord has just raised the rent on the premises by £100 a week. Many of the staff are on the minimum wage, set by the government, but this rose by 3 per cent last year. Gas and electricity bills have soared, up 50 per cent over the past two years. The government keeps putting up the tax on drinks, making drinks more expensive and less affordable.

The senior management of the night club last week held a crisis meeting because the figures showed that the club made a loss over the past three months, its first loss in four years. Every aspect of the club's finances was discussed. There was a lot of talk about how costs could be cut. However, the manager of the club felt the real problem was the declining numbers coming through the door. Perhaps they were booking the wrong DJs and playing the wrong music. Would more people come if there was better music? The manager, who had been there since the club opened, did not feel that changing the music would work. She wanted to experiment with the pricing. Perhaps they should lower the entrance fee from £5. One local nightclub had cut its entrance fee from £5 to £1. Or perhaps they should cut the price of drinks. If they were cheap enough, it would be bound to bring in more customers.

1. How much revenue is JustYou making on ticket sales on a typical Saturday night in recent months? Give the formula and show your workings. (4)
2. Explain why JustYou is currently making a loss. (3)
3. (a) Identify **three** costs that JustYou could cut fairly quickly if it wanted to. (3)
   (b) Explain what impact **two** of these cost cuts would have on the running of the business. (6)
4. Would cutting the entrance fee to £1 be the best solution to increasing revenues? Justify your answer. (8)

14 Break-even charts and break-even analysis

74

Case Study

Rollay Boxes is a company that manufactures stackable plastic storage boxes used in schools, offices and homes. It sells its boxes through office stationery suppliers, supermarkets and chain stores. The managing director of the company, Wayne Rollay, keeps a careful watch on the finances of the company and knows how many he needs to sell just to break-even.

Objectives

- Understand the principle of break-even.
- Appreciate how to draw and interpret break-even charts.
- Understand how to calculate the break-even point and the margin of safety.
- Appreciate how changes to price and costs affect the break-even point.
- Appreciate the value to a business of using break-even analysis.

Table 1 – Rollay Boxes: total revenue

	£ per year
Sales	Total revenue (average price, £2, x quantity sold)
20,000	40,000
40,000	80,000
60,000	120,000
80,000	160,000
100,000	200,000

edexcel ::: key terms

Break-even point – the level of output where total revenues are equal to total costs; this is where neither a profit nor a loss is being made.

Total revenue – the revenue earned by a business from the sale of a given quantity of products. It is equal to quantity sold x average price.

Break-even

The **break-even point** is very important for all businesses. It is the level of output where revenues just equal costs. Knowing the break-even point helps a business to understand how many products it needs to sell to just cover the costs of production. If revenues equal costs exactly, then the business is not making a profit. Nor is it making a loss. In most circumstances, selling more than the break-even level of output will mean the business makes a profit. If it sells less than the break-even point, then it will make a loss. The break-even level of output is so important because it is the tipping point between profit and loss.

To find the break-even point for a business like Rollay Boxes, it is necessary to calculate total revenues and total costs.

Total revenue

Total revenue is the amount of money earned by a business from selling its products. Rollay Boxes sells storage boxes to retailers like supermarkets. The total amount of cash it earns from this is its total revenue.

Total revenue can be calculated by multiplying the quantity sold by the average price at which it is sold. The average price is sometimes called the average revenue.

Total revenue = quantity sold x average price

The average price of a Rollay Box is £2. So, if the company sells 20,000 boxes, its total revenue is £40,000 (20,000 x £2). If it sells 100,000 boxes, its total revenue is £200,000 (100,000 x £2). How total revenue changes as the number sold changes is shown in Table 1. This is then plotted on a graph in Figure 1. The total revenue is always put on the vertical axis. The number sold is always put on the horizontal axis. The total revenue line is upward sloping because the more that is sold, the higher the total revenue.

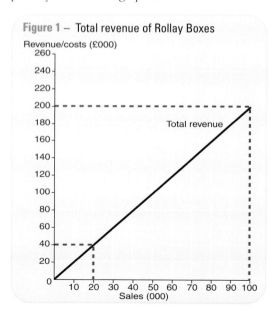

Figure 1 – Total revenue of Rollay Boxes

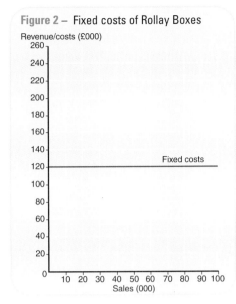

Figure 2 – Fixed costs of Rollay Boxes

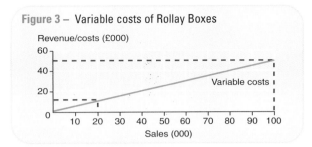

Figure 3 – Variable costs of Rollay Boxes

Total cost

Total cost is the sum of all the costs of the point at a given level of output. The costs of a business like Rolay Boxes can be split into fixed costs and variable costs.

Fixed costs **Fixed costs** are costs that do not depend on the amount produced. Rollay's fixed costs are not affected by however many boxes it produces. Fixed costs are costs such as the rent it has to pay for its factory, insurance and administration costs. These can change but are not dependent on the amount produced. The fixed costs for Rollay Boxes come to £120,000 per year. Fixed costs can be shown on a graph. In Figure 2, the fixed cost line is horizontal. However many boxes are produced, the fixed cost stays the same at £120,000.

Variable costs **Variable costs** are costs that change directly with the number of products made. They are directly related to the amount of boxes produced. The costs for Rollay to manufacture its boxes include raw materials like plastic, packaging and some types of energy and labour costs that are associated with production. It costs on average 50p for Rollay Boxes to manufacture a box. The more boxes produced, the higher will be the level of total variable costs. This is shown in Table 2 and then in Figure 3. If Rollay Boxes makes 20,000 boxes in a year, its variable cost will be £10,000 (20,000 x £0.50). If it manufactures 100,000 boxes, its variable cost will be £50,000 (100,000 x £0.50).

Total cost is fixed costs plus variable costs.

$$\text{Total cost} = \text{fixed cost} + \text{variable cost}$$

$$(TC = FC + VC)$$

Table 2 – Rollay Boxes: total variable costs

Production	Total variable cost (average cost, £0.50, x quantity produced)
	£ per year
20,000	10,000
40,000	20,000
60,000	30,000
80,000	40,000
100,000	50,000

Results Plus
Watch Out!

On a break-even chart, add the variable cost line on top of the fixed cost line to get the total cost line. Do not start the total cost line at zero unless there are no fixed costs.

edexcel ⠿ key terms

Total costs – all the costs of a business; equal to fixed costs plus variable costs.

Fixed costs – costs which do not vary with the amount produced, such as rent, business rates, advertising costs, administration costs and salaries.

Variable costs – costs which change directly with the number of products made by a business, such as the cost of buying raw materials.

Table 3 – Rollay Boxes: total revenue, total costs and profit/(loss)

Sales/ production	Total revenue (average price, £2 x quantity sold)	Total fixed cost	Total variable cost (£0.50 x quantity sold)	Total cost (fixed cost plus variable cost)	Profit/loss (total revenue minus total cost)[1]
					£ per year
20,000	40,000	120,000	10,000	130,000	(90,000)
40,000	80,000	120,000	20,000	140,000	(60,000)
60,000	120,000	120,000	30,000	150,000	(30,000)
80,000	160,000	120,000	40,000	160,000	0
100,000	200,000	120,000	50,000	170,000	30,000

1 Losses are shown by putting a bracket around the number.

75

Table 4 – Break-even analysis for Rollay boxes

			£ per year		
Sales/ production	Total revenue (average price, (£2 x quantity sold)	Total fixed cost	Total variable cost (£0.50 x quantity sold)	Total cost (fixed cost plus variable cost)	Profit/loss (total revenue minus total cost)[1]
20,000	40,000	120,000	10,000	130,000	(90,000)
40,000	80,000	120,000	20,000	140,000	(60,000)
60,000	120,000	120,000	30,000	150,000	(30,000)
80,000	160,000	120,000	40,000	160,000	0
100,000	200,000	120,000	50,000	170,000	30,000

1 Losses are shown by putting a bracket around the number.

If Rollay Boxes produces 100,000 boxes in a year, then its fixed cost is £120,000 and its variable cost is £50,000. So total cost is £170,000. Table 3 shows how total cost changes as production levels change.

The total cost line is drawn in Figure 4. The line starts on the left hand side of the graph where production is zero. When there is no production, Rollay Boxes still has to pay its fixed costs. The dotted line across the page shows these fixed costs that do not change as production increases. The variable cost is then added on top of this fixed cost line to give the total cost line. For example, at an output of 80,000 boxes per year, the

fixed cost is £120,000 and the variable cost is £40,000. So the total cost is £160,000. Note that if Rollay produces 0 boxes, its variable costs are zero but it still has to pay fixed costs of £120,000 so its total costs will also be £120,000.

Break-even

The break-even point is the level of output (or sales) where the business would neither make a profit or a loss. Total revenue exactly equals total costs.

Table 4 shows that the break-even point, where total costs equal total revenue, is at 80,000 boxes per year. If sales are more than this, the business will make a profit. If they are below this level, the business will make a loss.

Break-even charts

The information in Table 4 can be shown on a graph, called a **break-even chart**. This is shown in Figure 5. The break-even chart brings together the total cost and total revenue lines shown in Figures 1 and 4. The break-even point is

 edexcel key terms

Break-even chart – a graph which shows total revenue and total cost, allowing the break-even point to be drawn.

ResultsPlus Watch Out!

Get it the right way round. A rise in costs will raise the break-even level. A rise in prices will lead to a fall in the break-even level. Don't confuse 'price' and 'cost'.

ResultsPlus Watch Out!

Break-even analysis does not tell a business how many it **will** sell, only what it has to sell to break-even. For example, say a business is making a loss. It can see from a break-even chart that if it increased its prices **and** sold the same amount, it could break-even. But it then needs to take into account the fact that if it increased its prices, customers would almost certainly buy fewer products. Because of this price sensitivity, increasing prices might lead to even larger losses as sales fall faster in percentage terms than the increase in price.

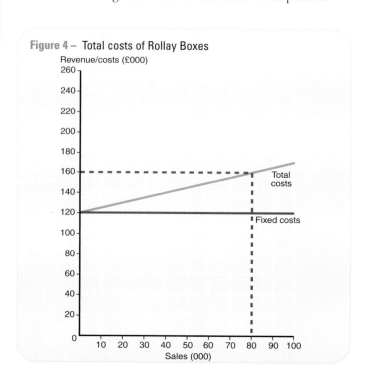

Figure 4 – Total costs of Rollay Boxes

where the total cost and total revenue lines cross. This is at a sales level of 80,000 and at a total cost and revenue level of £160,000. To the right of this point, Rollay Boxes will make a profit whilst to the left it will make a loss.

The number of sales above the break-even point is known as the **margin of safety**. It is the range of output over which a profit can be made. So if the level of sales were 90,000, the margin of safety would be 90,000 sales minus the break-even level of output, 80,000 sales, giving an answer of 10,000 sales. Rollay could see sales fall by 10,000 before it reaches a point where it starts to make a loss. This is a useful thing to know and helps the business with its planning.

Changes in price and costs

Break-even analysis is a useful planning tool for a business such as Rollay. If the business saw a change in its costs, or was considering a change in price, then it could use break-even analysis to understand the effect on its break-even point.

- If costs rise, the break-even point will rise too. This is shown in Figure 6. The total cost line rises because variable costs have risen from £0.50 per box to £0.80. At each level of output above zero, total cost is now higher. At 100,000 boxes, variable costs are now £80,000 (100,000 x £0.80) whilst fixed costs remain unchanged at £120,000. This makes a total cost of £200,000 when output is 100,000 boxes. The break-even level of output used to be 80,000 boxes. Now it is 100,000 boxes. The opposite is also true. If costs fall, the break-even level of output will also fall.

- If the price of the product increases, the break-even point will fall. This is shown in Figure 7. A rise in price from £2 per box to £3.50 per box will tilt the total revenue line upwards making it cross the total cost line at a higher point. If it charged £3.50 per box it would only need to sell 40 000 boxes before breaking even. The new break-even point is just 40,000 boxes. If it decided to reduce the price of each box to £1.70, the break-even point would rise. The total revenue line will tilt downwards, causing it to cross the total cost curve at a lower point. In Figure 7, the price falls to £1.70 per box. If Rollay decided to reduce the price of its boxes it would have to sell more boxes before it broke-even. The break even-point would rise to 100,000 boxes.

Contribution analysis

Drawing a break-even chart is not the only way to find the break-even level of output. The break-even point can also be calculated using **contribution analysis**. This means using the values for sales revenue, variable cost and fixed cost.

Assume the price of a Rollay box is £2. The variable cost of production per box is £0.50. Every time a box is sold, therefore, Rollay makes £1.50 above the variable cost of production. This £1.50 is called a **contribution**:
- first to paying off fixed costs;
- and then toward making a profit.

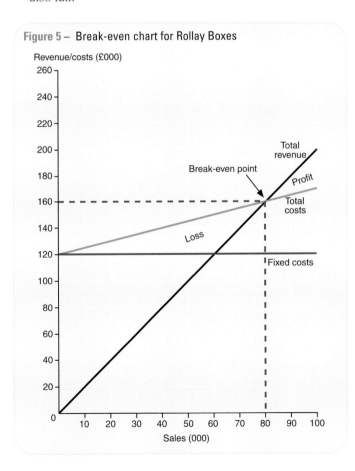

Figure 5 – Break-even chart for Rollay Boxes

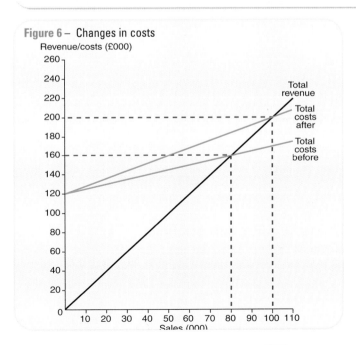

Figure 6 – Changes in costs

77

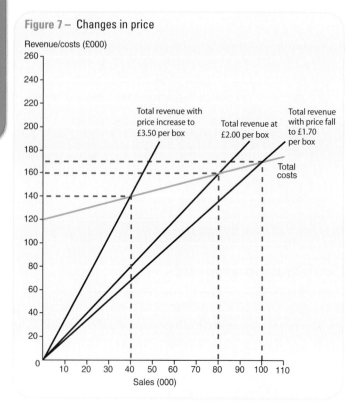

Figure 7 – Changes in price

The formula for contribution is:

Contribution = price per item sold - variable cost per item

The fixed costs of production for Rollay Boxes is £120,000. How many contributions of £1.50 does Rollay need to pay off the £120 000 and therefore to break-even? The answer is 80,000 (£120,000 ÷ £1.50). So Rollay Boxes needs to sell 80,000 boxes to break-even. Every box sold over 80,000 then makes a £1.50 contribution toward profit.

Calculating the break-even level of output using contribution analysis can be done using a formula:

$$\text{Break-even level of output} = \frac{\text{Fixed cost}}{\text{Contribution}} \quad \text{or} \quad \frac{\text{Total fixed cost}}{\text{Sales revenue per item - variable cost per item}}$$

With sales revenue at £2 per box, variable cost per box at £0.50 and total fixed costs of 120,000, the formula gives:

$$\text{Break-even level of output} = \frac{£120,000 \; (\text{Fixed cost})}{£1.50 \; (\text{Contribution of } £2.00 - £0.50)} = 80,000 \text{ boxes}$$

Using break-even analysis

The word 'analysis' means breaking down a complex issue or topic or situation into smaller, more manageable parts to better understand what is going on. Break-even analysis helps a firm to break down a number of things about its business to give it useful information that may help it in future planning

or taking action to correct problems. Break-even analysis has a variety of uses, therefore.

Understanding the past One use is to understand what has already happened. For example, assume Rollay Boxes made a loss last year. In its analysis of what went wrong, it would be very useful to know what had been the break-even level of output. This can be compared to the actual level of output. Was the problem that costs were too high? Was the price right?

Test yourself

1. A bookseller sells 1,000 books a month at an average price of £10 each. At the same time, the bookseller buys in 1,000 books a month at an average cost of £7 each. Buying books is the only cost which changes each month for the bookseller. Which **one** of the following is correct? Select **one** answer. Per month, total revenue is
   - A *£100 whilst fixed costs are £70*
   - B *£990 whilst fixed costs are £993*
   - C *£1,000 whilst variable costs are £70*
   - D *£10,000 whilst variable costs are £7,000*

2. Figure 8 shows a break-even chart for a business. The business is currently selling 15 million nuts at a price of 0.5p each. What is its margin of safety at this level of sales? Select **one** answer.
   - A *15 million sales*
   - B *5 million sales*
   - C *£75,000*
   - D *£25,000*

3. Figure 8 shows a break-even chart for a business. The fixed costs of the business rise from £40,000 to £60,000. What is the new break-even level of output of nuts? Select **one** answer.
   - A *5 million*
   - B *10 million*
   - C *15 million*
   - D *20 million*

Figure 8 – Break-even chart

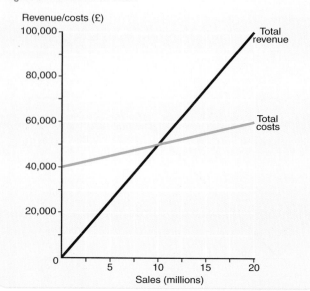

Achieving future targets Understanding the past helps in decision-making about the future. Businesses like Rollay Boxes set themselves targets and goals. Break-even analysis can help a business understand how those targets can be achieved. For example, Rollay Boxes has set itself the goal of making £60,000 profit. Using a break-even chart, it can see that it needs to sell 120,000 boxes to achieve that goal. The margin of safety shows how far above the break-even point is this goal. Break-even analysis also allows a business to ask 'what if?' questions. What if it decided to increase the price of boxes? What if the business could cut its production costs by 10 per cent? What would happen if the business gave its workers a three per cent pay increase this year?

Launching a new product Break-even analysis is essential in any decision about launching a new product. The business needs to know what the break-even level of output would be given certain assumptions about price, revenues and costs. Break-even analysis might show that there is little chance of a new product breaking even in the long term. In this case, the business should not launch the product.

Starting a new business Anyone starting a new business should use break-even analysis to see whether their business idea is viable. If break-even analysis shows that a new business is unlikely to break-even in the medium to long-term, then the business idea needs to be completely rethought.

Business plans Break-even analysis is an essential part of any business plan. If a business applies for a loan from a bank, the bank is likely to ask to see the business plan including its break-even analysis. A bank may well refuse a loan if there is no break-even analysis.

Over to you

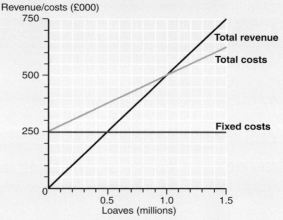

Figure 9 – Break-even chart for Stayfresh Bakeries

Stayfresh Bakeries bakes bread and sells it to wholesalers. On average, each loaf is sold for 50p. Figure 9 shows production in millions of loaves of bread.
1. What is the break-even point of sales? (1)
2. What is the current margin of safety (in quantity of loaves) if production is 1.2 million loaves? (1)
3. How much profit is the business currently making? (3)
   Draw the axes for a break-even chart running from 0 to 1.5 million loaves on the horizontal axis and 0 to £750,000 on the vertical axis. (You will find this easier if you use graph paper.)
4. Stayfresh Bakeries gives staff a pay rise and buys new machinery. This increases fixed costs by £50,000 a year. Plot the new fixed cost line on your diagram. (1)
5. The cost of flour goes up. This increases the variable cost of a loaf of bread by 8 per cent, from 25p per loaf to 27p. Plot the new total cost line on your diagram. (1)
6. Stayfresh Bakeries increases its prices by 4 per cent, from 50p per loaf to 52p per loaf to cover these increases in costs. Plot the new revenue line on your diagram. (1)
7. What has happened: (a) to the break-even point; and (b) to profit on sales of 1.2 million loaves? (4)
8. The aim of the company is to make £50,000 profit per year. One way is to increase the price of the bread sold and the other is to reduce the cost of the raw materials being used by sourcing a cheaper supplier. Which of these choices do you think is the most appropriate to reach the target profit level? Justify your answer. (6)

ResultsPlus
Build Better Answers

Elena Piazza owns a little trattoria (Italian restaurant) in Bath. It has 16 tables and can seat 45 people. She has several staff and her profit margins are steady. She is, however, slightly worried about rising food and fuel costs as this might have an affect on her break-even number of customers.
(a) Explain, with examples, **two** ways in which Elena might lower her break-even number of customers. (6)

Think: What is break-even? What affects the break even level?

■ **Basic** States up to two ways of moving the break-even number of customers. (1-2)

● **Good** Identifies two ways and offers some explanation behind them. For example 'One way is to reduce the raw

material costs (1) by buying cheaper ingredients for her meals which will means less being spent. (1) Another way is to get rid of some staff (1) which will lower her wage bill.' (1)

▲ **Excellent** Clear identification of two ways with a strong explanation of each. Links to the outcome from each method may be discussed. For example 'One thing that Elena could do is look at her fixed costs and see if she can reduce these. (1) She may be able to reduce the cost of her insurance by shopping around (1) however this might mean she has a reduced insurance protection on the business. (1) Another way is to look at the prices of the food and raise some. (1) This would raise revenue but may turn some customers away. However, it would depend on how far she increased her prices.' (1)

15 Financing growth

Case Study

ITV is one of the UK's largest media companies. It owns ITV1 which is the UK's largest commercial television channel in terms of audience share and advertising revenues. It also owns a number of digital television channels such as ITV2 and ITV3. ITV owns a large catalogue of television programmes which it sells worldwide to other television broadcasters and on DVD. The Internet is becoming increasingly important for ITV as more and more viewers watch ITV programmes online. In 2009, ITV also owned the Friends Reunited website.

Objectives

● Understand how to finance a business from internal sources (profit, asset sales).

● Understand how to finance a business from external sources (share capital, debt), including stock market flotation.

edexcel ⠿ key terms

Financing a business – how a business obtains money and other financial resources to start up, expand and if necessary pay off losses it has made.

Internal sources of finance – finance which is obtained within the business such as retained profit or the sale of assets.

External sources of finance – finance which is obtained from outside the business such as bank loans and cash from the issue of new shares.

Retained profit – profit which is kept back in the business and used to pay for investment in the business.

Equity or share capital – the monetary value of a business that belongs to the business' owners. In a company, this would be the value of their shares.

Financing a business

A business like ITV covers its ordinary day-to-day costs of production through the sale of its products. For ITV, much of its revenue comes from the sale of its TV air space to advertisers and its programmes. However, where did the money come from to start up ITV as a company? Where does it get the money to expand its business? What happens when the company makes a loss as it did in 2007 and 2008? These are questions about **financing a business**.

There are two ways to finance a business.

● **Internal sources of finance** come from within the business itself. Examples include retained profit and the sale of assets.

● **External sources of finance** come from outside the business. They include issuing new shares and borrowing money.

Internal sources of finance

There are typically two main internal sources of finance for a business like ITV. These are retained profit and the sale of assets.

Retained profit When a business makes a profit, it has to decide what to do with this profit. Typically, some of the profit is paid out to the owners of the business. For ITV, the owners are the shareholders - those who own a share in the company. Some of the profit is paid out to the government in tax. The tax on company profits is called Corporation Tax. However, businesses often keep back some of the profit. This is known as **retained profit**. This retained profit can then be used to finance investment in the firm. It can also be used to pay off losses if the business makes a loss in any one year. ITV has built up reserves of retained profit from years when it made a profit. It then uses this to finance its business. For example, in 2006, it partly financed the £175 million purchase of the website Friends Reunited from retained profit.

Asset sales Most businesses own assets. These could be buildings, equipment, land or other businesses. For example, Friends Reunited is a company which is wholly owned by ITV. In 2009, ITV said that it might sell Friends Reunited. The money raised could then be used to finance the growth of ITV. It could be used to help develop ITV.com, its website which customers can use to see recently broadcast ITV programmes.

External sources of finance

There are many types of external sources of finance but they fall into two main categories: equity and debt.

Share capital The **equity** of a business is the value of a business which belongs to its owners. In a small business start-up, for example, the owners might put £2,000 of their money into the business. For ITV, it is the value of the **shares** of the business, or its **share capital**. ITV can finance growth through the issue of new shares. For example, some of the money needed to buy Friends Reunited was raised through the issue of new shares in ITV. It is easier to issue new shares if a company is **listed** on a **stock exchange**. A stock exchange is a place where shares are bought and sold. If a company is listed on the stock exchange, it means that its shares are being traded on that stock exchange. ITV is listed on the London Stock Exchange. Companies listed on the stock exchange are called **public limited companies (or plc)**.

Private limited companies also have shareholders but they cannot issue new shares without the consent of existing shareholders and they are not listed on the stock exchange. Their owners, therefore, might find it difficult to raise extra capital to expand the business. One option open to a private limited company is to convert to a public limited company and thus be allowed to sell shares to the public. This is called 'floating the business'. This means that it has to carry out certain legal formalities and processes and be listed on the stock exchange. Once it floats the business, it can offer shares to the general public to buy. If shareholders in a plc want to buy and sell their shares they use the stock exchange to do so. This way, the business itself is not directly affected by the transfer of shares between buyers and sellers. The stock exchange acts as a market for those who want to buy and sell shares. PLCs find it easier to issue new shares than companies which are not listed. This is because any buyer of the new shares can easily sell them again if it is listed.

Debt Borrowing money is another form of external finance for a business. All types of business borrow money directly from banks.

- Some lending is through overdrafts. Businesses hold current accounts with banks. These accounts are used to receive and make payments. ITV, for example, is able to use cheques or electronic transaction processes such as BACs (Bank Automated Clearing) to pay some of its suppliers. An **overdraft** is money borrowed from a bank by drawing more money than is actually in a current account. The maximum that a bank allows a business to borrow in this way is called an **overdraft limit**.
- Businesses can also borrow money from banks through **loans**. A loan is typically repaid to the bank in regular instalments over a period of time. Overdrafts tend to be a short-term form of borrowing to cover changes in cash flow whereas loans tend to be longer-term.
- Large companies like ITV can also issue **bonds**. These are long term loans, normally between 5 and 25 years. The money is borrowed from a variety of institutions including banks, pension funds, insurance companies and private investors. Bond holders usually get a fixed rate of interest over the life of the loan but can trade them on the bond market.
- **Trade credit** is very important for some types of business. Trade credit is given by suppliers. When they sell goods to a business like ITV, they give time for the bill (or invoice) to be paid. Typically this time is 30 days but in practice is often much longer because businesses pay their invoices late.

Advantages and disadvantages of different types of finance

Different types of finance have advantages and disadvantages. Businesses like ITV therefore have to think about the costs and benefits of different types of financing and choose which is the best form of financing for a particular purpose. What is the money needed for? Different types of finance are better suited to some uses than others. For example, if ITV needed to boost its spending in the run up to Christmas, it would not take out a 25-year loan to pay for this. It should look,

Internal finance - sales of assets such as a factory.

External finance - shares.

Results**Plus**
Watch Out!

The size of a business tends to determine what types of finance are available. Very large companies have the widest choice of types of finance. A small sole trader has only a limited choice. Do not make the mistake, for example, of saying that a sole trader could issue shares on the stock exchange.

edexcel ⠿ key terms

Share – a part ownership in a business; for example a shareholder owning 25 per cent of the shares of a business owns a quarter of the business.

Overdraft – borrowing money from a bank by drawing more money than is actually in a current account. Interest is charged on the amount overdrawn.

Bonds – a long-term loan where typically interest is paid at regular intervals like a year and the loan is all repaid at the end of the life of the bond. Bonds are traded on stock markets.

for example, at borrowing money on overdraft that can then be quickly repaid. When ITV needed £175 million to pay for the company Friends Reunited, it did not attempt to raise this money on an overdraft. Banks, after all, can demand immediate repayment of money borrowed on overdraft. Instead, it issued new shares and borrowed money long-term.

Cost Different types of financing have different costs. Trade credit is usually interest free and so it is a cheap way of getting finance. Using retained profit is also often a cheap form of borrowing. However, it is not cost-free. The cost of spending part of the pool of past profits is the interest that is lost because the money would otherwise have been invested. Borrowing money means that interest has to be paid for the lifetime of the loan or overdraft. For example, in 2009, ITV had a £325 million bond on which it was paying 5.375 per cent interest per year. The bonds will have to be repaid in 2015.

If new shares are issued, shareholders expect to be paid dividends, their share of the profit. Shares never have to be repaid, so dividends will continue to be paid for the lifetime of the company. Issuing new shares also has a cost to existing shareholders. If there are now more shares, the profit of the company has to be divided amongst more shareholders. If the total profit given to shareholders does not change, each shareholder will now get less in dividends. This is called diluting the shareholding. Existing shareholders are therefore not always happy about their company issuing new shares.

Risk Different types of financing have different risks attached to them. Using retained profit is relatively risk free. So too is issuing new shares. Typically, companies can choose whether or not to pay a dividend to their shareholders. If the company has a bad year, it can choose not to pay a dividend. On the other hand, businesses usually cannot choose whether or not to make interest payments or repayments on bank loans and bonds. Businesses which have a lot of debt are likely to get into difficulty if they start to make large losses. They might then not have the cash to make payments on the loans.

ResultsPlus
Watch Out!

Companies only rarely issue large numbers of new shares. To issue new shares is a long and complicated process which needs the approval of existing shareholders. Getting a new loan, on the other hand, is usually much easier and quicker. Issuing new shares also only tends to happen when a company needs a large sum for expansion or when it is in real financial difficulties. Do not make the mistake of saying a company could issue new shares to pay for a small investment.

Availability of finance Not all types of finance are available to a business at any point in time. Small businesses, for example, will be too small to get a listing on a stock exchange. They will find it difficult to issue new shares. They are also too small to issue bonds. So what types of finance are available?

- All types of business can use retained profit with two exceptions. A start up business will have no retained profit. Nor will a business that has been making losses and has used up any retained profit it might once have had.
- Businesses can only sell assets if they own them and a buyer is willing to buy the assets.
- All businesses are likely to have access to bank overdrafts and loans. However, only very large companies are likely to be able to issue bonds.
- Trade credit is also likely to be available to most businesses. However, the amount of trade credit is limited by the amount a business buys from suppliers.
- Small businesses find it much more difficult than large businesses to get new equity. Even so, there is also a limit to how much money large businesses can raise in new shares. Investors might be unwilling to buy new shares in a company if they think there is too much risk attached.

Source: information from news.bbc.co.uk 12.6.2005, http://www.the register.co.uk 4.3.2009, http://www.itcplc.com.

Test yourself

1. A coffee shop company wants to expand by setting up five new outlets. It has decided to finance this through taking out a five-year loan from a bank. A disadvantage of taking out a loan is that it will

   A *have to pay dividends on the loan*
   B *have to pay interest on the loan*
   C *prevent the company from issuing new shares*
   D *reduce the availability of trade credit*
   Select **one** answer.

2. A recruitment agency floats itself on the stock market. This means that

   A *it borrows money from stock market traders*
   B *it recruits workers from the stock exchange*
   C *its sales on the stock market increase*
   D *its shares become available to buy and sell on the stock market*
   Select **one** answer.

3. Which **one** of the following is an internal source of finance for a business?

   A *retained profit*
   B *the issue of new shares*
   C *a loan*
   D *a bond*
   Select **one** answer.

Over to you

Weavephone is a UK mobile phone company. It has 8 million subscribers in the UK as well as 6 million in France and 9 million in Germany. The directors of the company have decided that it wants to establish an operation in India. The initial cost will be in excess of £200 million.

The directors have discussed a variety of ways of raising the £200 million. They have been advised that they could get a 5 year bank loan for the £200 million at a rate of interest of 7 per cent per annum. The money would have to be paid back in regular instalments each year. Alternatively, they might be able to issue a 15 year bond. They would have to offer 8 per cent interest but the money would only be repayable at the end of 15 years. Some directors favour a share issue. However, existing shareholders might not be very happy with a share issue even though the money would be used hopefully to generate more profits. The company has £300 million in retained profits. However, much of this has already been allocated to fund other investment projects over the next three years. Of course, some of these other investment projects could be cancelled and the retained profit diverted to pay for the expansion into India. One radical suggestion has been to sell off either the French or German part of the company. This would raise considerably more than £200 million and so would leave the company with a large amount of money to invest elsewhere.

1. Explain what is meant by (a) a share and (b) a bank loan. (6)

2. Why could the £200 million needed not be raised through increased trade credit? (3)

3. Analyse why issuing £200 million of shares would be a less risky option than getting a bank loan for the same amount. (6)

4. Do you think Weavephone should use its retained profit to fund the £200 million investment? Justify your answer. (8)

ResultsPlus
Build Better Answers

Limited companies sometimes need large amounts of capital in order to expand their businesses. Which of the following are **most likely** be disadvantages of issuing new shares? Select **two** answers.

A   Dividends have to be paid for the lifetime of the company
B   New share issue can raise the profile of a business
C   Interest payments may eat into the profit margins
D   Not all the shares may reach their selling price
E   Issuing new shares is a long and complicated process

Answer A and E

Technique guide: There is a number of choices available so first:

Think: What is a new share issue? Who is affected? What does it mean for the business?

Then: Consider each alternative and firstly look for the most obvious wrong answer.

C is clearly not the right answer as a share issue does not have an interest charge attached to it. ■

Decide: You are now left with four options.

Now: Go through these:

B is incorrect. An increased profile may lead to new investors or new customers which is a good thing. ■

D is incorrect. The price of the new share issue is fixed at the time of the sale and only goes up or down once released onto the stock market. ■

This leaves you with the correct answers of A and E. Shares are never repaid so they last for the life of the company and a share issue can be a long and drawn out process. ▲

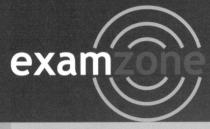
In this topic you have learned about: the key aspects of financial management such as credit terms and de-stocking.; the relationship between reducing outflows and increasing inflows; how profit increases from the reduction of costs and the increase of revenue; how and why changes in price impact on profit; how to draw and interpret break-even and how it can be used as a planning tool for businesses; how to finance a business from internal and external sources.

You should know…

☐ Cash flow and profit are not the same thing. A positive cash flow does not mean that a business has made a profit; a negative cash flow does not mean a business has made a loss.

☐ Cash flow is the movement of money into and out of a business.

☐ The main cash inflow is usually from customers paying for goods or services. Other inflows include interest received or rental payments. Outflows include wages and payment for materials.

☐ Cash inflows can be improved by de-stocking, the selling off of stocks, making customers pay for goods more quickly and hiring a 'factor' to recover payments owed. A long-term strategy to improve cash inflow is to take a loan.

☐ Cash outflows can be reduced by cutting the amount of raw materials being ordered, leasing equipment instead of buying or delaying payments to suppliers.

☐ Profit = total revenue (TR) - total costs (TC). Profit can be increased by reducing costs or improving revenues.

☐ Revenues can be increased by marketing goods better or making better products.

☐ Changes in price can affect revenues. There is a difference in the way 'price' and 'cost' are used in business studies compared to everyday use.

☐ A business must be careful not to cut costs and reduce the quality of the product or increase selling price too much.

☐ Break-even is the level of output where total revenue equals total costs.

☐ Total revenue = Quantity sold x Average price.

☐ Total cost is the sum of all the costs at any level of output.

☐ Total costs = fixed and variable costs (TC = FC + VC). Fixed costs are unaffected by changes to the amount produced. Variable costs change directly with a change in output.

☐ The break-even point will change if the costs change or the price of a product changes (or a combination of the two).

☐ Break-even analysis can be used to understand the past, forecast future actions, launch a new product, start a new business and develop a business plan.

☐ A business's finances come from internal or external sources of finance. Internal sources include retained profit or sales of assets. External sources include loans, grants, trade credit and share capital.

☐ The break-even formula is BE point = Fixed costs ÷ variable cost per unit - selling price.

☐ Selling price minus variable cost per unit is also called 'Contribution'.

☐ Different sources are suitable for different reasons. A business must think about the cost of the finance, the availability and the risk associated with it.

Support activity

- Make a record of your own personal cash flow for a week. Use this to make a forecast cash flow for the following week and month.

- Think about how you could improve your own personal cash flow. Make a list of all the ways that could reduce your costs or increase your revenue. From your list narrow it down to one way that you think would work for improving the inflow and one way for reducing the outflow.

- Discuss your list with another student in the class, and then discuss it as a class group. Are there any common areas of cost reduction or strategies to improve cash inflow? What might stop people from actually following these strategies?

Stretch activity

- Pick one business where you can readily identify the main sources of inflow and outflow.

- List as many as you can and then see if you can rank that list in order of financial size.

- From the list come up with realistic strategies that the business can undertake to improve its cash inflows.

- Now try and identify realistic strategies to reduce the costs without damaging the company image or product quality.

- Finally try to summarise your ideas and then explain why the business you have chosen might not have done these yet.

Amberley Freeman wants to open a hairdressers in St Albans. She thinks that there is a gap in the market for this as many of the current places seem to offer the same service and all look very similar. She checked 'Up my Street' and found out that the average income in the areas is relatively high. She is using the information she has collected to try to work out her break-even point.

(i) What is meant by the term 'break-even?' (1)
(ii) Explain **one** way in which break-even analysis might benefit a business. (3)

Think: What is break even? What is involved in arriving at a break even figure? Why does looking at these variables help a business to run more successfully?

Student answer	Examiner comment	Build a better answer
(a) It's when a firm doesn't make or lose anything.	■ A basic answer which indicates that there is neither profit or loss being made. It would be unclear if the candidate actually understands the full meaning.	△ Use the right terminology such as '... costs are covered by the revenue made' or use an example, such as 'If the total costs in a month for Amberley are £3,000 then she needs to sell £3,000 worth of services to cover those, therefore breaking even'.
(b) A business will be able to see how much they need to sell to cover the costs.	■ Simple answer which is correct but undeveloped and would not progress beyond 1 mark as a result. The command word is 'explain' and therefore requires some development of the point.	△ The question is worth three marks so expect to give one point as requested by the question and then offer some links to develop it. For example 'Analysis will help identify the level of sales needed to cover the costs after which a profit will be made. (1 mark) This helps the business to be able to plan ahead to manage its resources (1 mark) to ensure it can produce the required amount to meet and hopefully exceed its break-even target.' (1 mark)

Practice Exam Questions

Lyn Terry knew that there was an opportunity for expansion which gave her the opportunity to meet a customer need. She had worked in the shopfitting industry for 24 years and built up her own successful company, Sign 'O The Times. Lyn's business fitted out shops - installing lighting, shelving, equipment and display units for retail outlets. She felt her experience meant that she could read the market pretty well. Recently the retail market had been suffering with many more shops than normal closing down. However in the last 3 months things seemed to be picking up following a recent announcement by the government to support small businesses if they wished to open.

This had developed into a spate of applications to open various retail businesses right across the Midlands, where Lyn's shopfitting business was based. Requests for quotes for shopfitting had increased threefold and Lyn knew that it wasn't going to stop there, after all her business had a great reputation for quality products and service.

If she was going to cope with the demand then she would need to move to a bigger premises and employ more people. The amount of raw materials that she would need would also have to rise. Lyn tried to run her business on a lean production system but always carried buffer stock in case of emergency callouts or repairs.

To finance this expansion Lyn knew that she needed to make some difficult choices about where to get the capital from.

Estimates seemed to indicate that she would need around £75,000 for the expansion. She knew that internal financing would not cover everything she needed and she would have to look at some form of external financing.

(a) Which **two** of the following are **not** external sources of finance? (2)

A   Share capital
B   Bank loan
C   Government grant
D   Retained profit
E   Asset sales
F   Trade credit

(b) Lyn has decided to raise the internal finance for the expansion in one of two ways. She will use either retained profit or raise finance by selling assets.
Which of these choices do you think is the most appropriate source of finance for Lyn's expansion? Justify your answer. (6)

(c) The following **two** factors might affect Lyn's choice of source of finance.
(i) The cost of the finance and
(ii) the risks associated with the source of finance.
In your opinion, which of these **two** factors is the most important in making her choice? Justify your answer. (8)

Topic 3.4: Effective people management

Case study

Grace Williams has worked for a couple of years as the manager of a car hire outlet in Manchester. The company she works for has outlets covering the whole of the UK. It is part of a much larger company which has two divisions: car hire and travel sales.

Topic overview

This topic examines how the organisational structure of a business can be reflected in an organisational chart, the importance of organisational structures, how different businesses have different structures, the factors that affect motivation at work and how these relate to theories such as Maslow's hierarchy of needs, the impact of effective and poor communication in organisations, the barriers to effective communication and the various methods used to remunerate people and the effect that different payment systems can have on employees and organisations.

The car hire division has a chain of command which goes from the manager director down to the office cleaner. As manager, she was responsible for a staff of fifteen workers. Some were full-time staff, others part-time. She was paid a salary. On top of that, she received a bonus according to the turnover of her outlet. The more cars she could hire out, the higher would be her bonus. Her company wanted to motivate her to generate extra sales. On top of that, she received the fringe benefit of being able to use one of the cars for her own personal use if it was not being hired out to a customer.

Grace found the selling exciting. The key to getting extra sales was to visit businesses and persuade them to hire cars. She enjoyed having the freedom to create her own schedule and shape the way in which she worked. She also enjoyed getting the respect of more senior managers for the way in which she generated sales. However, Grace did not get very much satisfaction from managing the other workers at her outlet. She felt they did not include her and would rather she was away from the outlet making her sales pitches to business clients. Partly because of this, Grace was looking for another job either within the company or outside.

The company was fairly centralised in its organisation. It kept a tight control over most of what went on at the outlet. It determined how many staff were employed and what were their duties. There were fixed procedures for checking and cleaning cars before they were hired out to clients. The company decided what cars would be bought to loan out and how many cars would be allocated to each outlet.

There were fairly extensive manuals containing all company procedures which should be followed. It was up to Grace to make sure that all the workers in her outlet followed the procedures laid down. Talking to managers of other outlets, Grace found that some managers followed the procedures strictly. Other managers were more lax, allowing workers to do jobs in the way they thought best. These workers often did not know that there were company procedures because their manager had never told them about them. Some managers found the written procedures so complex that they did not even fully understand them themselves. Grace was someone who tried to make sure that procedures were always followed. Her subordinates found her sometimes too inflexible and this demotivated them.

1. Explain the structure of the car hire and travel sales business.

2. What motivated and demotivated the workers described in the case study?

3. To what extent do you think there was effective communication down the chain of command in the car hire company? Justify your answer.

4. Discuss whether a different payment system would have motivated Grace more.

What will I learn?

Organisational structure What is meant by a divisional structure for a company? How are business organisations structured through levels of hierarchy and chains of command? What is the difference between a centralised system of organisation and a decentralised system?

Motivation theory What is the significance of motivation in the workplace? How can Maslow's theory of the Hierarchy of Needs help you understand what motivates workers? How can this theory help businesses to release the potential of workers in their organisations? Does motivation come within a worker rather than from outside?

Communication What is the impact of insufficient or excessive communication on efficiency, staff and their motivation? What are the barriers to effective communication?

Remuneration What is the impact on staff of various payment strategies including time, piece rates and commission. What is the difference between full-time work paid by salary and freelance or temporary work? What is meant by fringe benefits? What is the impact on business of different payment systems?

How will I be assessed?

This is assessed through Unit 3, a written examination lasting 1 hour 30 minutes.

The paper is divided into three sections.

Section A is a mix of mainly multiple choice questions and short answer questions with one or more questions requiring an extended answer.

Sections B and C consist of short and long answer questions based on two scenarios, one for each section, given in the paper.

16 Organisational structure

Case Study

Tomkins plc is a multinational company that, in 2008, had sales and manufacturing operations in 24 countries and 142 sites. It owned most or all of 54 subsidiary and associate companies. It manufactures a wide range of industrial and automotive products as well as building products. For example, some of the parts in the engine of your family car might have been made by a Tomkins company. If you take a holiday in Florida in the USA, the bath in your hotel room might have been made by another Tomkins company.

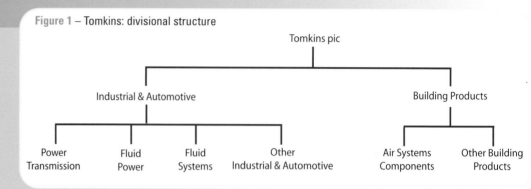

Figure 1 – Tomkins: divisional structure

Objectives

- Appreciate that businesses tend to be organised through a particular structure.
- Understand the importance of divisional structures within a business.
- Understand levels of hierarchy and chains of command within a business context.
- Compare centralised versus decentralised systems.

Divisional structures

One way in which Tomkins is organised is on a product basis. Tomkins is organised into two product divisions, Industrial & Automotive and Building Products as shown in Figure 1. Both divisions are organised into different areas again according to product. Within each product area, there is a number of subsidiary companies, each specialising in a particular product area. For example, the Building Products Division is organised into two areas, Air System Components and Other Building Products. Within the Air System Components area, there is a number of subsidiary companies including Air System Components Inc (a US company), Hart & Colley Inc (US), NRG Industries Inc (US) and Ruskin Air Management Ltd (UK).

Organising on a product basis allows Tomkins subsidiaries to specialise. Each company has expertise in manufacturing or selling a specific range of products. Workers in those companies have specialised knowledge which they can use. Each subsidiary also has capital equipment specifically designed for the manufacture or sale of the range of products.

This type of organisation also increases accountability. Each subsidiary has to draw up its own accounts and show how it is performing. It gives the management

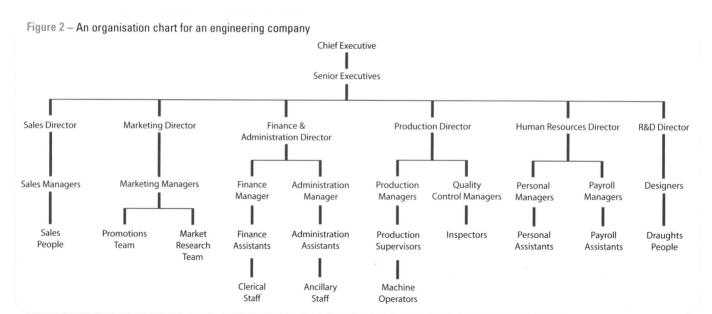

Figure 2 – An organisation chart for an engineering company

and workers of each subsidiary an incentive to perform better. It also helps the directors of Tomkins to identify those parts of the business which are doing well and those doing less well. The company can then make decisions based on this information.

Some large companies are organised on a regional basis. For example, all the businesses in North America might be organised into a North American division. Companies which organise themselves on a geographical basis may sell a fairly narrow range of products. It then makes sense for operations in a region to co-operate with each other. They can, for example, share their knowledge about the market in the region, its economic environment and government regulations.

Tomkins could have chosen to organise itself on a geographical basis. It could, for example, have chosen to group all its US companies into one division. However, it decided that this would be a less efficient way of organising itself than on a product basis.

Organisation

Throughout Tomkins, workers specialise in the jobs they perform. Each takes on a **role**, a given job of work. Some workers are administration or sales staff, some are skilled workers, whilst others are managers. Workers need to know:

- what jobs they are supposed to do;
- who is in charge of them;
- who they are in charge of;
- how they relate to the wider organisation.

This can be shown on an organisation chart.

Organisation charts

Figure 2 shows an organisation chart for an engineering company similar to those within the Tomkins group of companies. Within the company, there is a hierarchy. This is a series of layers in the organisation. At the top is the Chief Executive. Next in the hierarchy are senior executives who are responsible for individual departmental directors. These include the Sales Director, the Product Director and the R&D Director. At the bottom of the hierarchy are the machine operators and ancillary staff. Workers in a hierarchy have a line manager. This is someone immediately above the worker, to whom he or she reports.

Most businesses are organised by function. This means that they are organised according to what people in the organisation do. So, the department responsible for sales is led by the Sales Director whilst the Production Director is responsible for the production department.

Because there tend to be more people the lower down you go in the organisation, a hierarchy is often said to be a pyramid.

The chain of command

The person at the top of the organisational pyramid is in a position of authority over workers lower down the pyramid. So a Chief Executive has authority over Departmental Executives. He or she can give orders to workers lower down the hierarchy, their subordinates. For instance, they could tell the Finance & Administration Director to prepare a report on the latest cash flow position of the company. In the organisational pyramid, there is therefore a chain of command from the top to the bottom. The chain of command shows how orders and decisions are passed down throughout the organisation from those in senior positions to workers in other parts of the organisation. This is shown in Figure 3. The more layers in the chain of command, the longer it becomes. A short chain of command would have very few layers between the top of the chain and the bottom.

key terms

Organisation – the way in which a business is structured for it to achieve its objectives.

Organisation chart – a diagram which shows the internal structure of an organisation.

Hierarchy – structure of different levels of authority in a business organisation, one on top of the other.

Line manager – employee who is responsible for overseeing the work of others further down the hierarchy of an organisation.

Function – tasks or jobs. Organisation by function means that a business is organised according to tasks that have to be completed, such as production or finance.

Authority – the right to decide what to do in a situation and take command of it to be able to make decisions without referring to anyone else.

Subordinate – workers in the hierarchy who work under the control of a more senior worker.

Chain of command – the path (or chain) down which orders (or commands) are passed. In a company, this goes from the board of directors down to other workers in the organisation.

Figure 3 – Chain of command for an engineering company

Chief Executive

|

Senior Executive

|

Finance & Administration Director

|

Finance Manager

|

Finance Assistant

|

Clerical Assistant

The length of the chain of command

The length of the chain of command varies between business organisations. In a small independent hairdressers, for example, there might only be two layers in the chain of

edexcel ⠿ key terms

Delayering – removing layers of management and workers in a hierarchy so that there are fewer workers in the chain of command.

Empowerment – giving more responsibility to workers further down the chain of command in a hierarchy.

Downsizing – when a business employs fewer workers to produce the same amount through increases in productivity which can be achieved through delayering.

command: the owner manager and the hair stylists. In a large oil company like British Petroleum (BP) or Shell, there might 15 or 20 layers between the bottom of the hierarchy and the Chief Executive at the top.

The longer the chain of command, the more difficulties a business can face.

- Messages can get lost or distorted as they go up and down the chain of command, rather as in a game of Chinese whispers.
- Managing change can be another problem. In a sole proprietorship, like an independent hairdressers, change is simple. The sole trader decides to change and acts on that decision. In a large organisation, the chairperson might decide on change but it might be resisted further down the hierarchy. The longer the chain of command, the more people and groups there are who might have a reason to resist that change.
- Long chains of command can demotivate some workers who may feel alienated from the business. They may not feel part of the business. They may feel like outsiders, workers who do not belong in the business. As a result, they may not give their best. This can reduce efficiency and productivity.
- Lots of different layers can create a 'tribe mentality' where each layer focuses on its own affairs rather than on the business's aims and objectives as a whole and this can also lead to inefficiencies.

Groups, teams and delayering

Some large businesses try to resolve the problems of a long chain of command by flattening it - changing the way the business is organised by removing some of the levels of management and changing job roles. This is called **delayering**. They cut out large numbers of middle managers, pushing responsibility and decision making down the line.

This is often linked to more **group**, **team** or **cell** working. Workers may be organised into a small group or a team or a cell. There is likely to be a leader of the group, team or cell. But everyone else in the team may be at the same level in the hierarchy. The team is given a task or job. However, how the team members achieve that task may be up to them. In a factory, for instance, supervisors and quality control inspectors can be eliminated if workers are organised into cells and made responsible for their own work in terms of output and quality. They may even manage their own budgets in some cases.

This **empowerment** of workers can motivate them. However, it usually means that workers have to be better trained to cope with the extra responsibilities. Workers might have to be paid more because they are doing a more responsible job. Delayering should lead to workers becoming more productive. Fewer workers are needed to do the same amount of work. Businesses can then **downsize**, making workers redundant whilst producing as much as before.

Figure 4 – The span of control for a sales director

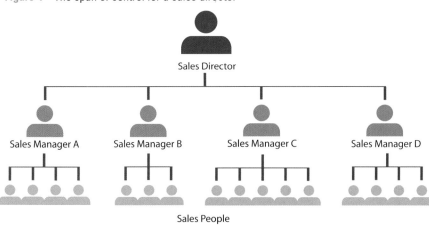

Some workers may be suspicious of attempts to reorganise and may not see it as an attempt to improve efficiency or improve motivation but simply as a cost-cutting exercise. Leaders have to demonstrate considerable skill to see through such changes.

Span of control

A Sales Director at a company responsible for a large sales team is unlikely to be able to organise or supervise every single worker in the Sales Department. This job would be too large. Instead, the Sales Director will only supervise some workers. In Figure 4, it is assumed that he or she controls four Sales Managers. Each Sales Manager then controls a number of other workers in the department.

The number of people that a worker directly controls is called a **span of control**. The span of control of the Sales Director is therefore four employees - the four Sales Managers.

The span of control: how big?

The span of control varies depending upon circumstances.

* The more complex the supervision task, the smaller the span of control. The supervision task can be complex if checking work is difficult and time consuming. It can also be complex if the workers that need supervising are not particularly good at their job.
* The span of control has to be small if it takes a lot of time to communicate with subordinates. If it takes half a day a week for a Sales Director to talk things through with a Sales Manager, then the Sales Director cannot be responsible for too many workers.
* The better the supervisor, the more people he or she can supervise.
* The more supervisors **delegate** their work, the greater can be the span of control. Delegation means passing down responsibility to subordinates to complete tasks. Delegation frees up a supervisor's time to supervise the work of more workers. It also empowers subordinates. Workers further down the chain of command are likely to be more motivated the greater the degree of delegation. This is because they are being shown trust and can use their own talents and skills more.

Centralisation

Tomkins, in part, is a **centralised** organisation. What this means is that many decisions about the company are made at head office. These decisions are then sent out to the rest of the business. Deciding on objectives for the company and working out strategies to achieve them is done from head office. Common systems and procedures are laid down so that costs can be minimised. The problem with centralised organisations is that they can be slow to make decisions and respond to the needs of the market.

So Tomkins is also in part a **decentralised** organisation. The power to make decisions is devolved or given to smaller parts of the organisation. For instance, decisions about pricing of whirlpool baths produced by its US subsidiary Lasco Bathware are not made at Tomkins headquarters in London but left to Lasco Bathware. Decentralisation encourages workers to change more quickly as the business environment changes. It gives power to those who are closest to customers, suppliers and to the market. A business like Tomkins needs to achieve the right balance between centralisation and decentralisation.

Source: information from www.tomkins.co.uk.

edexcel ⠿ key terms

Span of control – the number of people who report directly to another worker in an organisation.

Delegation – passing down of authority for work to another worker further down the hierarchy of the organisation.

Centralisation – a type of business organisation where decisions are made at the centre or core of the organisation and then passed down the chain of command.

Decentralisation – a type of business organisation where decision-making is pushed down the hierarchy and away from the centre of the organisation.

Test yourself

1. A business has a short chain of command within its organisation. Which one of the following is most likely to be an advantage of a short chain of command compared to a long chain of command?

Select one answer.

A The span of control of each worker in the chain of command is likely to be longer

B Each worker is likely to be more specialised in their job

C There are likely to be more supervisors in the chain of command

D Messages are less likely to be distorted as they go up and down the chain of command

2. A centralised company is most likely to be one where

A the parts of the company are located near the head office of the company

B all major decisions are made at the head office of the company

C the products made are very similar to each other

D the chain of command has been delayered

Select one answer.

3. In a company, Deepta is the line manager of John. This means that Deepta is

A able to delegate work to John
B subordinate to John
C lower down the chain of command than John
D lower down the hierarchy than John

Select one answer.

ResultsPlus
Build Better Answers

Draw **six** lines to link each key word about organisational structure on the left with its correct description on the right.

a. Authority
b. Delegation
c. Downsizing
d. Line manager
e. Organisation chart
f. Subordinate

(i) When a business employs fewer workers to produce the same amount through increases in productivity

(ii) A diagram which shows the internal structure of an organisation

(iii) An employee who is responsible for other workers and to whom other employee/s report

(iv) The right to decide what to do in a situation, take command of it and make decisions

(v) Passing down of authority for work to another worker further down the hierarchy of the organisation

(vi) Worker in the hierarchy who works under the control of a more senior worker

Answer:
a. - (iv)
b. - (v)
c. - (i)
d. - (iii)
e. - (ii)
f. - (vi)

Technique: you have 6 statements that clearly link to the concept of Organisational Structure. Look at the list and try and see if there are any clear links between the statement and the descriptions and likewise ones that do not match at all.

Think: What is organisation? What structures link to organisations? What is involved at each level?

Decide:
'...authority' links to being in command. So a. = (iv)

'Delegation' passes work down a chain, so b. = (v)

'Downsizing' sounds like getting smaller or reducing something. So c. = (i)

Managers often check on workers, therefore d. = (iii)

A chart sounds like a map or diagram. So e. = (ii)

This leaves the subordinate working under someone more senior. So f. = (vi)

Over to you

Charlie Sugden is one of 246 managers of a local chain of newsagents. The chain forms one of the two divisions of a company which also owns a number of local newspapers. The strategy of the company is to sell its own local newspapers aggressively through the newsagents whilst minimising sales of a rival local newspaper.

Charlie's job is not easy. He has to work very long hours. To help him, he asked his line manager to appoint an assistant manager. However, they have always said that his newsagents was too small to justify this.

So he has to struggle alone with the task of running the shop and its 46 workers. There are 30 youngsters delivering newspapers, both in the morning and the evening. Then there are 16 adult staff. All but two of them are part-time. Staff often complain about the low wages and how they do not feel appreciated by management. This is hardly surprising since Charlie often barely gets to know some of the staff before they leave.

All the major functions of the business are centralised. Head office deals with everything from buying stock to paying wages to adult staff to refits for the newsagents. Charlie is responsible for the day to management of the shop and recruiting the youngsters who deliver the newspapers.

Charlie would like to be able to make more decisions at shop level. For example, he would like to be able to recruit adult staff. He thinks that the people at Head Office who do this often do not understand his local needs. So they recruit people who are unsuitable and do not stay. Equally, he feels he could sell more if he could have more choice about what is stocked in the newsagents.

1. Using examples from the passage, explain what is meant by (a) 'two divisions of a company and (b) 'centralised' organisation. (6)

2. Explain how the appointment of an assistant manager to Charlie would affect the chain of command. (3)

3. (i) Identify **one** problem that may occur because of the size of Charlie's span of control. (1)
   (ii) Explain how this problem might affect the business. (3)

4. Do you think a less centralised organisation would benefit the company? Justify your answer. (6)

17 Motivation theory

Case Study

Beaverbrooks is a chain of jewellery shops. Founded in 1919, it still very much has the feel of a family run business. The managing director is Mark Adlestone. He is the grandson of one of the three brothers who founded the business. Explaining his philosophy, he says: 'We look after people as is if we were a family. We really do listen to our people. Our people become part of a family that has been in love with this business for 90 years. Our passion for jewellery is only matched by our passion for our people.' Beaverbrooks management style means that its 800 staff are highly motivated. In 2009, the company was voted the UK's number one company to work for in the Sunday Times 100 Best Companies to Work For award.

Objectives

● Understand the meaning of the term 'motivation'.

● Understand the significance of motivation in the workplace with specific focus on Maslow's Hierarchy of Needs and its potential in organisations.

● Appreciate that motivation can also come from within.

edexcel ⋮⋮⋮ **key terms**

Motivation – in work, the desire to complete a task.

The importance of motivation

Motivation refers to the extent to which an individual gives their best at all times when working for a business. Most companies will want to find ways of encouraging workers to do this because it means that the business's aims and objectives are more likely to be met and, as a result, customer needs will also be met.

A company like Beaverbrooks needs to **motivate** its workers. A well motivated workforce has a lot of benefits for a business.

- A well motivated workforce is likely to be more committed to the business and want it to do well. Demotivated workers may not be fully committed to the business and as a result may not carry out their jobs as well as they could. They may, for example, spend a lot of time talking to each other about things that have nothing to do with work. They may take much longer breaks than they should. Such an approach to work is likely to mean that they are less productive and the business might be less efficient than it would like to be. In addition, demotivated workers might present a bad image to customers and this might not help to encourage customer loyalty and repeat purchase.

- Motivated workers tend to produce better, higher quality work. They are interested in what they are doing. They take a pride in the quality of what they do. This helps the business achieve its quality standards and meet its aims and objectives.

- Motivated workers are often more flexible. They are prepared to do a variety of tasks. They are more willing to learn. This increases their productivity - the output per worker per period of time.

The motivation of its staff is key to the success of a company like Beaverbrooks. The company says: 'Our work ethic is as important to us as ever and we pride ourselves on making our working environment open, positive and motivated.' The high level of motivation of Beaverbrook workers helps it to provide the best customer service possible. This helps increase sales and revenues. Worker motivation also helps it to be efficient as a company, keeping costs down. Higher levels of efficiency, increased sales and lower costs contribute to higher profits for the company.

Maslow's Hierarchy of Needs

To understand what motivates workers, it is important to understand what makes them take a job and what makes them want to work. One explanation that can help is Maslow's Hierarchy of Needs. A H Maslow was an American researcher who suggested in the 1950s that people have a number of different needs. These needs can be put into order of importance to produce a **hierarchy of needs**. This hierarchy is shown in Figure 1.

Physiological needs At the bottom of the hierarchy are physiological (physical) needs. People have physical needs such as to eat, to be warm, and to be in good health. To satisfy these needs, people must have food, clothes, shelter and heating. Workers at a business like Beaverbrooks are motivated to work because they want to earn the money to buy these items. Therefore, the amount of money workers are paid might act as a motivator in that it enables workers to satisfy these needs.

Safety needs People want their environment to be safe. For example, they do not want road accidents to occur, or for people to fall ill, or for savers to lose all their money on the stock exchange. When working for a business, people want to know they are physically safe. So health and safety at work are important. They also want to know that their job is secure and they will not be made redundant. They want to know that they will be paid regularly and they want to know how much they will paid. If Beaverbrook, for example, wants to motivate its workers, it must create this environment of safety. Workers become demotivated when they work for a business where there is a poor health and safety record, or where there is job insecurity.

Love and belonging People want to feel accepted as part of a group, like a family at home or a team in a workplace. They want to be trusted and be able to support others. Beaverbrooks as a company is particularly successful at creating a sense of family. For example, most promotion comes from within the 'family' of workers at Beaverbrooks. Workers as a 'family' are encouraged to raise money for

Results Plus
Watch Out!

In Maslow's hierarchy of needs, one factor which affects motivation can often be put into two or more categories. For example, pay satisfies physiological needs. But it is often very important for self-esteem needs. The higher the pay you receive, the more you feel respected for what you do. Belonging to a team gives many workers a sense of love and belonging. But it can also satisfy their safety needs - they feel more secure because they are not working on their own. Training can increase the self-esteem of a worker. However, going on a training course can also increase their sense of belonging in their place of work. It may also allow them to achieve self-actualisation if there is a creative element to the course.

Figure 1 – Maslow's hierarchy of needs

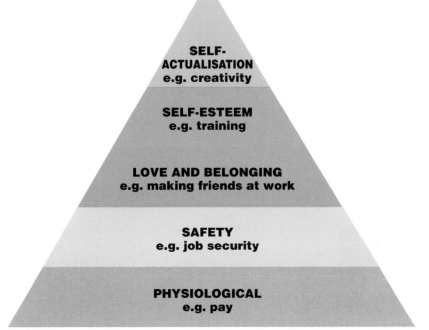

edexcel ::: key terms

Hierarchy of needs – placing needs in an order of importance, starting with basic needs.

96

charity. The company gives away an extra £1 to charity with every £1 that its own workers raise. Most importantly, the management of the company spend a lot of time listening to its workers in order to improve every aspect of how the company is run.

Self-esteem needs People want to feel that others respect them for what they can do. They want to respect themselves too, feeling that they have achieved something and are good at a task. For example, at Beaverbrooks, workers can develop a sense of self respect through getting involved with local

Needs include working in a safe environment, feeling part of a group and being respected.

charities. Workers can be given time off work to develop their work for charities. The company also has very strong policies on issues such as bullying at work or racism to combat anything which would lower the self-esteem of workers.

Self-actualisation This is the highest order need, according to Maslow. It is the ability to realise your full potential. For instance, at Beaverbrooks all workers are encouraged to fulfil their own potential. The company says: 'We believe in encouraging each member of every team to develop their knowledge and skills to achieve their full potential, whatever that may be'. So workers are encouraged to apply for the Management Development Programme, a programme of training which will allow workers to apply for store management positions.

Maslow suggested that once one need was satisfied it ceased to act as a motivator. This implies that if workers have satisfied a particular need then offering more of that need will not necessarily act as a motivator.

Using Maslow's hierarchy of needs in the workplace

Maslow's theory suggests that there is a number of different reasons why people come to work. They have a job because they need the money to survive. This is their **basic need**. However, they also want to satisfy their **higher order needs** such as self-esteem needs and self-actualisation needs.

Some businesses strongly believe that the most important motivator of workers is pay. These businesses tend to use pay systems that directly link pay and the amount of work that is achieved. For a machinist in a clothing factory, for example, the worker might be paid piece rates - an amount for every garment they machine. For a worker in a City bank, most of their pay (their bonus) might be linked to how much profit they have made for their bank from trading on the stock exchange.

A company like Beaverbrook, on the other hand, believes that workers need to be motivated in a number of different ways. If possible, all aspects of their needs should be met through work. The best way to motivate workers is therefore to give them opportunities to do this. Because Beaverbrooks operates in a fiercely competitive environment, it cannot afford to give its workers big salaries and bonuses. Almost half of Beaverbrooks 800 workers earn less than £15 000 a year. Only 52 earn more than £35,000 a year. It therefore relies on fulfilling the other needs of workers to motivate its staff.

Motivation comes from within

A business like Beaverbrooks can only have a limited influence on the motivation of its workers. This is because motivation is something that also comes from within an individual worker. Some workers are more motivated than others. They have more enthusiasm for work and they seem to work harder.

How much motivation comes from within workers themselves and how much comes from the environment which a business creates is a matter of debate. A very good employer like Beaverbrooks seems to have a significant impact on motivation of staff. Working in teams where there are motivated workers also increases the motivation of less committed staff. However, ultimately, there will always be differences in motivation of workers in the same business.

In 2008 a survey by the City & Guilds organisation suggested that the amount people get paid is not a main motivator - despite many businesses and leaders believing it is. A survey they published suggested that having an interest in the job itself was the main motivator followed by relationships and friendships with work colleagues, a good work-life balance and flexible working arrangements. This sort of research has been supported elsewhere but many managers and business leaders might be misled into using money or payment as a motivator even when it may not be the most effective way to motivate staff. Professor Cary Cooper, a researcher into organisational psychology at the University of Lancaster, said: 'The City & Guilds Happiness Index provides a call to action for the business community to rethink its reward and recognition strategies and consider employees' needs on an individual basis. It marks the end of an era for organisation wide human resources policies. From now on a flexible approach is needed if businesses are to create a happy, and by association productive, workforce.' Such research might give managers cause to think more carefully about the way in which they motivate workers.

Source: information from www.timesonline 8.3.2009; www.beaverbrooks.co.uk

Test yourself

1. The physiological needs of a worker are most likely to be needs for

   A **self-actualisation**
   B **job security**
   C **food and shelter**
   D **love and belonging**

   Select one answer.

2. Gina owns and runs a veterinary business employing 10 workers. Henry is one of her workers. Henry spends all day, every day, doing the same job, cleaning areas where animals are kept. Which of Henry's needs is least likely to have been met? Select one answer.

   A **Self-actualisation needs**
   B **Physiological needs**
   C **Safety needs**
   D **Security needs**

3. A business has made 20 per cent of its workforce redundant over the past 6 months. Amongst the remaining staff, rumour has it that there is another round of redundancies to come shortly. Using Maslow's hierarchy of needs, this is most likely to demotivate staff because they will feel that

   A **their needs for self-actualisation are not being met**
   B **their safety needs are not being met**
   C **their self-esteem needs are not being met**
   D **their physiological needs are not being met**

   Select one answer.

Over to you

Woods is a national chain of shoe shops. It is looking for a full time shop assistant for one of its stores. It has interviewed the five candidates below. Some of the comments made at the interviews are shown next to each candidate.

Rachael Boswell – You are offering good pay and I need the money. I'm very keen on doing overtime. I'm sure the job will be OK. I've done a number of different jobs before. Some of them have been much worse than this. I've had some terrible managers in my time. I hope the one you put me with will be better.

Sean McDermott - I know my qualifications aren't very good. I messed around at school a lot. Then I had some awful work placements. But the last one in a shop was great. It really opened my eyes. I want to get on. I want to go right to the top. I want to be in charge and make big decisions. I know this sounds stupid because this is just a job at the bottom of the ladder. But you've got to start somewhere, haven't you?

Efia Charles - Being at home all day can be very depressing. I used to work in a shop before I had the children. I'm really looking forward to getting out of the house and back to work again. I really enjoyed the friendships with the rest of the staff. You always had a few awkward customers and a lot of the work was rather boring, but some customers were really nice. What are the opportunities for promotion?

Belinda Tombs - It looks as though my branch is going to go. They call it 'rationalisation'. I've been looking around because I could see this coming. There's nothing worse than turning up every day thinking that this is the day when you'll get your redundancy notice. My boss says she'll give me a good reference. I pride myself on being a good worker. I like everything to be perfect. My boss says I'm too much of a perfectionist. I don't really need the money.

Josh Nichols - I've just got married. My wife says I've got to settle down and get a decent job. She works in a shop too and says its OK. It will bring in the money and that is what's most important isn't it? What are your overtime rates? I expect I'll get used to dealing with the public. Do you give free uniforms or anything like that?

1. What is meant by 'motivation'? (1)

2. Explain **one** factor that is likely to motivate:
   (a) Josh Nichols
   (b) Efia Charles. (6)

3. On the evidence of the interview comments, which candidate would you choose for the job? Justify your answer. (6)

ResultsPlus
Build Better Answers

Why does a chef become a chef? For many people it is not always about the pay. Often other things motivate people to work.

(a) Identify **one** reason, apart from pay, why people work (1)

(b) Explain **one** reason why a motivated workforce is good for a business (3)

Think: What is motivation? What helps motivate people? What motivates me? Why would I do a job? What does motivation bring for a business?

■ **Basic** Gives one reason why people work but does not explain any benefits. Such as 'People work because they enjoy the feeling of being in a team situation. (1)

● **Good** 'One reason that people work is to feel good about themselves. (1) This is good for a business as it makes them work harder.' (1)

▲ **Excellent** 'One reason why people work is to reach a personal goal or target. (1) Motivation helps a business as people who are motivated want to go to work and have an interest in the job they are doing. (1) If they enjoy their job then they will probably work better, producing better quality goods at a faster rate. (1) This not only increases productivity but also increases the chance of securing and retaining customers.' (1)

18 Communication

Case Study

Barclays is one of the largest banking organisations in the UK. It employs around 155,000 staff in more than 50 countries around the world. With more than 48 million customers, effective communication is vital for the success of such a large company.

Objectives

- Understand the meaning of communication.
- Appreciate the impact of insufficient or excessive communication on efficiency.
- Appreciate the impact of poor communication on staff and the motivation of staff.
- Understand the barriers to effective communication.

Senders and receivers

There are always two parties to any **communication**

- The **sender**. An example would be Barclays sending out bank statements to its customers. It might be an employee giving financial advice to a small business. It might be the head of the personnel department giving instructions to other heads of department about how to deal with a staff problem.
- The **receiver**. This may be a shareholder getting a copy of Barclays Annual Report through the post. It may be a customer receiving confirmation of a loan. It may be heads of department receiving instructions from the head of personnel.

The receiver may give **feedback**. The shareholder getting a copy of the Annual Report may, for instance, write a letter to the company commenting on its performance. Figure 1 shows feedback that may take place in a banking business.

Internal and external communication

Some communications are internal to the business. Examples of **internal communication** would be:

- one bank teller talking to another bank teller;
- the branch manager sending a memo (or memorandum, typically a short letter-type communication giving instructions or asking for information) to branch staff;
- a company director requesting her personal assistant to arrange some appointments;
- a copy of a customer mortgage application being faxed from a Bristol branch to a Cornwall branch;
- a bank teller receiving training from the branch manager.

Other communications are **external**, where Barclays communicates with people or organisations outside the business. Examples would be:

- a customer services agent talking to an account holder;
- the chairperson discussing company progress with a major shareholder;
- a building company faxing Barclays to confirm a specification for repairs.

edexcel ⋮⋮⋮ key terms

Communication – messages passed between a sender and a receiver, through a medium such as a letter or a email.

Feedback – response to a message by its receiver to the sender.

Internal communication – communication within the business organisation.

External communication – communication between the business and an outside individual or organisation like a customer, a supplier or a tax inspector.

Figure 1 – Sending and receiving a message

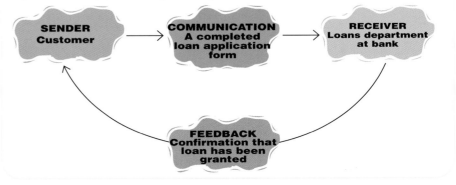

• an advert designed to show potential customers products and services the bank has on offer.

Channels of communication

Information passes along **channels of communication**. These are channels which are recognised and approved by the business and by employee representatives such as trade unions. There are two main types of **formal communication**: horizontal and vertical communication. These are shown in Figure 2.

Horizontal communication Horizontal communication occurs when workers at the same level in a business communicate formally with each other. One branch manager might consult with another branch manager about the details in a report they have both been sent, for example. These are shown in figure 2.

Vertical communication Vertical communication is communication up and down the hierarchy of the business. For instance, a worker at a Barclays call centre might seek authorisation to waive (cancel) a customer's bank charges from a supervisor. Or the chief executive of Barclays might send a note to a personnel secretary asking for a venue to be booked for the next meeting of the board of directors.

Often, communication does not get passed along official channels in the organisation. **informal communication** is called communication through the **grapevine**. For instance, a manager in the foreign currency department may have a friend who works in mortgages. When they chat and exchange gossip about what is going on in the company, they are passing on information through the grapevine.

Channels of communication should be clearly laid down by a business. If they are not, then vital information can get sent to the wrong people, or get lost. Communication through the grapevine can sometimes be a problem because messages may get distorted and exaggerated the more people they go through. On the other hand, the grapevine can be very useful. A manager may know that to do his job properly, he needs as much information as possible. This might mean getting more information than he 'officially' receives.

In general, the fewer the number of stages through which a communication passes (i.e the shorter the chain of communication), the less likely it is that a message will be misinterpreted. One of the possible advantages of a small company compared to Barclays is that, with very few people employed, it may be easier to communicate effectively. This is why Barclays has to work hard to maintain the effectiveness of its communication systems.

Communication skills

There is a number of key factors which make a communication effective.

Information What is communicated must be accurate. It must be complete, giving all the information necessary. It must also be simple and clear, so that the receiver can understand the information as quickly and easily as possible.

Sender and receiver The message must be sent **from** the right people **to** the right people. An e-mail sent to all employees dealing with details about a new product which is received only by those working in the London branches may be an example of poor communication.

Time and place Communication must take place at the right time and right place. A 2008 Barclays advertising leaflet might be useless if it is sent out in 2010 because the interest rate is likely to have changed, for example. A notice about fire safety which nobody can read because it is pinned too high up is in the wrong place. An

Poor communication is a major problem in any business. The source of the problem tends to be either in the person giving the message, the person receiving the message or an inappropriate method of communication being used.

Figure 2 – Horizontal and vertical communication

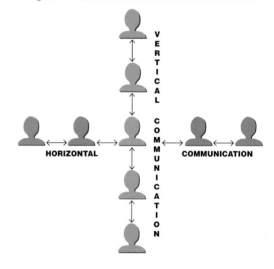

edexcel ⠿ key terms

Channel of communication – the path taken by a message, such as horizontal communication, vertical communication or grapevine communication.

Formal channels of communication – channels of communication that are recognised and approved by the business and by employee representatives such as trade unions.

Informal communication or communication through the grapevine – communication through channels that are not formally recognised by the business.

In business communication can be a formal meeting or an informal discussion between workers who attend the same leisure centre.

urgent letter from head office mustn't arrive at branches three weeks later.

Method The method of communication must be right. Methods include face to face communication, memos, telephone calls and the use of information technology.

Barriers to communication

Not all communication is effective. There is a number of reasons why communication breaks down.

- The person sending the communication might not explain themselves very well.
- The receivers might not be capable of understanding the message because they lack understanding of technical jargon.
- The receiver might not hear the message because he or she is not paying attention or chooses to focus in on part of the message, but not all of it.
- Messages can get distorted if they go through many people.
- Equipment might break down or not be working very well. A fax machine or a telephone may have a fault or the signal on a mobile phone might be poor or disappear.

Some of these problems are caused by **insufficient** communication. There is not enough communication taking place to get a message across. Some problems are caused by **excessive** communication. Too much is being said or written and the message gets lost because too many words, symbols or gestures are being used. Some problems are caused by **contradictory** communication. The message is saying two different things at the same time and so it is unclear what is being said.

The importance of good communication

Good communication is essential to any business. For instance, at Barclays:

- accurate advertising brochures avoid disappointed customers;
- a clear instruction by a manager makes it more likely that a task gets done;
- an accurate e-mail from the personnel department might help clear up a misunderstanding.

Poor communication can lead to a variety of problems.

Dissatisfied customers Poor communication leads to problems with the quality of products provided to customers. For example, a customer might try to sort out a problem with their bank account by calling a helpline. If the problem is not sorted quickly and easily, the customer will be left dissatisfied. A dissatisfied customer is someone who might not buy other products from the business and become a customer of another bank.

Problems with suppliers Poor communication with suppliers can lead to the wrong products being bought and delivered. This is wasteful and can lead to problems with production.

Misunderstanding amongst staff Poor internal communication leads to misunderstanding between workers. This leads to problems with the quality of work done. It also means that jobs are not done as quickly as they might have been and mistakes are made. Workers are therefore less efficient.

Motivation Poor communication often leads to demotivation of staff. For example, workers become frustrated and demotivated if they do not understand what they have been told to do. They become demotivated if they know the quality of their work is poor. Poor communication is one of the causes of a 'them and us' attitude. Frustrated workers blame problems on 'them', who could be more senior managers, fellow workers or even customers. If there were better communication, workers would be likely to see the real causes of a problem. Better communication then would allow the problem to be solved.

Source: information from group.barclays.com.

Test yourself

1. Mohammed works for an insurance company. He gets so many emails from other members of staff that he often does not bother to look at them if he thinks they will not be important. Sometimes, though, this means he misses out on information that is important. This is a problem caused by
   - **A excessive communication**
   - **B insufficient communication**
   - **C channels of communication**
   - **D informal communication**
   Select one answer.

2. Which one of the following is most likely to be a barrier to effective communication? Select one answer.
   - **A A full colour advertising brochure**
   - **B An early morning meeting between two workers**
   - **C A poorly worded letter**
   - **D A memo sent down the chain of communication**

3. Insufficient communication within a business is most likely to lead to
   - **A increased efficiency of staff**
   - **B demotivation of staff**
   - **C face to face communication with staff**
   - **D external communication between staff**
   Select one answer.

Over to you

Nick works in a call centre run by a mobile phone company. He deals with enquiries about customers' phone bills. Most customers are polite and it is easy to deal with whatever they have phoned up about. However, at least once an hour, he gets an aggressive phone call or one about a problem he cannot resolve easily.

The aggressive phone calls are the worst. Often, the caller clearly is not prepared to listen to the answer he gives. They are so worked up about their problem that nothing he says seems to help. Nick finds it tough being on the receiving end of these phone calls and some days he wonders why he does not just quit his job. When he started the job, he had two days of training. A one hour session was given over to how to deal with aggressive phone calls. However, the company does not seem to want to know about how these phone calls make him feel now or any day. Instead, he just has to joke about the calls when he is with workmates in the rest room during his breaks or lunch hour.

Breaks and lunchtimes are also the times when everyone has a go at the management. All the call operators get the phone calls from customers who have unusual problems with the service the mobile phone company provides. For Nick, the worst one is when customers ring up and say they have paid a bill months ago but are still being sent reminders to pay up. What is more, they have already phoned the company or sent them a letter explaining the situation. Nick was taught on his training to say that the company would look into the matter. At the end of the phone call, he presses a key that sends a message to someone else in the company saying that the

customer has this problem. Clearly, though, it is fairly random whether something is done about it. There are just too many customers who say they have already rung up more than once and never got a reply. Nick gets very frustrated that management do not seem to care whether customers get a response.

Nick also gets very cross about the amount of time customers have to wait to get through to speak to someone about their problem. On the wall of the call centre, there is a big digital display which says how many customers are 'on hold' and the amount of time they can expect to wait to get through. Management keep on telling call centre staff that it is their problem if the waiting time is too long. They should be more efficient and spend less time talking to each customer. The staff taking the calls know the problem is that the company will not employ enough staff to deal with all the calls. It is all very demotivating.

1. Identify **three** examples of communication from the passage. (3)

2. Explain, using examples from the passage, how bad communication can (a) damage the relationship between a business and its customers; (b) demotivate workers; (c) create inefficiency in the workplace. (9)

3. Would all the problems at the call centre be solved if workers received better training? Justify your answer. (8)

ResultsPlus
Build Better Answers

Paul DeKort was very excited. He had just received an email from his graphic designer with the latest drawings for his proposed new product, the 'ChromeDome' which was a new type of glove especially designed to help polish metal golf clubs to keep them in top condition. When he opened the email however he found that he couldn't access the drawings as his computer system was incompatible with the designer's software. Frustrated, he had no option but to wait for the plans to arrive as hard copies with a courier the following day. Which of the following is the **most likely** result of the failure in communication that Paul has faced? Select **one** answer.

A. Misunderstanding of the message
B. Lost profits
C. Increased costs
D. Increased motivation
E. Time wasted

Answer E

Technique guide: There is a number of choices available so first:

Think: What is communication? What are the outcomes of poor communication? How might Paul have been affected in this instance?

Then: Consider each alternative.

Go through these:

A is incorrect. Paul did not get a chance to see the communication as he could not open it to find out if he understood it or not. ■

B is unlikely. The product is only in the design stage and as yet is not making any profits. ■

C is unlikely. The delay is minimal so costs will not rise. ■

D is clearly wrong. Motivation is not a factor involved here, especially not improved motivation. ■

E is correct. The inability to open the attachment has resulted in time being lost. ▲

19 Remuneration

Objectives

- Understand the impact on staff of various payment strategies, including time, piece rate, commission; full-time salary versus freelance or temporary work; fringe benefits.

- Understand the impact on business of different payment systems.

edexcel ⠿ key terms

Payment systems – methods of organising the payment of workers, such as piece rates or salaries.

Manual or blue collar workers – workers who do mainly physical work like an assembly line worker.

Wages – tend to be paid to manual workers for working a fixed number of hours per week plus overtime.

Overtime – time worked over and above the basic working week.

Basic pay – pay earned for working the basic working week.

Non-manual or white collar workers – workers who do non-physical work, like an office worker or teacher.

Salary – pay, usually of non-manual workers, expressed as a yearly figure but paid monthly.

Commission – payment system usually operated for sales staff where their earnings are determined by how much they sell.

Bonus – addition to the basic wage or salary, for instance, for achieving a target.

Payment systems

The Co-operative employs nearly 90,000 workers in total. They are employed across the business from managers at head office in Manchester to check out assistants in a Co-operative supermarket to farm workers.

The Co-operative uses a number of different **payment systems**. These are different ways of paying workers.

Time-based systems **Manual workers** or **blue collar workers** are workers who tend to do manual work. At The Co-operative food stores, their job title is customer service assistant. They do jobs like stacking shelves, operating tills, serving customers and cleaning. Manual workers in the UK have tended to be paid **wages** on a time based system. They are paid 'so much' per hour worked. If they work longer than the agreed basic working week, such as 38 hours, they usually get **overtime**. This is often paid at a higher hourly rate, such as time-and-a-quarter or double time. This means that they are paid 1.5 or 2 times the **basic pay** per hour for every hour of overtime worked. For instance, say a worker's basic working week was 38 hours. They are paid at £8.00 an hour. So their basic pay per week would be £304. The company pays time and a half for overtime at the weekend. So overtime pay rates at the weekend are £12 an hour (1.5 x £8). If workers do four hours overtime one weekend, they would earn an extra £40 in total (4 x £12). The **gross earnings** or **gross pay** for the basic working week plus 4 hours overtime at the weekend would then be £152 (£304 + £48).

Salaries **Non-manual workers** or **white collar workers** tend to be paid **salaries**. A non-manual worker is one who does non-physical work, like an accountant or purchaser at The Co-operative or a teacher. Salaries tend to be paid monthly rather than weekly as with wages. Salaried workers are paid for doing a particular job. No overtime is usually paid because salaried workers are expected to work for as long as it takes to do their job. Salaried managers at The Co-operative are likely to work for more hours than the basic weekly hours of manual workers.

Results-based systems Some workers are paid according to how much they produce. Workers on **piece rates** are paid for every item they produce; the more they produce the more they get paid . Sales staff may be paid on **commission**. For every sale they achieve, they get paid a certain amount. Some sales staff are paid totally on commission, and so if they sell nothing, they get paid nothing. Others are paid a **bonus**. Bonuses are given as a reward for doing well and or achieving specific targets that may either be set by the company or agreed with the worker as part of the performance review. Non-sales staff may be given bonuses if, for instance, their department achieves a particular target for work. This is called a group bonus.

Temporary and freelance work

Some of the workers employed by The Co-operative are **part-time workers** rather than **full-time workers**. This means they are not employed for the full working week. As a result, they will get a fraction of the full-time weekly or monthly pay. For example, a part-time worker who works three days a week might get three fifths (0.6) of the weekly pay of a full-time worker who works five days a week.

Temporary workers are workers who are employed on a **temporary contract**. They might be employed on a daily, weekly or monthly basis. Businesses like The Co-operative use temporary workers to cover emergencies or peaks in work. A temporary worker might be employed to cover for someone who has gone on maternity leave. Or they might be employed in the run up to Christmas when demand is exceptionally high.

Freelance workers (usually self-employed workers) are workers who are paid by a business to perform a particular task. They are suppliers of services to a business. Freelance workers submit invoices to the business for payment like any other supplier. In some industries, freelance workers tend to be highly specialised, skilled workers. For example, a business might contract a freelance worker to write a report on a particular problem for it. In the construction industry, a lot of ordinary workers are freelance. Building firms like to employ them because it saves them paying so much tax and helps them to keep costs under control. If there is no work then the freelance worker is not needed unlike a full-time worker who may still have to be paid.

Other forms of payment

Workers can be paid in other ways than money. **Fringe benefits** are payments in kind (not in the form of money) over and above the wage or salary paid to a worker. For example, many workers benefit from a subsidised company pension scheme. The employer puts money into a pension scheme on behalf of its workers. Some businesses offer a range of other financial fringe benefits such as free or subsidised private health care, insurance or Pay-as you-earn savings schemes, subsidised meals, sports club membership or therapies such as reflexology or massages. Company cars are another example of a fringe benefit. Retail businesses typically offer a discount to their workers on anything bought within their stores.

The more senior the position you hold in a company, the more fringe benefits you are likely to receive. The managing director is likely to receive a range of fringe benefits including a company car and pension benefits. Workers at the bottom of the company may receive no fringe benefits at all.

Fringe benefits are often given for tax reasons. The business pays less tax and other contributions in providing £1,000 worth of fringe benefits than it would if it paid an extra £1,000 in wages to a worker. Similarly, a worker may find there is a tax gain in receiving a fringe benefit rather than cash.

Fringe benefits are also used to motivate workers. The company car, for instance, is very important to many workers (although it is now seen as less of a 'perk' because of the way the government taxes this type of benefit). Offering a company pension scheme gives many workers a sense of security and belonging.

Which payment system?

The Co-operative has to make decisions about which payment systems to use for different groups of workers. There is a number of factors that determine which payment system is used.

What is possible? Which payment system is used depends partly on what is possible. The Co-operative might find it very difficult to use piece rates for a store

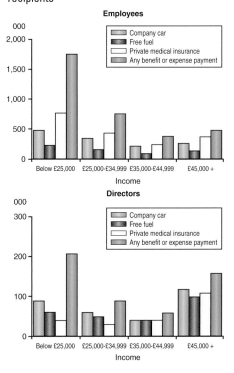

Figure 1 – Taxable fringe benefits received by employees and company directors, number of recipients

Source: adapted from www.statistics.gov.uk

manager, for instance, because it is so difficult to measure output. Equally, The Co-operative paying its cleaners on a commission basis would not be possible either because they do not sell anything. Even sales staff might not be paid commission if sales are a team effort rather than the result of the work of one individual. One reason why The Co-operative employs part-time staff is because so many people want to work part-time. It could not fill all of its posts if it insisted that all its workers work full-time. Equally, some workers expect certain types of payment. It would be almost impossible to find the right candidate for the job of chief executive of a large company without offering a large salary, bonuses and a range of fringe benefits.

Tradition In many workplaces, today's payment system is very similar to how it was 10 or 20 years ago. Workers often dislike changes to their payment system. Usually this is because they are worried they will earn less than before under a new system. For example, many manufacturing businesses have moved from piece rate systems to time systems over the past twenty years. This is often because businesses want workers to produce quality products working in teams. However, the fastest workers under piece rates are likely to earn less under the new time based system. They are likely to resist the change.

Tax and other employment costs Some payment systems are used because they reduce the tax bill of both employers and employees. Fringe benefits are an example of this. Businesses can also save on other employment costs, such as pension costs and National Insurance payments, by putting

ResultsPlus
Watch Out!

Bonuses are not necessarily paid just to individuals for their performance. Bonuses can also be given to whole teams of workers or even to all the workers in a business if their collective performance has been good.

ResultsPlus
Watch Out!

Workers in the same place of work are often paid using different payment systems. Workers doing manual jobs tend to be paid on a time-based system whilst managerial workers tend to be paid salaries, for example. Also, workers are sometimes paid using a mixture of payment systems. So a worker might be paid on a time-based system but on top of that also receive a bonus or commission. Some salaried workers are also paid overtime in certain circumstances.

work out to freelance (self-employed) workers.

Motivation Payment systems can be used to motivate workers. Piece rates, for example, can encourage workers to work hard. The more they produce, they more they get paid. The same is true of bonuses and commission. When sales representatives are paid a substantial commission for every sale they make, there is a large incentive for them to make as many sales as possible. However, piece rates, bonuses and commissions can also damage a business. Piece rates may encourage workers to work fast but this might lead to more mistakes and lower quality. Bonuses and commissions linked to sales can lead to overselling. Someone selling mortgages (loans to buy a house) may get a commission for every mortgage sold. But this encourages the sales person to give mortgages to people who are a poor risk and might be unable to keep up the repayments on a house. Any type of individual reward system also is likely to damage team work. For example, why should a shelf stacker in a supermarket work hard if they know that their supervisor gets a bonus every time their team of shelf stackers achieves its targets? To get round this problem, some businesses pay bonuses to whole teams of workers, or to a whole workplace or even to all the workers in a business.

Source: adapted from The Co-operative website.

Test yourself

1. Brandon is a worker who is paid on commission. This is most likely to mean that he is paid according to how much

    A time he works
    B he sells
    C he produces
    D work is done by his team

    Select **one** answer.

2. Emma is paid piece rates. Her employer is most likely to do this to

    A motivate her to work hard
    B save the company paying tax
    C increase the sales of the company
    D minimise the salary they pay her

    Select **one** answer.

3. Which **one** of the following is most likely to be an example of a fringe benefit? Select **one** answer.

    A Commission
    B Salaries
    C Bonuses
    D Company cars

Over to you

OilcoDistribution is an oil company which delivers fuels such as petrol and diesel from oil refiners to customers such as garages and homes.

In 2008, OilcoDistribution agreed a two-year pay deal with its tanker drivers. The drivers received a 3.5 per cent increase in 2008 with a further 1.0 per cent increase in 2009. OilcoDistribution used a time-based system to pay the drivers. Before the pay increases, the tanker drivers earned £370 a week (the equivalent of £10.00 an hour) for a basic 37 hour week. Most drivers in addition earned around £50 a week extra in overtime, working 4 hours at time and a quarter. The pay deal included a £500 annual bonus for drivers who agree to do immediate maintenance on their tankers following training.

As part of the deal, tanker drivers have agreed to the installation of in-cab computer systems. These will be linked to depots and a central control centre which will be able to monitor the position of road tankers at any point in time. They will also be able to tell the tanker drivers to follow different routes if there is traffic congestion. Deliveries may be rescheduled to the following day if congestion is so severe that drivers are running well behind time. OilcoDistribution expects the computer system to raise efficiency by reducing journey times and increasing the number of deliveries that can be made in an eight hour working day.

OilcoDistribution has also renewed an agreement made eight years ago that it will not make any tanker drivers redundant from a depot if at the same time it is contracting out work to other companies. Currently, if there is too much work for OilcoDistribution drivers to do on any one day, the company hires tankers and tanker drivers from other companies to complete the work. OilcoDistribution pays per delivery made rather than by the day. Where tanker drivers own their own road tanker, OilcoDistribution is effectively paying piece rates to these drivers.

1. (a) How much per hour were tanker drivers at OilcoDistribution paid before the signing of the two year pay deal? (1)
   (b) How much in pounds were drivers paid for working one hour of overtime? (1)
   (c) Given that the average driver worked 4 hours overtime a week, how much did the average driver earn per week? (2)
   (d) How much per hour did a tanker driver earn in 2008 after the new pay deal came into effect? (2)

2. Explain the difference between the 'time-based system' of payment used by OilcoDistribution for its drivers and the 'piece rate' system it used for the work it contracted out to other companies. (3)

3. Do you think the 2008 pay agreement will have motivated tanker drivers working for OilcoDistribution? Justify your answer. (6)

4. Assess whether OilcoDistribution would find it better to make all its drivers redundant and rely on a system of contracting out oil deliveries to other companies. Justify your answer. (6)

Results Plus
Build Better Answers

(a) Using an example, explain **one** advantage to a business of using fringe benefits to supplement employees' salaries. (3)

Think: What is a fringe benefit? What types of fringe benefits exist? How do they help employees and affect a business?

■ **Basic** States an advantage of fringe benefits, such as discounts on company products. (1)

● **Good** Identifies an advantage and offers some limited development. For example 'One example of a fringe benefit is offering discounts on company products and services. Staff might be encouraged to buy them, which could increase sales.' (1)

▲ **Excellent** Clear identification of fringe benefit and how that benefit might be an advantage to the business. For example 'One fringe benefit is discounts on company products and services. (1) Discounts may encourage staff to buy company goods, which aids revenue figures. (1) Staff may provide word of mouth advertising to others about the quality and value of the products. This could further increase product use and boost sales, which is of benefit to the business.' (1)

In this topic you have learned about: the link between roles and organisation structures; the needs for effective motivation and the problems that poor motivation can cause; the different types of communication; the advantages and disadvantages of good and poor communication; the variety of ways in which you can remunerate a worker; the opportunities to reward by means other than pay and the motivational aspects of pay systems.

You should know...

- [ ] The roles of workers can be shown on an organisation chart.
- [ ] Most businesses are organised by function.
- [ ] Workers in a hierarchy have a line manager. The hierarchy can be associated with a pyramid shape.
- [ ] There is a chain of command within a hierarchy. The length of the chain of command can effect the success of communication.
- [ ] To reduce communication problems businesses sometimes undertake delayering.
- [ ] The number of people that a worker directly controls is called a span of control.
- [ ] Businesses can be centralised or decentralised depending on where decisions are made.
- [ ] A motivated workforce has many benefits - harder working staff, higher work quality and greater flexibility.
- [ ] Abraham Maslow developed the hierarchy of needs to help explain factors that can motivate workers.
- [ ] Motivation can be helped by a firm but also comes from within a worker.
- [ ] Communication involves sender and receivers.

- [ ] Some communication is internal. Other communication is external.
- [ ] Communication can be both formal and informal.
- [ ] Communication passes along channels.
- [ ] There are horizontal and vertical lines of communication.
- [ ] Effective communication is due to several factors - clarity, to and from the right people, sent at the right time, using the right method.
- [ ] Communication can fail due to barriers.
- [ ] Good communication is vital to avoid dissatisfaction amongst customers, staff and suppliers.
- [ ] Poor communication can lead to demotivation.
- [ ] There are several different payment systems - time-based, results-based and salary.
- [ ] Workers may be full-time, part-time, temporary or freelance.
- [ ] Fringe benefits are forms of non-monetary payment.
- [ ] Which payment system to use depends on what is available, the tradition of the company, what motivation you desire and tax and cost issues.

Support activity

- Write a list of a variety of jobs that are carried out at your school/college.
- From this list identify the roles that fulfil these jobs.
- Next, identify how many people undertake these roles
- Finally draw an organisation chart showing these positions within the school/college

Stretch activity

- Find four job adverts, either in the newspaper or online.
- Identify the motivating factors of each job. Outline what makes them motivating. Is there anything in the adverts that you feel is demotivating?
- Choose one position within a firm that you know or understand (or your own school/college) and try and write a job advert with a job description and person specification. Try and make your advert, description and specification as motivating as possible for potential candidates. Finally, write a report discussing why you think your work demonstrates a motivational aspect.

Disaster! The new promotional material had just arrived and Bjorn Johansson the marketing manager, had unpacked it. To his horror the wording on the poster was wrong. It should have read 'Fiveaday - the new way to get your kids to eat their greens' instead it read 'Liveaday - the new way to eat their greens!' Not only was the message wrong it even got the name of the new product wrong. Bjorn felt that the only way this could have happened is if the communication between his department and the printers had become confused. He certainly had not received any feedback from the printers when he sent the information over.

(i) What is meant by the term 'feedback' (1)

(ii) Explain **one** effect of the poor communication on the business. (3)

Think: What is involved in communicating a message? What actions do individuals need to take when sending messages? What are the effects on a business of these actions? What is the difference between good and poor communication?

Student answer	Examiner comment	Build a better answer
(a) It's when you get a message back after sending one	■ A very simple answer that has merit only in the fact that it identifies information coming back from a sent message and would question if the candidate actually understands the full meaning.	▲ Use clear phrases such as 'response to a message by its receiver to the sender' or use an example such as 'Bjorn may have expected feedback from the printers such as a question regarding the name of the product.'
(b) A business will be affected as customers and suppliers might get confused or be sent the wrong messages, and this might mean a loss of sales.	■ A basic response which, whilst correct, does not begin to explain in depth.	▲ Identify one outcome then link the reasons for this outcome together. For example 'There is a clear link between customers and suppliers, poor communication and the firm. Customers may not return to purchase again if they are not communicated with effectively and this may affect future sales. Suppliers on the other hand may deliver the wrong materials or refuse to deliver at all, affecting the production of a business.' Using examples would also help develop the answer if the explanations are weak, such as 'a customer might not know a product was available if it is not advertised right' or 'in Bjorn's case the product delivered is wrong due to poor communication between the marketing department and the printers.'

Practice Exam Questions

Caroline and Neil Kirby have run their chicken farm for several years. The farm is made up of several functions. They rear chickens to sell on to the local abattoir, they have hens that lay eggs which are sold onto a national supermarket chain, and they have an on site farm shop selling a wide range of local produce. Their next venture is to develop a tourist attraction which they wish to call ChickStop. It is based on the petting zoo model where visitors can come and handle chickens, see baby chicks being born, help organise chicken races and also see how a modern farm works. They will also have other animals such as goats, rabbits and guinea pigs for the visitors to play with.

They will need to employ several new members of staff and possibly re-assign some current ones. What they are keen to do is ensure that their staff are well motivated in order to give the visitors the best possible experience when they come. Motivation is a high priority for Caroline and Neil.

(a) Which **two** of the following are **not** benefits to a business such as ChickStop of good staff motivation? (2)

A   Profits will be higher
B   Quality of work improves
C   A government grant might be available
D   Suppliers will be more willing to supply
E   The employees' physiological needs will be met
F   The staff will be more flexible.

(b) Abraham Maslow developed the hierarchy of needs.
  (i) Identify **two** parts of the Hierarchy of Needs. (2)
  (ii) Outline how the **two** parts you have identified in (i) above could be provided by a business to its workers. (4).

(c) How effective do you think that using the hierarchy of needs will be for Caroline and Neil, the owners of the business, in improving motivation of their workers? Justify your answer. (8)

Topic 3.5: The wider world affecting business

Case study

Blist is a major world oil company. It is involved in all stages of the oil industry from exploration to extraction to refining to selling petrol on garage forecourts.

Topic overview

This topic considers how the wider world affects businesses. It examines the meaning and nature of ethics in business and the trade off between ethics and profit, how businesses are affected by environmental issues and controls, how income differentials can affect international trade and the ways in which export and import controls, legislation, regulation and taxation affect international trade and businesses.

Over the past thirty years, it has been forced to become more environmentally conscious. Governments and environmental pressure groups have led to changes in operating policies. The company has had to spend billions of pounds to upgrade equipment, minimise air and water pollution and deal with the waste created from its oil facilities. Since oil is a non-renewable resource, the company has also been investing in new renewable energy technologies such as wind turbines and solar panels. It hopes that once oil runs out, it will be well placed to survive as a major world energy company.

Environmental concerns, however, continue to pose major ethical issues for the company. Shareholders are always demanding higher profits. On the other hand, going beyond what legal minimum environmental standards demand adds to costs. One issue that the company repeatedly faces is about different operating standards in different countries. Environmental standards are lower in Nigeria or India than in the UK or the United States. The ethical dilemma is whether the company should operate to the same environmental standards in Nigeria as in the UK even though this would increase costs.

Another issue concerns taxation. Different countries impose different levels of taxation on a company like Blist. It tries to minimise its tax bill by shifting as many resources, revenues and profits to low tax countries and away from high tax countries as is possible. However, some pressure groups have criticised its practices as being unethical. They argue that many poor developing countries lose out because they have relatively high tax rates.

Blist operates across the globe in both developed and developing countries. Its main customers are in developed countries because these countries generate most of the world's income. As developing countries become richer, this will change. Developing countries will provide much larger opportunities for Blist to expand its sales operations. Some countries, however, have strong protectionist policies that keep Blist out of their markets. For example, Blist is unable to sell fuel directly to motorists in both India and China because of their policies. The company continues to press governments to lower or abolish tariffs and quotas and other protectionist measures so that it can operate more freely across the globe.

1. Using Blist as an example, what is meant by 'ethics' in a business context?

2. What impact does an oil company like Blist have on the environment (a) in the short term and (b) in the long term?

3. Explain why Blist would like to see the removal of all protectionist policies on oil and other energy products.

4. What impact does regulations and taxes have on the way in which Blist operates?

What will I learn?

Ethics in business What is the meaning of the term 'ethics' in business? Why are moral issues that affect a business organisation often complex? What are the possible trade-offs between ethics and profit? What are the potential effects of pressure group activity on a business?

Environmental issues How do businesses affect the environment? What short-term environmental effects, such as traffic congestion, air pollution, noise pollution and water pollution, do businesses have on the environment? How are businesses responsible for recycling? What long-term environmental effects, such as global warming and resource depletion, do businesses have on the environment?

Economic issues affecting international trade What are the extremes of income distribution on an international scale? What is the effect of import protection and export subsidies on business?

The impact of government and the EU What impact do regulation and taxation have on businesses? What are the benefits and drawbacks to businesses of minimum wages, maternity/paternity rights and health and safety regulations?

How will I be assessed?

This is assessed through Unit 3, a written examination lasting 1 hour 30 minutes.

The paper is divided into three sections.

Section A is a mix of mainly multiple choice questions and short answer questions with one or more questions requiring an extended answer.

Sections B and C consist of short and long answer questions based on two scenarios, one for each section, given in the paper.

20 Ethics in business

Case Study

Marks & Spencer is one of the UK's largest retailers. In 2008, it sold over £9 billion worth of products. In 2007, it launched 'Plan A', a five year programme costing £200 million to take forward its environmental and ethical business practices. The detailed 100-point plan covers climate change, waste, raw materials, fair trade and healthy living. Chief executive, Sir Stuart Rose, said: 'We think this is the right thing to do because our customers, employees and, increasingly, shareholders are asking us to. We believe those people will embrace a responsible business.'

Objectives

● Appreciate the meaning of the term 'ethics' in business.

● Understand the complexity of moral issues affecting organisations.

● Understand the possible trade-offs between ethics and profit.

● Appreciate the importance of the potential effects of pressure group activity.

The ethical business

Businesses, like people, have to make **ethical** choices. They have to decide whether an activity or decision is morally right or wrong.

Ethics is becoming more important to businesses today. Many large businesses want to show that they are ethically responsible on a range of issues from production to suppliers, workers, customers, competitors, products, the environment and local communities.

Production

Marks & Spencer is a retailer. It produces a service, buying goods in bulk from suppliers and selling them individually to customers from its stores. Like any business, it has choices about how to produce. One choice is about the amount of waste it produces and what it does with its waste. Financially, it should choose the cheapest option, but this might not be the most environmentally friendly option. Marks & Spencer has chosen, as part of Plan A, to reduce the amount of waste it creates and to recycle more. It also has decided to stop sending any waste from its stores to landfill sites because landfill sites are seen as environmentally bad.

Suppliers

A business like Marks & Spencer has ethical choices about how it treats its suppliers and what it will buy from suppliers. Financially, to maximise profit, a business should pay its suppliers the lowest prices possible. However, these prices may not be 'fair'. For example, many producers in Developing Countries receive low prices for their products from buyers in rich countries like the UK. Marks & Spencer takes part in the Fair Trade scheme. It buys Fair Trade products that give producers a higher price for what they make, grow and sell. Marks & Spencer is aiming to increase both the range of Fair Trade products it offers and the amount sold as part of its Plan A programme.

Marks & Spencer works closely with suppliers on a variety of other ethical issues. For example, it has banned its farming suppliers from using 60 types of pesticide, with another 19 more on the list within three years. Animal welfare is another important issue. Marks & Spencer now only buys eggs from suppliers that are free range.

edexcel ⠿ key terms

Business ethics – ideas about what is morally correct or not, applied in a business situation.

Workers

Different businesses treat their workers in different ways. Some pay their workers as little as possible and only give them their minimum legal rights in the workplace. Other businesses, like Marks & Spencer, have a different attitude to workers. They see workers as important stakeholders in the business to whom they have a moral responsibility. This means they have a duty to look after them properly.

Marks & Spencer has set itself targets for training and career development, to allow its employees to realise their work potential. The company is committed to reducing accidents in the workplace. It has a variety of occupational health schemes designed to help employees with physical and mental health problems.

Customers

Businesses need customers to survive. If there are no customers, there will be no sales. However, different businesses have different attitudes to customers. A company like Marks & Spencer attempts to listen to its customers and give them what they want. Plan A, Marks & Spencer's five year plan on environmental and ethical business practices, partly came out of what its customers wanted from a retailer. Some businesses will not sell to certain customers on ethical grounds. For example, the Co-operative Bank will not offer any services to arms manufacturers and dealers. Many businesses won't export to countries like Burma that have governments that do not give their people basic human rights.

Competitors

Businesses have to decide how far they can go in trying to win customers from their competitors. Marks & Spencer has always set itself high standards in this area. Some other businesses, though, are faced with more difficult ethical problems. Arms manufacturers, for example, have in the past commonly given bribes to secure contracts with overseas governments. Today, giving bribes is illegal for any UK company, but bribery still takes place. Is this ethical? Is it ethical for a children's charity to receive a donation from a cigarette manufacturer?

The product

A business like Marks & Spencer has to decide what products to make. Marks & Spencer has adopted a strong ethical stance towards its products. For example, because it believes that GM (genetically modified) crops could damage the environment, it doesn't sell any products containing GM ingredients. 85 per cent of all clothes sold at Marks & Spencer can be washed at low temperatures. This saves on energy bills for customers and on dry cleaning, which is less environmentally friendly than washing clothes at home. Many businesses have to make choices about what to sell. For example, should a shop sell replica guns? Should adult magazines be sold in a newsagent where children will also shop? Should chewing gum and fast food producers take full responsibility for the cleaning up of the waste from their products?

The environment

All businesses have an impact on the environment. Some businesses, like coal mining companies or companies operating land fill sites, have a major impact on the local environment. Owners of coal, gas and oil fired power stations making electricity are major contributors to greenhouse gases. Service industry businesses like Marks & Spencer have less direct impact on the environment but it is still likely to be negative. Businesses therefore have to decide whether to put the environment as a major objective. Most businesses, for example, can cut the amount of waste they generate, or increase the amount of waste which is recycled. They can cut energy use and reduce the number of miles travelled by suppliers, workers and customers. Marks & Spencer, for example, is committed to buying more food locally to cut down the number of miles travelled by their products. Other businesses are allowing workers to work from home. This helps reduce congestion and pollution.

Local communities

Many businesses have little or nothing to do with their local communities apart from providing jobs, and perhaps selling goods. Some argue, however, that businesses should do more than this. Some businesses support local charities. Other businesses

ResultsPlus
Watch Out!

It is very easy to think that either all businesses have no ethical standards or that they are all busily trying to save the planet through recycling and other schemes. The truth is somewhere in between these two extremes. Most businesses at least try to stay within the law. They see the law as providing a moral standard about how to behave. Some businesses go beyond the legal minimum. However, watch out for businesses that use their ethical practices as a marketing tool to attract customers.

are prepared to pay more when building new premises to put up a beautiful building, or landscape the area. Some businesses will get involved with local schools or sponsor sports clubs whilst others might sponsor a road or a roundabout. Marks & Spencer is a large company and it supports charities in the developing world. When the coast of Sri Lanka was hit by a tsunami (a large wave) in 2005, which caused widespread destruction, it gave £250,000 to help rebuild homes in the country.

Possible trade-offs

Most businesses would argue that there is a trade-off between ethics and profit. Acting ethically raises costs, they would argue. For example, buying products from Fair Trade farmers in the Third World is more expensive than buying them through normal channels. Improving workers' conditions costs money. Supporting local charities adds to costs.

On the other hand, some businesses raise their sales by using their ethical policies as a marketing tool. Companies like Marks & Spencer, The Co-operative Bank and The BodyShop openly advertise their ethical practices. It helps bring in customers and therefore increases revenue. Also, acting ethically can be an important motivator for workers in a business. If they feel part of an ethical business, they may be willing to work harder. This would help reduce costs. For these businesses, acting ethically might even raise profit. However, if every business were to become an 'ethical business', these sorts of advantages would disappear for any single business.

Pressure groups

Pressure groups are organisations that support causes such as workers' rights, the environment, animal welfare and world poverty. Examples of pressure groups are trade unions, Greenpeace, the RSPCA (Royal Society for the Prevention of Cruelty to Animals) and Oxfam.

Pressure groups try to get businesses to change what they are doing. Trade unions want businesses to pay higher wages to workers. Greenpeace wants businesses to operate more environmentally friendly policies. Oxfam campaigns for better working conditions for workers in Developing Countries who may be making products for sale in the UK.

Most businesses are not directly affected by pressure group activities. Most businesses, for example, do not employ workers that belong to trade unions. Very few businesses are subjected to campaigns against them by environmental pressure groups or pressure groups working to reduce poverty. However, when businesses are affected, they need to make a decision about how to respond.

- Businesses can do nothing. Businesses can hope the issue will cease to be important and the pressure group will go away.
- Businesses can work against the pressure group. For example, the US company WalMart, the world's largest supermarket chain, has a policy of not working with trade unions in its US stores. Oil companies in the past have

The Fairtrade Foundation is the independent non-profit organisation that licenses use of the FairtradeMark on products in the UK in accordance with internationally agreed Fairtrade standards.

Pressure groups can influence business and government decisions.

opposed the activities of environmental pressure groups like Greenpeace. Sometimes, businesses are successful in their fight with pressure groups. Sometimes, they get such bad publicity that they are forced to give in to at least some of their demands.

- Businesses can work with pressure groups. Marks & Spencer, for example, works with the World Wildlife Fund (WFF) on a variety of environmental issues. It works with Oxfam on clothes recycling. It also works with the Fairtrade Foundation on buying more clothes made from Fairtrade cotton.

Most pressure groups try to put forward their point of view legally. Some, however, believe that the only way to get business to change is by taking more extreme action. Some animal rights groups have taken extreme action to prevent what they see as cruelty to animals. This can include releasing animals from laboratories, threatening workers and staff at businesses that work with animals, causing damage to property and even, in one case, stealing the dead body of a relative of a business that bred hamsters which were used in scientific experiments. There is an ethical dimension here too. How far should a pressure group go to make their point and persuade a business to change its practices? Do the means (illegal action) justify the ends (a change in a businesses behaviour)?

Source: information from www.marksandspencer.com ; Marks & Spencer, Annual Report and Accounts, http://www.guardian.co.uk, 7.5.2009, http://news.bbc.co.uk 15.1.2007, http://www.telegraph.co.uk 22.1.2008, http://www.talkingretail.com 4.2.2008.

Test yourself

1. A pressure group campaigns to get supermarkets to reduce the amount of packaging they use. This pressure group is **most likely** to be

   A a trade union
   B the government
   C customers of the supermarket
   D a charity with environmental aims

   Select **one** answer.

2. A company comes under pressure to reduce the amount of waste it produces. It is **most likely** to refuse to do this if

   A this would reduce its profits
   B customers also refuse to reduce their waste
   C the government brings in new laws about waste
   D trade unions support waste reduction

   Select **one** answer.

3. Which one of the following is **most likely** to be an ethical issue for a company selling cosmetics on the high street? Whether or not to

   A open a new shop
   B increase the size of its overdraft
   C buy products which have been tested on animals
   D use red packaging rather than green packaging for a product

   Select **one** answer.

ResultsPlus
Build Better Answers

The Internet allows people to find out and share more information about the behaviour of businesses. One effect of this is that more people are aware of business ethics.

Which of the following **best** describes the phrase 'business ethics'? Select **one** answer.

A. The right to decide what to do in a situation and take command of it
B. Ideas about what is morally correct or not, applied in a business situation
C. Measures that reduce the price of goods sold abroad
D. Organisations that lobby on behalf of causes
E. The impact on the pollution in the local area

Answer B

Technique guide: There is a number of choices available so first:

Think: What is business? What are ethics? What is involved in business ethical decisions?

Then: Consider each alternative.

Go through these:

A is incorrect. This describes someone who has authority in a business.

C is incorrect. This describes export subsidies. ■

D is clearly wrong. These are the actions of pressure groups. ■

E is unlikely. This is an outcome of an unethical action. ■

B is correct. This discusses moral choices in a business context. ▲

Over to you

Nike is the world's number one trainer brand. It does not manufacturer anything. It specialises in designing trainers and selling them. All its production is done by independent companies around the world. In 2008, around 800,000 workers were employed in factories making Nike trainers. 80 per cent of these were young women aged 18-24 in developing countries.

Nike has been a target for pressure groups. It started in 1992 when a campaigner produced a report about working conditions in factories making Nike products. The report exposed a variety of labour abuses including forced overtime by workers and bad working conditions. Student groups in America, key buyers of Nike products, began boycotting Nike products. They called for Nike to make changes to where and how it bought its products.

At first, Nike tried to ignore the protests but quickly realised that it could lose sales if it did not act. The problem was that it had its products made in factories in developing countries because it was cheap to do so. Making factories improve their labour standards would be costly, time consuming and difficult.

Today, Nike is one of the few companies that publishes the location of every factory where its products are made. This means that pressure groups can gather information on the factories to expose problems. However, Nike is committed to making sure that conditions of work in those factories are fair to workers. Even so, as it admitted in a 2001 report, making Nike trainers will continue to be 'tedious, hard and doesn't offer a wonderful future' for Nike factory workers in the developing countries. To make its factories adopt Western style conditions of work, including pay levels, would mean that it was unable to compete against other companies. Nearly all the large branded clothing manufacturers, clothes retailers and supermarket chains buy most of their clothes and shoes from low wage countries. Companies such as Primark, Asda and Tesco have all come under criticism for buying products from 'sweatshop' factories in developing countries.

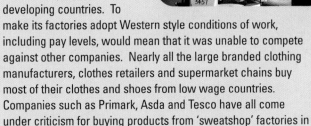

Source: information from www.mailonline 7.12.2006, www.wikipedia.org; www.oxfam.org.au; www.nikebitz.com

1. Explain (a) why Nike buying products from a factory in the developing world is an ethical issue and (b) why some pressure groups are interested in this issue. (6)
2. Explain why there is a possible trade-off for a company like Nike between behaving ethically and earning more profit. (3)
3. Do you think that companies like Nike, Primark or Asda should worry about criticisms from pressure groups? Justify your answer. (8)

21 Environmental issues

Case Study

Amazon is the world's largest Internet seller of books. It also sells a range of other products including CDs and DVDs, electronic equipment and furniture. The company is at the cutting edge of technology in offering download services for television programmes and films. Amazon was founded in 1994 in the USA by Jeff Bezos. Today it operates throughout the world as well as in Europe and North America.

Objectives

- Understand how business activity affects the environment.
- Appreciate the importance of short-term environmental effects, such as the impact on traffic congestion, air, noise, smell and water pollution and recycling.
- Appreciate the importance of long-term environment effects such as climate change and resource depletion.

Businesses and the environment

Amazon's core business is the sale of books. It buys books from publishers, stores them in a warehouse and then sells them to customers. It uses the post to get the books from the warehouse to the homes of customers. The supply chain for the business is quite long. It starts with forestry businesses that cut down trees to make paper, the manufacture and dying of paper, printing and binding of books, the transport of books and other products from manufacturers to warehouses and ends up with a personal delivery by the mail service. All of this has an impact on the environment. The impact can be divided into short-term effects and long-term effects.

Short-term effects

Producing and selling books has a number of different short-term effects on the environment.

Traffic congestion When books are distributed, there is an impact on traffic congestion. The growth of Internet sales of consumer products has meant a growth in the number of miles travelled by delivery vans. Every time an Amazon book is delivered to the door of a customer, it helps contribute to congestion on the roads. Traffic congestion means increased travel times for everybody using the roads. In addition, vehicles operate less efficiently on roads that are congested. They use more fuel per mile travelled. This contributes both to climate change and the using up of non-renewable resources as explained later on in this unit. Most business activity contributes directly or indirectly to traffic congestion because goods have to be delivered from supplier to customer. Equally, customers often have to come to a seller like a supermarket chain to buy products.

Air, noise, smell and water pollution Businesses contribute directly and indirectly to air, noise, smell and water pollution. For example, Amazon relies on computers for its Internet sales. Computers work on electricity and electricity generation contributes to air pollution. Coal fired power stations emit a range of harmful gases. Vans used to deliver books from Amazon cause noise pollution to local residents. Paper manufacturing, essential for the production of books sold by Amazon, uses water intensively and creates waste water. This water has to be treated if it is not to pollute the environment. Some businesses give off odours (smells) as part of their production processes and this can affect local communities. For example, when cellophane was produced in Somerset, the town of Bridgewater was affected by a pungent smell from the factory located nearby. Pet food manufacturers have been criticised in the Midlands for the odour their production gives off. Farming also produces odours that some people find unpleasant.

edexcel key terms

Supply chain – the processes that are involved in the route taken by a product from the raw materials needed to create it right through to the final customer.

Long-term effects

Producing and selling books has a number of long term effects on the environment.

Climate change One of the major challenges facing the world today is climate change. This is caused by the emission of too many greenhouse gases such as CO_2 (carbon dioxide) and methane gas. The increase in the emission of greenhouse gases has been caused by increased industrial activity across the world. For example, as the world industrialises and grows richer, more and more coal and gas-fired power stations are being built. In developing countries like China that have been growing very fast, the number of new power stations is likely to double or treble over the next twenty years. Burning fossil fuels creates greenhouse gases. These trap the warmth coming from the earth and act as a blanket for the earth's environment. Hence, average temperatures are rising. This will cause major problems such as rising sea levels and changes to where crops can be grown in the world.

Resource depletion Resource depletion refers to the use of resources in production which reduces the amount of resources available. Many of the resources used in the production and distribution of books are **renewable**. This means they can be reused in the future. For example, trees used to make paper are a renewable resource because new trees can be planted to replace trees which have been cut down. Electricity generated by wind power is a renewable resource because the wind keeps blowing over time. However, coal, oil and gas are **non-renewable** resources. The oil that is used to make the diesel that powers most delivery vans cannot be replaced once it is used. Estimates vary about how much oil there is in oil reservoirs round the world. Every day, millions of barrels of oil are used throughout the world for production, fueling cars, heating, energy generation and so on. At current levels of useage, oil is likely to run out within the next few hundred years if not before. Amazon, like most other businesses, through its supply chain contributes to the depletion of non-renewable resources.

Many businesses, including Amazon, are now more aware of the effect of their operations on things like climate change and congestion. Many have put in place steps to try to reduce the effect of their business operations on the environment. In addition governments force businesses to reduce their environmental impact through laws, regulations and taxes. Laws, such as planning permission for building or limits on pollution, restrict the activities of business. Environmental or 'green' taxes are also used to change the behaviour of businesses. Putting a tax on petrol, for example, discourages businesses from using petrol. Many businesses in England have to pay a landfill tax which makes them pay for disposing of waste in landfill sites. Amazon's activities are restricted throughout the world by different government environmental regulations and taxes.

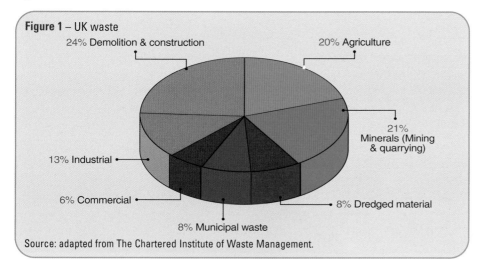

Figure 1 – UK waste

- 24% Demolition & construction
- 20% Agriculture
- 21% Minerals (Mining & quarrying)
- 13% Industrial
- 6% Commercial
- 8% Municipal waste
- 8% Dredged material

Source: adapted from The Chartered Institute of Waste Management.

Environmental problems - air pollution, water pollution and waste.

In the UK, Amazon, like most other businesses, is affected by laws and regulations on waste management and recycling. Figure 1 shows what waste is created each year in the UK. The three largest sources of waste are the construction industry, agriculture and mining and quarrying. Between them, they account for two thirds of all waste generated.

In law, waste is anything that is discarded by households, businesses or government organisations. Waste management describes the whole process of how waste is treated at every stage. This includes:
- how waste is collected and stored at the place where the waste is generated;
- how it is transported from that place;
- what happens to the waste once it arrives at a disposal site.

Waste management is about reducing the amount of waste generated in the first place. It is also about recycling. Many types of waste can be reused. For example, old newspapers and books can be recycled into new paper. Old pieces of wood can be recycled into animal bedding or garden landscaping products. Glass can recycled into new glass or used in the production of bricks, sports turf and fibreglass insulation.

Recycling does not come without a cost though. Converting waste products into something that can be used again also takes up resources and costs money. To be worthwhile (to make it economically viable) the benefit of recycling has to be greater than the cost. For waste to be recycled on an economic basis, it usually needs to be sorted at the point where the waste is generated. So households need to sort their rubbish into different types - garden waste, landfill rubbish and recycling, for example. On a construction site, different skips for wood, bricks and general waste need to be provided. At a warehouse site like Amazon's, waste paper needs to be separated from other waste.

Increasingly, manufacturers are being forced to design their products in a way which will allow them to be recycled. The European Union, for example, has regulations which affect the manufacture of vehicles such as vans used to distribute Amazon books. Vehicles must now be made so that they are easy to dismantle into different waste products at the end of their life. Dangerous substances must not be used. Recycled materials must be used in the production of vehicles.

In an ideal world, there would be a waste management cycle which led to no waste being generated. All waste would be recycled into new products. However, at the moment this is not technically possible. It would also be far too expensive.

Customer demands

Customers are putting pressure on some businesses to be more environmentally friendly. For example, magazines are now usually printed on recycled paper because some of their readers have asked for this. Supermarkets are stocking more organic products because organic food is seen by customers as being 'greener'. Businesses which can persuade customers that they are more environmentally friendly than their competitors can gain a competitive edge. They can use their environmentally friendly reputation as part of their **public relations**.

Business opportunities

Environmental concerns can represent a business opportunity. There are many new businesses which have been created to make energy saving or renewable energy products. Solar panel producers and wind farm electricity companies are examples. Other businesses create products which reduce pollution. When designing its warehouses, for example, Amazon used the latest technologies to minimise energy useage and waste. Equipment it uses, from light fittings to fork lift trucks, represent opportunities for companies to sell environmentally friendly 'green' products to Amazon.

Results Plus
Watch Out!

It is often very difficult to come to balanced decisions about environmental issues. Environmental pressure groups tend to put the worst case scenario forward. Businesses tend to argue that the environmental impact of their activities is fairly small. Always try to sort out the facts from opinions. Usually, the truth is somewhere in between the positions of environment pressure groups and businesses.

Test yourself

1. Matthew Henfield owns a farm and raises cattle for meat. His cattle produce methane gas which is a greenhouse gas. This contributes to the long term environmental problem of

   A resource depletion
   B global warming
   C noise pollution
   D water pollution

   Select **one** answer.

2. A firm of solicitors is considering replacing some old energy intensive heating equipment with ones that are far more energy efficient. Which one of the following environmental problems is this **most likely** to help reduce? Select **one** answer.

   A resource depletion
   B noise pollution
   C water pollution
   D traffic congestion

3. The government introduces tighter business regulations on recycling waste. This is **most likely** to mean that

   A all waste will now be recycled
   B all businesses will see their costs of production rise
   C some businesses will have an incentive to redesign their products
   D some businesses will reduce their spending on recycling

   Select **one** answer.

Over to you

EDF, a French company, is one of the world's largest producers of electricity. In France, it owns and runs a large number of nuclear power stations. In the UK, it owns the power cables and other infrastructure that link homes and businesses to power stations in the London and the South East of England. It also owns British Energy, the UK company that owns most of the country's nuclear power stations.

EDF has plans to be at the forefront of building new nuclear power stations in the UK. The British government has decided its ageing existing nuclear power stations, that traditionally provide nearly 20 per cent of British electricity, must be closed and replaced by new nuclear power stations.

The government is committed to reducing greenhouse gas emissions, a long-term environmental problem. The great advantage of nuclear power is that it creates few greenhouse gases, unlike gas and coal fired power stations. Also, unlike gas, coal and oil, which are non-renewable resources, there are abundant supplies of raw materials to run the power stations.

Environmental pressure groups, however, bitterly oppose British government plans. They do not want companies like EDF building new nuclear power stations. Friends of the Earth, for example, argue that nuclear power stations pollute the local environment when inevitably accidents occur. Nuclear waste is difficult and costly to treat or store. Nuclear waste is also radioactive for up to 1000 years. Nuclear waste will have to be looked after for generations to come. There are also fears about

what would happen if a nuclear power plant were attacked, for example by a terrorist group.

Pressure groups like Friends of the Earth want all existing nuclear power stations to be closed. Future energy needs should come from renewable energy sources like wind power. The UK government argues that it is impossible to build enough renewable energy installations to replace the output of current nuclear power stations.

EDF is currently building wind farms to provide green renewable energy. However, it also sees a profitable opportunity to build and run new nuclear power stations. It wants to use all the expertise it has built up in running nuclear power stations to expand its operations.

With information from http://www.nce.co.uk/; http://www.edfenergy.com; http://www.foe.co.uk; http://news.bbc.co.uk

1. Explain, using nuclear power as an example, what is meant by (a) non-renewable energy; (b) a long-term environmental problem; (c) pressure groups. (9)

2. Analyse the impact of EDF on the environment. (6)

3. Discuss whether EDF should put more of its resources into building renewable energy installations and abandon plans to build new nuclear power stations. (8)

Results Plus
Build Better Answers

Draw **six** lines to link each term about environmental issues on the left with its correct definition on the right.

a. Climate change
b. Congestion
c. Non-renewable resources
d. Business opportunities
e. Legislation, regulation and taxation
f. Air pollution

(i) The emission of gases into the atmosphere by things such as factories, power stations and aircraft
(ii) Changes in weather systems caused by pollutants affecting sea levels, ice melts and so on
(iii) Items that, once used, cannot be re-made or used again
(iv) Measures that can be undertaken by government to slow down or halt the environmental damage that businesses cause
(v) The increase in the number of vehicles and vehicle miles on the road due to increasing numbers of deliveries
(vi) Areas that may be developed by business to take advantage of the consumers growing concern about the environment

Answer

a. - (ii)
b. - (v)
c. - (iii)
d. - (vi)
e. - (iv)
f. - (i)

Technique: you have 6 statements that clearly link to the concept of the environment. Look at the list and try and see if there are any clear links between the statement and the descriptions and likewise ones that do not match at all.

Think: What do we mean by the environment? What concerns are there? Are there any opportunities?

Decide:
'...weather systems, so a clear link to 'climate'. So a. = (ii)

'Congestion' indicates increased traffic, so b. = (v)

Resources that can't be re-made links to 'non-renewable'. So c. = (iii)

'...opportunities' can also be seen as 'areas for development', so d. = (vi)

'Legislation, regulation and taxation' are all government control measures. So e. = (iv)

This leaves air pollution being caused by increased emissions into the atmosphere. So f. = (i)

22 Economic issues affecting international trade

120

Case Study

Tata Motors is India's largest automobile company. The company is the world's fourth largest truck manufacturer and the world's second largest bus manufacturer. Founded in 1954, it has since grown strongly in its home market in India and more recently in export markets. Since 2004, it has expanded internationally, buying a number of overseas companies. In 2008, it bought Jaguar Land Rover, a UK based vehicle manufacturer that makes up-market Jaguar and Land Rover cars.

Objectives

● Appreciate the extremes of income distribution internationally.

● Understand the effect of import protection and export subsidy on businesses.

Income distribution across the world

The world's income is distributed very unevenly. Look at Figure 1. In the United States, average income per person per year was $45,850 in 2007. This is equivalent to roughly £30,000. 'Per person' does not just include workers. It means everybody in the population including babies and people aged 100+. In contrast, in Ethiopia, average income is just $780 or roughly £500 per person. The average American has an income that is sixty times the size of the average Ethiopian. The average income of the UK is $34,370. This is not as high as in the United States. However, it is still 44 times as high as in Ethopia. In India, the home country of Tata Motors, average income is only $2,740 per year.

Table 1 shows average incomes for three groups of countries: low income countries such as Ethiopia, middle income countries such as China and high income countries such as the UK. High income countries are also often called developed countries. Low and middle income countries are often called developing countries. Table 1

Table 1 – Average income per head (US$) and population

	Average income per head ($US)	Total population (million)
Low income countries	$1,494	1,296
Middle income countries	$5,952	4,260
High income countries	$36,100	1,056

Source: adapted from World Bank, World Development Report 2009.

edexcel ⠿ key terms

Developed countries – countries with a relatively high income per person.

Developing countries – countries with a lower income per person than developed countries.

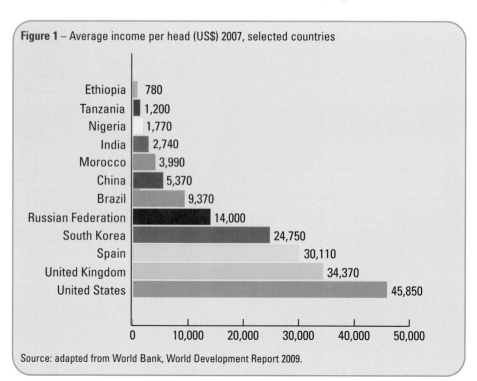

Figure 1 – Average income per head (US$) 2007, selected countries

Country	Income
Ethiopia	780
Tanzania	1,200
Nigeria	1,770
India	2,740
Morocco	3,990
China	5,370
Brazil	9,370
Russian Federation	14,000
South Korea	24,750
Spain	30,110
United Kingdom	34,370
United States	45,850

Source: adapted from World Bank, World Development Report 2009.

also shows how many people live in low, middle and high income countries. Most people, 54 per cent of the world's total, live in middle income countries. 16 per cent of the world's population lives in high income countries. 20 per cent live in low income countries.

Income, wages, products and trade

The level of development of an economy affects its imports (what it buys from abroad) and its exports (what it sells abroad).

Average incomes Average incomes in high income countries are tens of times higher than in low income countries. This helps explain why high income countries like the UK and the USA spend far more on imports than low income countries. In the UK, because of our high average income, the average person is buying products made from across the world. We buy clothes made in China, toys made in India and take holidays in Spain and the Caribbean. The average person in Ethiopia buys hardly any products made outside the country. For UK businesses, this means that they are far more likely to sell their products to European or North American customers than they are to developing countries such as India or China. For Tata Motors, the customers for Jaguar cars and LandRover vehicles made in the UK are far more likely to be living in rich developed countries than poorer developing countries.

Wages and prices UK businesses and consumers can take advantage of low wages paid to workers in developing countries. Many products such as clothing are now made mainly in developing countries. Companies like Primark and Tesco offer very low prices on clothing because they buy from suppliers in developing countries. Developing countries are therefore a source of cheap imports for rich developing countries.

Quality and technology of products Price is only one of the factors that persuade customers to buy a product. The quality and the level of technology of the product is important too. Many products made in developing countries are too poor quality or not sufficiently technologically advanced to be sold to customers in rich developed countries. For example, Tata Motors does not sell the vehicles it currently makes in India to countries like the USA and India. Although they are very cheap compared with cars made in developed countries, they often do not conform even to the minimum safety standards laid down by governments in developed countries. In contrast, developing countries tend to buy high quality, high technology products from developed countries. These could be anything from fashion brands such as Gucci to luxury cars such as Mercedes to machinery using the latest technology made in Germany.

So businesses in developed countries tend to sell high priced, high quality products to developing countries. Businesses in developing countries tend to sell lower quality, less technologically advanced but cheaper products to developed countries.

Import protection and export subsidy

A company like Tata Motors is affected by import protection and export subsidies. Nearly every country in the world operates protectionist policies. These are measures designed to reduce the amount of imports coming into a country and in doing so help to give an advantage to domestic firms, not only in selling products in the country but also in exporting products.

Import protection Import protection is designed to reduce imports being bought from abroad. There are many different types of import protection. One is tariffs or customs duties. These are taxes on imported goods. The Indian government, for example, imposes 60 per cent tariffs on imported cars. This means that a Jaguar car

ResultsPlus
Watch Out!

Do not get tariffs and quotas mixed up. Tariffs are taxes on imported goods. Quotas are restrictions on the physical number of goods that can be imported.

edexcel ⣿ key terms

Import – an import is the purchase of a good or service from a foreign business that leads to a flow of money out of the UK. The UK buyer will have to change pounds into the seller's currency to make the transaction.

Export – an export is the sale of a good or service to a foreign buyer that leads to a flow of money into the UK. The foreign buyer will have to change their currency into pounds to complete the purchase.

Protectionist policies – measures designed to reduce foreign products coming into a country but give an advantage to domestic firms to sell products at home or export products.

Tariffs or customs duties – taxes put on goods imported into a country which make them more expensive for buyers.

sold to India for £10,000 would cost £16,000 to import. £6,000 is the amount of tax levied on the car as an import. High taxes on imported cars help reduce the number of foreign cars in the Indian market. Indian tariffs benefit Tata Motors because they face less competition from foreign motor manufacturers in the Indian market. Tata Motors is therefore able to sell more cars in India. There are many other forms of import protection.

Quotas are limits on the physical number of goods that can be imported over a period. For example, a country might impose a quota of 100,000 cars imported from Japan. This means that Japanese car producers like Toyota and Honda can only sell 100,000 cars to that country in a year. Safety standards can be a hidden form of import protection. A country might impose safety standards for products that are unique to that country. This discourages foreign firms from selling to the country because they would have to produce special products just for that one market. This would make the cost of production too high.

Export subsidies Many countries operate a system of export subsidies. The government might give firms that export products money (a subsidy) which helps to reduce the cost of production. The effect is to reduce the price of these goods sold abroad. It therefore makes the country's exports more price competitive and so sales may be higher. Export subsidies can be simply the opposite of a tax. Round the world today, for example, many governments subsidise the exports of agricultural products like wheat or cotton. This gives their farmers an advantage over competitors in other countries. There are many other types of export subsidy, though. One common subsidy in car manufacturing is for governments to give grants to car makers developing new cars. This lowers research and development costs. As a result, the cars can be

sold at a cheaper price.

Import protection and export subsidies mean that some businesses gain and other businesses lose out. Some businesses see their sales increase. Other businesses are prevented from selling their products in some countries. Tata Motors, for example, benefits from import tariffs put on cars coming into India. At the same time, it loses out on sales to other countries that also put tariffs on cars coming into their country. South Korea is one country that protects its main car manufacturer, Hyundai, through protectionist policies. One of the many reasons why Tata Motors, in 2004, bought Daewoo Commercial Vehicles Company, South Korea's second largest manufacturer of commercial trucks, was to get round South Korean import restrictions. Buying a South Korean company meant that Tata could sell trucks into the South Korean market.

Source: information from www.tatamotors.com; Garry Pursell, Nalin Kishor, and Kanupriya Gupta: Manufacturing Protection in India Since Independence, 2007; World Bank, World Development Report 2009.

edexcel ⋮⋮⋮ key terms

Quotas – limits on the physical number of goods that can be imported over a period.

Export subsidies – measures that reduce the price of goods sold abroad.

ResultsPlus
Watch Out!

The UK government no longer has the legal power to impose quotas and tariffs on goods coming into the UK. Decisions about these matters are now made at EU (European Union) level. Quotas and tariffs therefore affect all businesses across the EU.

Test yourself

1. The UK is **most likely** to be described as a

   A *low income country*
   B *poor country*
   C *developed country*
   D *developing country*

   Select **one** answer.

2. Which **one** of the following would be **most likely** to be an example of import protection? Select **one** answer.

   A *A tariff*
   B *Low wages*
   C *Low taxes*
   D *New technology*

3. Which **one** of the following is the best definition of an export subsidy?

   A *A tax imposed on goods leaving the country*
   B *A payment made to a business for selling goods to foreign customers*
   C *A payment given by the government to businesses when they sell goods abroad*
   D *A tax on goods which have received a subsidy from government*

   Select **one** answer.

Over to you

The price of shoes in shops from Clarks to Primark and New Look to Tesco has fallen over the past ten years. This is because most shoes sold in the UK today are imported from South America and the Far East. Producers in China and Vietnam can make shoes at a fraction of the cost of traditional footwear manufacturers in Europe because of the low wages paid to staff.
Imports have hit European footwear manufacturers very hard. Up until 2005, European manufacturers enjoyed some protection because of a strict quota system for the import of shoes from outside the European Union (EU). Despite this protection, footwear production fell by 30 per cent between 2001 and 2005 with the loss of 40,000 jobs in the industry. In 2005, quotas were abolished. This led to a significant increase in imports of shoes into the European Union and the UK. This had little impact on UK footwear manufacturers. Almost all of the industry had already been closed down due to fierce competition from overseas producers. However, both Italy and Portugal still had a large footwear production industry. They wanted protection reintroduced. In October 2006, the EU announced it was putting tariffs on the imports of some types of shoe from China and Vietnam. Imports from China of approximately 174 million pairs of shoes would have a 16.5 per cent tariff put on them. Imports from Vietnam would have a 10 per cent tariff.
Since then, Italian and Portuguese footwear manufacturers have continued to put pressure on the EU to keep the tariffs in place. However, retailers like Clarks and Tesco have argued against keeping the tariffs. It raises their costs and leads to reduced sales of shoes.

Source: adapted from www.telegraph.co.uk 4.10.2006.

1. Using examples from the passage, explain the difference between a quota and a tariff. (3)

2. Explain why Italian footwear manufacturers want the EU to keep its protectionist policies on footwear imports. (3)

3. Analyse how **one** stakeholder in the UK might lose out from tariffs on footwear. (6)

4. Do you think that exports of shoes from the EU should be subsidised? Justify your answer. (8)

ResultsPlus
Build Better Answers

The EU imposed quotas on Chinese made textiles, leading to the so-called 'Bra Wars'. These quotas imposed a physical limit on the amounts of textiles that could cross into the European Union trading zone.

Which **two** of the following best describe the advantages of import protection measures such as quotas or tariffs? Select **two** answers.

A   Domestic firms are protected from imports into the market
B   Customers get a greater choice of products
C   High tariffs discourage consumers from buying imported goods
D   Safety standards will improve
E   The quality of the products in the market will rise

Answer A and C

Technique guide: There is a number of choices available so first:

Think: What is protection? What is a quota? What is a tariff? Who do they affect? What is the impact on the customers?

Then: Consider each alternative and firstly look for the most obvious wrong answer.

B is clearly not the right answer as protectionism tends to reduce the amount of products in the market. ■

Decide: You are now left with four options.

Now: Go through these:

D is incorrect. Safety standards will remain as they are without competition unless new laws are brought in to improve them. ■

E is incorrect. There may well be less of an incentive for domestic firms to improve their products as there is less competition. ■

This leaves you with the correct answers of A and C. Domestic firms are now not subject to increased competition and are proteted, whilst the high tariffs placed on goods and services makes them more expensive and discourages purchases from customers.

23 The impact of government and the EU on business

124

Case Study

McBride is Europe's leading manufacturer of own label household cleaning and personal care products. This includes fabric conditioners, dishwasher tablets, soap and shampoo. It manufactures products for leading retailers like Tesco and Sainsbury in the UK and for other supermarket chains in Europe. In 2009, it had 18 manufacturing plants across the European Union including the UK, Spain, Italy, France, Belgium, Luxembourg and Poland. Like any business operating within the European Union, McBride has to conform to regulations and taxes in each of the countries in which it operates.

Objectives

● Understand the impact of regulation and taxation on businesses.

● Appreciate the benefits and drawbacks of minimum wages, maternity and paternity rights and health and safety regulations on stakeholders and businesses.

The UK government and the EU

McBride is a UK company that operates across the European Union. In 2009, the UK was one of 27 member countries of the EU shown on the map in Figure 1. The European Union was founded in 1957. The number of countries in the EU has grown over time as Figure 1 shows. More countries, such as Croatia and Turkey, are in negotiations about joining in the future.

Being part of the European Union means that some of the decisions that used to be made at national level are now made at EU level. For example, tariffs and quotas that limit imports into a country are decided at EU level. There are EU product safety regulations that apply to all products sold in the EU. There are also many EU regulations that affect businesses and workers.

Figure 1 – The European Union, population and income

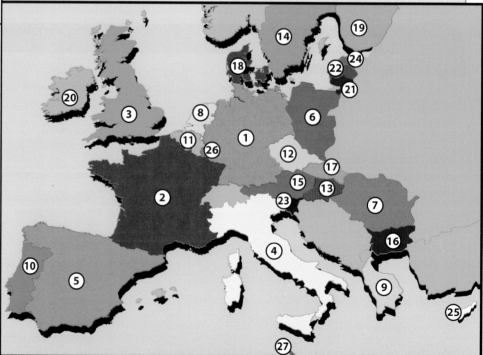

	Country	Population (millions)	National Income (€bn)*	Income as % of EU average	Date Joined
1.	Germany	82.4	2076	117	1958
2.	France	63.4	1529	112	1958
3.	United Kingdom	60.2	1530	118	1973
4.	Italy	58.8	1378	109	1958
5.	Spain	45.0	895	103	1986
6.	Poland	38.1	428	52	2004
7.	Romania	22.3	168	36	2007
8.	Netherlands	16.4	422	119	1958
9.	Greece	11.2	211	89	1981
10.	Portugal	10.6	167	74	1986
11.	Belgium	10.5	272	122	1958
12.	Czech Republic	10.3	162	74	2004
13.	Hungary	10.0	146	68	2004
14.	Sweden	9.0	228	117	1995
15.	Austria	8.2	229	130	1995
16.	Bulgaria	7.8	63	39	2007
17.	Slovakia	5.4	78	67	2004
18.	Denmark	5.4	156	134	1973
19.	Finland	5.3	138	122	1995
20.	Ireland	4.2	147	162	1973
21.	Lithuania	3.5	43	60	2004
22.	Latvia	2.2	26	54	2004
23.	Slovenia	2.0	38	88	2004
24.	Estonia	1.3	19	69	2004
25.	Cyprus	0.8	15	84	2004
26.	Luxembourg	0.5	27	273	1958
27.	Malta	0.4	6	76	2004

*Calculated at 1 Euro = $1.3

Source: adapted from wikipedia.org.

The European Union has helped create a **single** or **common** market. Goods can be traded freely between member countries. There are no tariffs or quotas on trade between member countries. McBride, for example, does not have to pay taxes on its cleaning products from its plant in Burnley in Lancashire when it sends them to a customer in France. By reducing barriers it should be as easy for McBride to sell British made products to a supermarket in London as to one in Rome or Paris. It should also be as easy to hire a worker in London to work in Lancashire as to hire the same worker to work in Poland.

The European Union is still changing. For example, most member countries now use the same currency, the euro. The UK and a few other member countries still have their own national currencies. In the long term, though, it is likely that every country will use the euro as their currency.

Taxation

Tax rates are still set by individual governments in the EU. For example, the tax rate on profits earned by companies is different in the UK than in Ireland or in France. Taxes affect both businesses and consumers.

- Taxes reduce the amount that businesses and consumers have to spend. For example, taxes on company profits mean that businesses have less money to pay out to shareholders in dividends. They also have less to keep back to use for investment in the company. Taxes like income tax reduce the take-home pay of workers. Taxes like Value Added Tax (VAT) on goods increase the price of goods and mean that businesses sell fewer goods than they would if there were no taxes.
- Taxes affect the way in which businesses and consumers behave. For example, taxes on employing workers (Employers' National Insurance contributions (NICs) in the UK) discourage businesses from employing workers. Very high taxes on cigarettes discourage smokers from buying so many cigarettes.

Businesses like McBride are affected by different tax rates in different European countries. Some companies, for example, have located themselves in Ireland to take advantage of low taxes on company profits. Some companies have moved from Germany to Eastern Europe because the taxes that German companies have to pay for employing workers are so high. For a company like McBride that has manufacturing plants across the EU, tax is one of the factors that affect its decision making.

Regulation

All businesses have to deal with government regulations. Sometimes government regulations are called '**red tape**' (because it ties things up and is difficult to unravel) and many businesses dislike them. Regulations cover every aspect of a business. McBride has to comply with thousands of different regulations. Here are some examples.

- It has to submit its financial accounts, audited by independent accountants, to Companies House each year.
- All its vehicles have to be insured.
- Its products sold to consumers must conform to the Trades Descriptions Act.
- It has to dispose of waste materials in accordance with waste disposal regulations.
- It can only locate its offices and factories in areas or buildings that have been designated by local authorities for commercial use under planning regulations.

Regulations are designed to protect different stakeholder groups in a business. For example, submitting accounts that are publicly available is designed to protect both businesses that buy and sell to the company and shareholders. Vehicle insurance means that if any vehicle is involved in a crash, any third parties (those not directly involved in the crash but who may be affected by it) that suffer losses will be compensated. Waste disposal regulations protect the environment.

Complying with regulations is costly for a business like McBride. Without

EU regulations give parents maternity and paternity rights.

ResultsPlus
Watch Out!

New regulations tend to be seen as bad by business because it costs them money to implement them. However, there should be benefits to society, such as improved working conditions or a cleaner environment. Always think carefully about whether the benefits to society of a new regulation are larger than the costs to business or smaller. This will tell you whether it is a good regulation or a bad regulation.

edexcel ::: key terms

Protectionist policies – measures designed to reduce foreign products coming into a country but give an advantage to domestic firms to sell products at home or export products.

Tariffs or customs duties – taxes put on goods imported into a country which make them more expensive for buyers.

regulations, there would be cheaper ways of doing business. Some complain that businesses in developing countries have an unfair competitive advantage compared to European firms because their regulations are nowhere near as strict. Being able to dump untreated waste into a river at no cost, for example, is cheaper than having to dispose of waste in an environmentally friendly way.

Some regulations are the same across the EU. So McBride has to follow the same regulations in its Polish factory and its UK factories. Some regulations differ. McBride has to know what are the regulations in each country in which it operates. This increases its costs. However, some businesses take advantage of this to shift operations to countries where regulations are relatively low.

Minimum wages

One set of regulations that affects McBride is minimum wage regulations. Minimum wages are the lowest wage that a business can legally pay a worker. Most countries in the EU set a minimum wage. However, the level of the minimum wage is not fixed by the EU. It is set by each national government. For example, in 2009, the monthly minimum wage for a 40 hour week in the UK was approximately £1,000 whereas in Slovakia it was just £250.

Minimum wages tend to reflect wage levels in a country. Average wages in the UK are much higher than in Slovakia or Poland. The higher the average wage, the more likely it is that the government will have set a relatively high minimum wage. This is an opportunity for businesses because some can locate their production facilities in low minimum wage countries. Their costs of production will then tend to be lower than at production facilities in high wage countries. It is also a threat for businesses that have to compete against firms that are located in low wage countries.

Pressure groups representing businesses in a country tend to argue that minimum wages are too high and that they should certainly not be increased. This is because high minimum wages tend to increase costs and hit profits. However, trade unions lobby (try to persuade) governments to have higher minimum wages. They argue that low paid workers are paid too little. They use the ethical argument that low paid workers deserve to be paid more.

Maternity and paternity rights

EU regulations give all workers minimum maternity rights. For example, the minimum maternity leave is 14 weeks. This means that working mothers who have a child are entitled to have 14 weeks paid leave. Individual countries are free to have their own regulations which give more rights than the EU minimum. Some countries like Sweden have much more generous maternity rights than countries like the UK. There are currently no equivalent EU rights for fathers, although some individual countries such as Sweden have generous paternity rights. This means that McBride workers have different rights depending on the country in which they are employed. In addition, individual employers may give more generous maternity and paternity rights than the legal minimum in a country.

Pressure groups representing businesses tend to argue against any extension in maternity and paternity rights. Employers often have to pay most of the cost of maternity pay. Work is also disrupted when a woman goes away on maternity leave. Employers by law have to keep her job open to her if she chooses to come back after maternity leave. Employers often appoint a temporary worker to fill the post. This can be disruptive if the temporary worker is not as good at the job as the person who has gone on maternity leave. The disruption can be particularly bad for small businesses who may only have a few employees. On the other hand, pressure groups representing workers such as trade unions argue that women who choose to have a child should not be penalised at work. Again, this is an example of a moral debate as well as an economic one.

Health and safety regulations

All countries in the EU have health and safety regulations. These set down minimum standards for the working environment. For example, there are regulations about

- how long employees can be made to work without a break;
- the storage of dangerous chemicals;
- the level of heating in a workplace;
- the amount of ventilation in a factory.

The regulations are meant to prevent workers from having accidents or falling ill due to their work.

Health and safety regulations impose costs on businesses. Business pressure groups often argue that health and safety regulations are excessive. They are very costly for businesses to implement but too often have little impact on the health and safety of workers. On the other hand, trade unions often argue that employers ignore the health and safety needs of their workers.

Health and safety regulations are often difficult to enforce. There are too few health and safety inspectors to check all premises on a regular basis. A large company like McBride sets itself high standards in terms of health and safety. Small businesses employing a few workers often ignore many aspects of health and safety regulations. This lowers their costs but it increases the likelihood of industrial accidents.

edexcel ⠿ key terms

Minimum wage – the lowest payment per hour, day or week that can be given to a worker for their work.

Source: information from www.mcbride.co.uk.

Over to you

According to the British Chambers of Commerce (BCC), a pressure group that represents UK businesses, the cost since 1998 of new regulations to British industry now stands at £76 billion. Of this 1998-2008 total, £53 billion was the result of conforming to EU regulations and £23 billion for conforming to UK specific regulations.

Director General of the British Chambers of Commerce, David Frost, said: 'Businesses are facing the toughest economic environment for a generation. Company cash-flow is being squeezed and unemployment is growing as a result. The government needs to get serious about reducing the massive burden of regulation on business. Cutting unnecessary burdens and announcing a moratorium (stop) on new regulations set to come in this year, is one way of providing instant and inexpensive help to British firms.' Business groups like the British Chambers of Commerce would like to see a reduction both in the number and the impact of the 104 new regulations that have come into force since 1998.

However, not everyone agrees with the BCC. For a start, the £76 billion is the cost over 12 years. The actual cost for the year in 2008 of regulations introduced between 1998 and 2008 was £10.8bn. The costliest piece of red-tape according to the BCC is the Working Time Regulations. These limit the amount of time a worker can work to 48 hours a week and give workers a holiday entitlement of 4 weeks a year. This, according to the BCC, increased costs to UK businesses by £2.2 billion in 2008. However, most people would agree that limiting working hours to 48 and giving workers holiday entitlement is something positive which may improve productivity and also benefits society. Also very costly are a number of energy saving regulations. For example, the cost to industry of being forced to run fuel efficient, less polluting, vehicles is nearly £1 billion per year. However, almost everyone agrees that we need to reduce pollution and carbon emissions from vehicles over time. This is a benefit to society, and not a cost. Brendon Barber, general secretary of the TUC which represents the interests of trade unions, said: 'Of course regulations need to be well-drafted and suit today's conditions, but too often what the BCC call a burden on business the rest of us would call basic rights in a modern civilised society. I suppose we should be grateful that the BCC haven't added in the cumulative costs of the abolition of slavery and stopping children cleaning chimneys.'

Source: information from www.britishchambers.org.uk; www.mirror.co.uk 27.3.2009; The Observer, 11.5.2008.

1. Using examples from the passage, explain what is meant by (a) red-tape and (b) pressure groups. (6)
2. Explain **two** reasons why businesses would like to see regulation cut. (6)
3. Do you think that all regulations governing how businesses operate in the UK should be removed? Justify your answer. (8)

ResultsPlus
Build Better Answers

In 1999 the UK government introduced the National Minimum Wage.

(a) Define the term 'minimum wage'. (1)

(b) Outline **three** possible benefits of a national minimum wage to a business. (3)

Think: What is the minimum wage? What does it do for workers? What does it do for businesses?

■ **Basic** Gives a basic definition of 'minimum wage' but fails to give any benefits. Such as 'The minimum wage is a set hourly rate that workers must get paid in the UK'. (1)

● **Good** 'Minimum wage is the lowest payment per hour, day or week that can be paid to a worker. (1) Advantages of this are that if you pay more, workers may stay in their jobs (1) and people might be more wiling to actually work and take up jobs on offer.' (1)

▲ **Excellent** 'Minimum wage is the lowest payment per hour, day or week that can be given to a worker for their work. (1) One advantage is that businesses will train and support their workers instead of relying on a cheap source of labour. (1) Another is that workers with better pay will spend a lot of it in the local area, adding to the local economy (1), and finally the worker will be more willing to work, taking up jobs and remaining in the job for longer.' (1)

Test yourself

1. The government increases the minimum wage. This is **most likely** to harm a business that employs low paid workers because
   A fewer workers will want to work for the business
   B its average cost of production will rise
   C its cash-flow position will improve
   D workers will have to pay higher taxes
   Select **one** answer.

2. The UK government increases rates of tax on company profits at a time when other EU governments have kept their tax rates the same. This is **most likely** to lead to some
   A companies changing their location within the EU
   B workers in the UK demanding high wage rates in compensation
   C EU customers buying more goods from UK businesses
   D suppliers buying more goods from outside the EU
   Select **one** answer.

3. Increased maternity rights are **most likely** to be a burden on businesses because
   A more women will want jobs
   B they cannot temporarily employ anyone to replace a woman who has taken maternity leave
   C the average cost of employing women will rise
   D fewer women will apply for vacancies
   Select **one** answer.

In this topic you have learned about: ethics and moral issues and how, in business, they are often highly complex; businesses' actions and how they have a significant effect on the environment; the wide variances of world income distribution; import protection and export subsidies and how they can have significant effects on businesses; how UK and EU regulations can make, break, help and hinder businesses and taxation and other ways in which governments can change business behaviour.

You should know...

☐ Businesses have to make ethical choices.

☐ Ethical considerations in decision-making are becoming more and more important in many businesses.

☐ Ethical choice affects the products made, suppliers used, workers employed, customers' treatment, competitors' actions, the environment and local communities.

☐ There is a trade-off between ethical behaviour and profits.

☐ Pressure groups try and get businesses to change their habits and actions.

☐ Some question whether businesses 'do the right things' for 'the right reasons' - is it just a marketing exercise?

☐ Businesses actions can have a dramatic effect on the environment such as pollution, congestion, climate change and use of scarce resources.

☐ Governments can help curb this by using legislation, regulation subsidies and taxation.

☐ Customer demands, the work of pressure groups and potential opportunities in new markets are helping to change the actions of some businesses.

☐ The world's income is very unevenly distributed.

☐ High income countries are also often called developed countries.

☐ Low and middle income countries are often called developing countries.

☐ The level of a country's development affect its import and export levels.

☐ If a country wishes to reduce imports it may choose to develop import protection strategies.

☐ If it wants to boost exports it will try some strategies to help exports.

☐ The European Union has helped to develop a single market by removing barriers to trade.

☐ Tax rates are still set by individual governments. They affect the behaviour of consumers and businesses.

☐ Regulations can also be known as 'red tape' and they are designed to protect different stakeholders, these include minimum wages, maternity and paternity rights and health & safety regulations.

☐ Regulations impose additional costs on businesses to comply.

☐ The minimum wage is the lowest wage that a business can legally pay its workers.

Support activity

- Think of two businesses - one which you think is an ethical one and one which you feel acts in a more unethical manner. Write down the way(s) each one operates or behaves that have led you to make these choices.

- Discuss your choices with the rest of the class - how many similarities are there? What are the differences?

- What could be done to stop unethical firms from acting in the way that they do? Would this be fair for all stakeholders? Write a list of some solutions and once again share them with the class. What similarities are there this time? Why?

- Some people argue that businesses may promote their ethical behaviour as a marketing exercise. Do you agree? Discuss your views with the rest of the class.

Stretch activity

- Choose one business to research; try and make it different from anyone else's choice in the class.

- Find out as much as you can about their ethical stance and what they try and do to be as ethical as possible. You could use the Internet and look at their company web page or search for news articles about the company.

- Write a report on their actions and also give recommendations as to what they could and should do in the future to improve their ethical position.

South West Water (SWW) has been forced by planning inspectors to upgrade plans for a sewage plant discharging into the sea off Cornwall . SWW wanted to treat some sewage but not all of it meaning that some raw sewage would be dumped into the ocean. The county council rejected SWWs plans following a public enquiry. The objections were led by the local pressure group Tintagel Against Inferior Sewage Treatment (TAIST). A national pressure group, Surfers Against Sewage (SAS) also supported TAIST's stance. They both worked together to produce evidence which was presented at the enquiry. In addition, SAS dressed up as characters from King Arthur's court outside the enquiry venue to further make the point that the level of sewage disposal being proposed by SWW was no different to that which would have happened in King Arthur's day. They called their protest 'Sir Campaignalot'. SAS campaign director Richard Hardy said 'It seemed a no-brainer really, but we needed the legendary campaigning skills of King Arthur and the magic of Merlin to see this proposal rejected. The biggest thumbs up though has to go to TAIST, who have done a fantastic job in showing just what a local grassroots community group can do.'

Source: adapted from www.bbc.co.uk/news.

(i) What is meant by the term 'pressure group'? (1)

(ii) With reference to the case study, explain **one** way in which a pressure group can influence a business's activities (3)

Think: What does a pressure group do? What is their desired outcome? Who is involved in issues that pressure groups champion?

Student answer	Examiner comment	Build a better answer
(a) A group of people who want to change something for the better.	■ A basic answer that is right, but only by the fact that the student identifies the desire to change something. There is a lack of use of appropriate terminology - remember that this is a business studies exam and you are meant to use terms, concepts and terminology appropriate to the subject.	▲ Clear and definitive terminology will help the answer. Clarity of wording is key and may be backed up with an example such as '... are groups who lobby on behalf of various causes such as Surfers Against Sewage, the National Union of Teachers or Tescopoly.'
(b) A pressure group can make a business be more ethical by telling people what they are doing wrong.	■ A simple answer which has a basic element of understanding but no explanation in any depth. The case study has not been used at all and so there are no application skills being demonstrated.	▲ You would be expected to state the way and then develop the point to make links. Examples help to clarify explanations and you should use the case study to help you. For example 'Pressure groups like SAS can highlight improper actions through the media to make these actions public. SAS dressed up in costumes to draw attention to the fact that SWW's plans would mean raw sewage would be dumped in the ocean. This helps to get publicity for their cause through the media.'

Practice Exam Questions

Globalisation has drastically changed the face of world business. It is undeniable that UK consumers have benefited greatly from such a movement. Better choices of goods are available, with many at a lower price. This in turn has benefited UK businesses, allowing them to enjoy greater sales levels than ever before and higher profit margins. To do this however there is often a trade-off between acting ethically and taking advantage of lower input costs to realise the additional profit that is available. For some consumers this is not a problem and they will continue to buy goods at a lower price, whilst for others the feeling is that the line is crossed too often and with too big a step. Primark is one such company that shows this divide. In 2008 it was reported that it was using an Indian sub-contractor who employed child labour in its factories. Things didn't get better for Primark as it was also investigated for using a UK supplier who used illegal workers and also paid its staff below minimum wage levels. Primark responded by sacking three of its Indian sub-contractors and holding a full investigation into the dealings with the UK supplier in relation to its non-compliance with Primark's own work and ethical policies. In addition to this pressure has been put onto Primark by groups such as No-Sweat and Save the Children to halt the use of child labour in the manufacture of its garments.The use of other firms (sub contractors) in less developed countries to manufacture clothing by firms like Primark is a common way to reduce input costs. There are possible disadvantages to firms such as Primark of doing this.

Source: information from www.bized.co.uk, www.bbc.co.uk/news

(a) Which **two** of the following might be the effects on a firm like Primark of using sub-contractors who behave unethically? (2)
   A The firm's reputation may be damaged
   B The firm's costs will rise
   C The firm will be able to apply for the Fairtrade certification
   D The media may report the firm in a positive manner
   E The firm will be taxed more on its sales
   F Pressure groups might lobby the firm

(b) A business like Primark can respond to the pressure placed on it by pressure groups in different ways.
   • One choice is to ignore the pressure groups and hope that the issue will fade away
   OR
   • Work with the pressure groups to improve the situation.
   Which of these choices do you think is the most appropriate choice for Primark? Justify your answer (6).

(c) In your opinion, can a business like Primark make high profits and also be ethical at the same time? Justify your answer. (8)

Welcome to examzone

Revising for your exams can sometimes be a scary prospect. In this section of the book we'll take you through the best way of revising for your exams, step-by-step, to help you prepare as well as you can.

Zone In!

Have you ever had that same feeling in any activity in your life when a challenging task feels easy, and you feel totally absorbed in the task, without worrying about all the other issues in your life? This is a feeling familiar to many athletes and performers, and is one that they strive hard to recreate in order to perform at their very best. It's a feeling of being 'in the zone'.

On the other hand, we all know what it feels like when our brains start running away with us in pressurised situations and can say lots of unhelpful things like 'I've always been bad at exams', or 'I know I am going to forget everything I thought I knew when I look at the exam paper'.

The good news is that 'being in the zone' can be achieved by taking some steps in advance of the exam. Here are our top tips on getting 'into the zone'.

UNDERSTAND IT

Understand the exam process and what revision you need to do. This will give you confidence but also help you to put things into proportion. These pages are a good place to find some starting pointers for performing well at exams.

DEAL WITH DISTRACTIONS

Think about the issues in your life that may interfere with revision. Write them all down. Then think about how you can deal with each so they don't affect your revision.

FRIENDS AND FAMILY

Make sure that they know when you want to revise and even share your revision plan with them. Help them to understand that you must not get distracted. Set aside quality time with them, when you aren't revising and when you aren't worrying about what you should be doing.

COMPARTMENTALISE

You might not be able to deal with all issues. For example, you may be worried about an ill friend, or just be afraid of the exam. In this case, you can employ a useful technique of putting all of these things into an imagined box in your mind at the start of your revision (or in the exam) and mentally locking it, then opening it again at the end of your revision session.

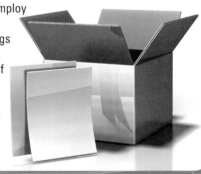

BUILD CONFIDENCE

Use your revision time not just to revise content, but to build your confidence for tackling the examination.

DIET AND EXERCISE

Make sure you eat well and exercise. If your body is not in the right state, how can your mind be?

 More on the Active Teach CD

Planning Zone

The key to success in exams and revision often lies in the right planning. Knowing what you need to do and when you need to do it is your best path to a stress-free experience. Here are some top tips in creating a great personal revision plan.

First of all, know your strengths and weaknesses. Go through each topic making a list of how well you think you know the topic. Use your mock examination results and any further tests that are available to you as a check on your self-assessment. This will help you to plan your personal revision effectively by putting a little more time into your weaker areas. Importantly, make sure you do not just identify strengths and weaknesses in your knowledge of the content but also in terms of exam technique – what aspects of the assessment objectives are you weakest on, for example?

Next, create your plan!
Use the guidelines across the page to help you.

Finally, follow the plan!
You can use the sections in the following pages to kick-start your revision and for some great ideas for helping you to revise and remember key points.

MAY

SUNDAY

29

Cut your revision down into smaller sections. This will make it more manageable and less daunting. In Business Studies you could follow the order of topics and sub-divisions within topics in the specification, which is clearly divided up already. Revise one at a time, but ensure you give more time to topics that you have identified weaknesses in.

MONDAY

Be realistic in how much time you can devote to your revision, but also make sure you put in enough time. Give yourself regular breaks or different activities to give your life some variance. Revision need not be a prison sentence.

TUES

review
tion 2
lete tw

7

Find out your exam dates. Go to www.edexcel.com to find all final exam dates, and check with your teacher.

13

14

Make sure you allow time for assessing progress against your initial self-assessment. Measuring progress will allow you to see and celebrate your improvement and these little victories will build your confidence for the final exam.

Make time for considering how topics interrelate. For example, in Business Studies, try to see where all the parts of the specification fit together. A business has to deal with lots of things all at once and cannot separate them out easily. You have to show that you are aware of all these factors. For example, a business might plan a marketing strategy but has to take into account the fact that interest rates might change and affect sales or that exchange rates may affect both costs and revenues if the business trades abroad.

Review s
comple
practic
ques

Draw up a calendar or list of all the dates from when you can start your revision through to your exams.

Make sure that you know what the assessment objectives against which you will be measured are and what they mean. Get to know the command words that will give you a guide as to what assessment objectives you are expected to demonstrate.

xam
Day!

More on the Active Teach CD

27

28

Know Zone

In this section you'll find some useful suggestions about how to structure your revision for each of the main topics. You might want to skim-read this before starting your revision planning, to help you think about the best way to revise the content. Different people learn in different ways – some remember visually and therefore might want to think about using diagrams and other drawings for their revision. Others remember better through sound or through writing things out. Some people work best alone, whereas others work best when bouncing ideas off friends on the same course. Try to think about what works best for you by trialling a few methods for the first topic.

Remember that each part of the specification could be tested, so revise it all.

Writing revision plans

A useful technique to help you revise important points is to summarise topics into short points. It can be difficult to remember lots of information from textbooks or the notes you have taken during your course. To make notes on a topic:

● read the topic carefully;

● highlight the key points in the topic;

● identify the important information in each point;

● decide how to summarise each point into a short sentence so that it is easy to remember.

Below is an example of how this could be done for Unit 3 – 'Product life cycle' from Topic 3.1.

Topic 3.1, Unit 3, Product life cycle - revision points

● The Product Life Cycle charts the stages through which a product passes over time. It has six separate stages.

1. Development
2. Launch
3. Growth
4. Maturity
5. Saturation
6. Decline

● During growth sales and profits should be rising.

● Maturity sees a peak in sales and the profit generated can now be used to fund other products.

● Businesses try and maximise the length of the maturity phase by undertaking extension strategies.

● Saturation is where competitors bring out rival products which draw sales away from a company.

● The cash flow during the development and launch phase of a product is likely to be negative as the product needs lots of support.

● During the growth phase the cash flow is likely to me small but positive. In maturity, saturation and decline the cash flow is likely to be positive.

● Product portfolio analysis will help a business answer questions about their current and potential products.

● One key product analysis tool is the Boston Matrix. The Boston Matrix is a measurement tool that allows a business to measure the relevant success of a product in its market according to market share and market growth. It has four distinct sections.

1. Cash Cow (low growth; high share).
2. Star (high growth; high share).
3. Problem Children (high growth; low share).
4. Dog (low growth, low share).

More on the Active Teach CD

Memory tips

In the examination you will need to remember important facts, information and data that will help you to answer questions. Some of these will simply be a list of terms such as:

● the types of variable cost;

● the methods of improving cash flow;

● the stakeholders in a business.

Others might be a list of phrases such as:

● the advantages of Just In Time for a business;

● the factors influencing effective customer service;

● the ways in which legislation affects a business.

Different people remember in different ways. You might use some of the following methods to help you.

Memory tips - Mnemonics

This is a word that is made up from the first letters of the terms you want to remember. Some well know phrases in business and economics are:

● PESTLE – the Political, Economic, Social, Technological, Legal and Environmental factors affecting a business;

● SWOT – the Strengths, Weaknesses, Opportunities and Threats facing a business;

● the 4 Ps of the marketing mix – Price, Product, Promotion and Place.

You can make up your own mnemonic for a topic. For example, to remember Maslow's hierarchy of needs use the mnemonic PSLSS – Physiological, Safety, Love and belonging, Self-esteem, Self-actualisation (try to remember it as 'Peaceless').

Memory tips - Visual presentation

Some people remember if the information is a picture or diagram. Below is an example of a diagram that could be used to remember Maslow's hierarchy of needs.

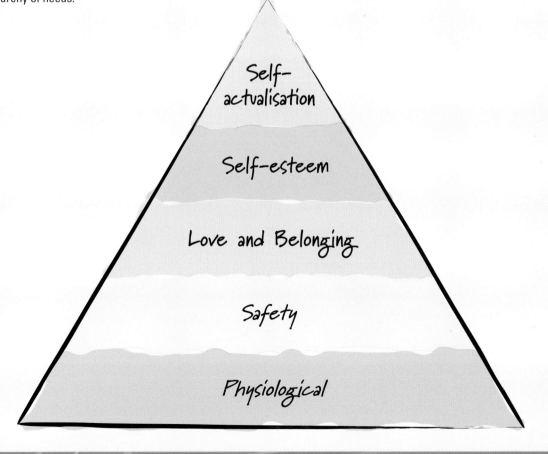

Know Zone

Memory tips - Mindmaps

A mindmap is a diagram that records words and ideas and shows connections. At the centre of the map, or page, is the main word or idea. Flowing out from this main word or idea is a number of key words and ideas linked to the main word. Mindmaps are used in business. But you can also use a mindmap for your revision. Below is a mindmap outlining how to improve cash flow.

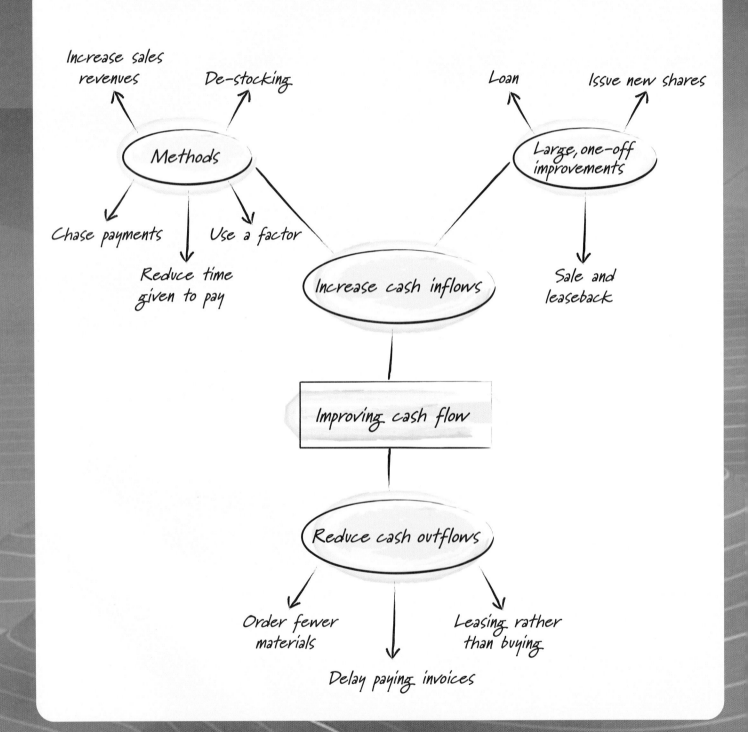

Don't Panic Zone

Once you have completed your revision in your plan, you'll be coming closer and closer to The Big Day. Many students find this the most stressful time and tend to go into panic-mode, either working long hours without really giving their brain a chance to absorb information, or giving up and staring blankly at the wall. Some top tips are shown here.

◉ Test yourself by relating your knowledge to business issues that arise in the news – can you explain what is happening in these issues and why?

◉ Get hold of past papers and the mark schemes for the papers. Look carefully at what the mark schemes are expecting of the candidate in relation to the question.

◉ Get hold of a copy of the Examiner's Report from the previous exam series. It contains lots of useful advice about where candidates performed well and where the main mistakes were. Learn from these. The Examiner's Report and past papers are often available on the awarding body Website – check with your teacher.

◉ Do plenty of practice papers to hone your technique, help manage your time and build confidence in dealing with different questions.

◉ Relax the night before your exam – last minute revision for several hours rarely has much additional benefit. A runner doing a marathon is unlikely to practice the night before by going for a quick 15 mile run. Your brain needs to be rested and relaxed to perform at its best.

◉ Remember the purpose of the exam – it is for you to show the examiner what you have learnt and understood about business. It is not a means of trying to trick you.

Last minute learning tips for Business Studies

The week before the exam should be spent going through past papers. Look at each question carefully and compare question types. Make sure that you are familiar with the different types of question and you know the style needed to answer each question.

There will be **multi choice** questions or **objective test** questions. These ask you to make a choice from a series of options, such as 'Which **one** of the following is an export from the UK?' **or** 'Which of the following is **not** a reason for taxation in the UK? Select **one** answer.'

There will be questions assessing your **knowledge** and **application** skills, such as 'What is meant by the term "stakeholder"?' and 'Identify **two** effects of a strong pound in the passage.'

Certain questions will test **analysis** and **evaluation** such as 'Explain how a fall in interest rates might affect a business' or 'To what extent can pressure groups affect a business? Justify your answer.'

Try to devote some time to actually writing out the answers in the time period allowed to refine your skills. You can check your answers against the mark scheme to see how you would have performed. Make sure you understand what the command words are for each question and how they relate to the assessment objectives. For example, an 8 mark question might consist of 2 marks for knowledge, 2 for application and 4 for analysis and evaluation.

Remember that you can get full marks by answering in the space provided on the exam paper - it is not the amount you write but the quality and the extent to which you demonstrate the assessment objectives being targeted.

On the night before the exam, relax, give your brain a rest and try and do something you enjoy. Get to bed at a reasonable hour so that you can get a good night's sleep and be refreshed for the exam.

More on the Active Teach CD

Exam Zone

About the exam paper

The assessment for Unit 3 is through an examination which will last for one and a half hours. Students are required to answer all questions. There will be a total of 90 marks. The examination will be divided into three sections which include a variety of questions including:

● multiple choice questions;

● short answer questions;

● extended answer questions.

Sections B and C will consist of questions based on scenarios given in the examination.

Understanding the language of the exam paper

Which of the following is... Select one answer	You need to identify the correct response from a selection of options.
Which two of the following are...	You need to identify the two correct responses from a selection of options.
Which of the following is most likely to...	The key is 'most likely' – this means that there could be more than one option that is possible; you have to decide which is the most likely.
Which of the following is not...	This is a question asking you to spot the negative option from a list – read each option carefully.
Fill in the blanks	This may require you to complete some calculations in a table, for example.
What is meant by...	This requires you to give a definition of a key term in business studies – an example to help support the definition is usually worth giving also.
Identify...	This type of question requires only a one word answer or a short phrase or sentence – it is associated with knowledge and understanding and often requires the student to extract information from a context.
State...	Similar to 'identify' – again usually only requires a one word answer.
Describe...	Give the main characteristics of a topic or issue.
Explain...	Describe the issue, term etc, giving reasons or features.
Analyse...	Break down the topic or issue into manageable parts to help explain what is going on, how something works, what relationships may exist and what assumptions might be made.
Assess...	Offer a judgement on the importance, significance, relevance and value of something, with reasons why you have made such a judgement.
Do you think...	Asking you to make a judgement – which requires support and reasons to be given for the judgement.
What is the most important...	Another question asking you to make a judgement and offer support for the judgement. Explain why one factor is more important than another and why.
To what extent...	Is the issue very, very important/significant/, quite important/significant, moderately important/significant, not very significant/important at all – and why?
Evaluate...	Arrive at a judgement – with some support for your reasoning.
Justify...	Offer support and reasons for the judgement you have made – and why.
Write a report...	A report might consist of advantages and disadvantages, key features, summaries and judgements about the value of one option against others.

Exam Zone

Meet the exam paper

This diagram shows the front cover of the exam paper. These instructions, information and advice will always appear on the front of the paper. It is worth reading it carefully now. Check you understand it. Now is a good opportunity to ask your teacher about anything you are not sure of here.

Print your surname here, and your initial afterwards and sign the paper. This is an additional safeguard to ensure that the exam board awards the marks to the right candidate.

Here will be the school's centre number.

Ensure that you understand exactly how long the examination will last, and plan your time accordingly.

Make sure you are aware of how many marks are given for each question and write to justify these marks.

Here you fill in your personal exam number. Take care when writing it down because the number is important to the exam board when writing your score.

In this box, the examiner will write the total marks you have achieved in the exam paper.

Make sure you understand what you are allowed to take into the exam and what you are not.

Make sure that you understand exactly which questions you should attempt and the style you should use to answer them.

Write your name here

Surname

Other names

Centre Number

Candidate Number

Edexcel GCSE

Business Studies

Unit 3: Building a Business

Time: 1 hour 30 minutes

Paper Reference

5BS03/01

You do not need any other materials.

Total Marks

Instructions

- Use **black** ink or ball-point pen.
- **Fill in the boxes** at the top of this page with your name, centre number and candidate number.
- Answer **all** the questions.
- Answer the questions in the spaces provided
  – *there may be more space than you need.*

Information

- The total mark for this paper is 90.
- The marks for **each** question are shown in brackets
  – *use this as a guide as to how much time to spend on each question.*
- Questions labelled with an **asterisk** (*) are ones where the quality of your written communication will be assessed.
  – *you should take particular care with your spelling, punctuation and grammar, as well as the clarity of expression, on these questions.*

Advice

- Read each question carefully before you start to answer it.
- Keep an eye on the time.
- Try to answer every question.
- Check your answers if you have time at the end.

Turn over ▶

N35641A

©2008 Edexcel Limited.
2/2

Edexcel GCSEs in Business

Sample Assessment Materials

© Edexcel Limited 2008

27

edexcel
advancing learning, changing lives

 More on the Active Teach CD

Zone Out

This section provides answers to the most common questions students have about what happens after they complete their exams. For much more information, visit www.examzone.co.uk

About your grades

Whether you've done better than, worse than or just as you expected, your grades are the final measure of your performance on your course and in the exams. On this page we explain some of the information that appears on your results slip and tell you what to do if you think something is wrong. We answer the most popular questions about grades and look at some of the options facing you.

When will my results be published?

Results for summer examinations are issued on the middle two Thursdays in August, with GCE first and GCSE second.

Can I get my results online?

Visit www.resultsplusdirect.co.uk, where you will find detailed student results information including the 'Edexcel Gradeometer' which demonstrates how close you were to the nearest grade boundary. Students can only gain their results online if their centre gives them permission to do so.

I haven't done as well as I expected. What can I do now?

First of all, talk to your subject teacher. After all the teaching that you have had, tests and internal examinations, he/she is the person who best knows what grade you are capable of achieving. Take your results slip to your subject teacher, and go through the information on it in detail. If you both think that there is something wrong with the result, the school or college can apply to see your completed examination paper and then, if necessary, ask for a re-mark immediately. The original mark can be confirmed or lowered, as well as raised, as a result of a re-mark.

How do my grades compare with those of everybody else who sat this exam?

You can compare your results with those of others in the UK who have completed the same examination using the information on our website at: http://www.edexcel.com

What happens if I was ill over the period of my examinations?

If you become ill before or during the examination period you are eligible for special consideration. This also applies if you have been affected by an accident, bereavement or serious disturbance during an examination.

If my school has requested special consideration for me, is this shown on my Statement of Results?

If your school has requested special consideration for you, it is not shown on your results slip, but it will be shown on a subject mark report that is sent to your school or college. If you want to know whether special consideration was requested for you, you should ask your Examinations Officer.

Can I have a re-mark of my examination paper?

Yes, this is possible, but remember that only your school or college can apply for a re-mark, not you or your parents/carers. First of all, you should consider carefully whether or not to ask your school or college to make a request for a re-mark. You should remember that very few re-marks result in a change to a grade - not because Edexcel is embarrassed that a change of marks has been made, but simply because a re-mark request has shown that the original marking was accurate.

Check the closing date for remarking requests with your Examinations Officer.

When I asked for a re-mark of my paper, my subject grade went down. What can I do?

There is no guarantee that your grades will go up if your papers are remarked. They can also go down or stay the same. After a re-mark, the only way to improve your grade is to take the examination again. Your school or college Examinations Officer can tell you when you can do that.

Can I resit a unit?

If you are sitting your exams from 2014 onwards, you will be sitting all your exams together at the end of your course. Make sure you know in which order you are sitting the exams, and prepare for each accordingly – check with your teacher if you're not sure. They are likely to be about a week apart, so make sure you allow plenty of revision time for each before your first exam.

 More on the Active Teach CD

Index

Page references which appear in colour are defined in the Key Terms sections in each chapter.